D1270107

# THE OLD CHINA BOOK

Fig. 24. ALMSHOUSE, NEW YORK. *A. Stevenson.*

Fig. 25. COLUMBIA COLLEGE. *A. Stevenson.*

# THE OLD CHINA BOOK

INCLUDING

## STAFFORDSHIRE, WEDGWOOD, LUSTRE,

AND

## OTHER ENGLISH POTTERY AND PORCELAIN

BY

## N. HUDSON MOORE

TUDOR PUBLISHING COMPANY
NEW YORK

*Reprinted February, 1936*
*Reprinted, 1937*
*Reprinted, 1942*

PRINTED IN THE UNITED STATES OF AMERICA
BY J. J. LITTLE & IVES COMPANY, NEW YORK

# PREFACE.

THIS little book has been compiled to meet the wants (expressed in hundreds of letters) of those who own old china, particularly old English china, and would like to know more about it, and to stimulate others to whom the fascinations of china collecting are as yet unknown.

There are many more to whom we hope to appeal :— those who are interested in their country's history during that strenuous time when the colony cast aside its mother's hand and took its first steps alone. It may well stir our patriotism to look on the plain buildings our ancestors were content to view as " Beauties " ; to note the primitive methods of transportation both on land and sea ; to revise our knowledge of such famous victories as McDonough's, or Bunker Hill, and to study the rugged features of those who worked and died to make our country what she is. All this and more may be found within the limits of a collection of " Old Blue."

Quite apart from the peculiar interest of the Staffordshire wares are those lovely English porcelains and pottery of the late eighteenth century. They well repay study, and many of us may rejoice to find that we are harbouring angels unawares.

Some of the illustrations have been used in articles on this subject, and thanks are due to the *Delineator*, *House Beautiful*, and the *Ledger Monthly* for permission to reproduce them.

To the editors of " Old China " the writer is indebted for a number of cuts, particularly the fine English views, which are being eagerly sought. Numerous photographs were taken expressly for this book, and obligations are expressed to the Boston Museum of Fine Arts, Concord Antiquarian Society, to Mrs. Frederick Yates, Mrs. A. K. Davis, Anthony Killgore, Esq., Mr. William M. Hoyt, and many others, who kindly put their private collections at the writer's disposal.

# ILLUSTRATIONS.

## CHAPTER I.

1. Salt glaze plate.
2. Tortoise-shell covered mug.
3. Queen's ware jug.
4. Willow pattern platter.

## CHAPTER II.

5. View of City of Albany.
6. "Chief Justice Marshall" (steamboat).
7. "Cadmus."
8. Wood and Caldwell jug.
9. Catskill, N. Y.
10. Lake George, N. Y.
11. Castle Garden and Battery, N. Y.
12. West Point, Newburg, Catskill Mt. House.
13. Landing of the Pilgrims.
14. Landing of Pilgrims pitcher.
15. Erie Canal plates.
16. Table Rock, Niagara.
17. Falls of Montmorency.
18. Woman of Samaria.
19. Marine Hospital, Ky.
20. Limehouse Dock.
21. Warwick Castle.
22. Ely.
23. Mill at Charenton.
24. Columbia College.
25. Almshouse, N. Y.
26. New York from Brooklyn Heights.
27. New York from Brooklyn Heights (platter).
28. Landing of Lafayette.
29. States platter.

30. Pittsfield Elm.
31. Syntax tray. Advertisement for a Wife.
32. Syntax plate. Bluestocking Beauty.
33. The Valentine. Wilkie design.
34. Lumley Castle, Durham.
35. Boston State House.
36. Nahant.

CHAPTER III.

37. Capitol at Washington.
38. Almshouse, N. Y.
39. Boston Hospital.
40. Capitol at Washington (Fish tray).
41. Octagon Church, Boston.
42. Mount Vernon and two cup-plates.
43. All Soul's College and St. Mary's Church, Oxford.
44. Battery.
45. Battle of Bunker Hill.
46. Lawrence Mansion, Boston.
47. So called—Lawrence Mansion.
48. Capitol, Washington.
49. City Hotel, N. Y.
50. Scudder's American Museum.
51. Harvard College.
52. Columbia College.
53. Harewood House.
54. Franklin's Tomb (cup and saucer).

CHAPTER IV.

55. Arms of Rhode Island.
56. Arms of Pennsylvania.
57. Arms of New York.
58. Arms of Delaware.
59. Tomb (sugar bowl).
60. Mitchell & Freeman's China House.
61. Columbus plate.
62. St. George's Chapel.
63. Branxholm Castle.

64. Hancock House.
65. State House, Boston.
66. U. S. Hotel, Philadelphia.
67. Richard Jordan's residence.
68. Louisville, Ky.
69. Sandusky, Ohio.
70. Albany, N. Y.
71. Baltimore Almshouse.
72. Fulton steamboat.
73. Eulogy plate.
74. Utica inscription.
75. Lovejoy plate.
76. Burning of Merchant's Exchange, N. Y.

CHAPTER V.

77. Medallion pitcher.
78. St. Paul's Chapel.
79. Windsor Castle.
80. Jefferson and Clinton, Boston Hospital.
81. Lafayette.
82. Niagara.
83. Franklin.
84. Perry.

CHAPTER VI.

85. Butcher's Arms pitcher.
86. Butchers Arms pitcher.   Reverse side.
87. Black-printed ware.
88. Apotheosis jug.
89. Washington map jug.
90. Washington jug.
91. Monument jug.
92. Washington jug.
93. Masonic jug.
94. Death of Wolfe.
95. Commodore Preble pitcher.
96. Sunderland jugs.
97. Printed tea-set.

## CHAPTER VII

98. Bow pickle leaf and creamer.
99. Chelsea.
100. Crown-Derby, Falstaff.
101. Bristol, Flora.
102. Bristol pottery.
103. Leed's ware.
104. Old Worcester cup and saucer.
105. Old Worcester plate.
106. Plymouth, Harlequin.
107. Corner cupboard of Lowestoft.
108. Rose-sprigged Lowestoft.
109. Blue-banded Lowestoft.
110. Certified Lowestoft.
111. Spode.
112. Mason's stone.
113. Herculaneum porcelain.

## CHAPTER VIII.

114. Black basaltes tea-set.
115. Nelson teapot.
116. Silver lustre tea-set.
117. Silver lustre cake-basket and vases.
118. Group of jugs.
119. Lustre mug and goblets.
120. Group of lustre jugs.
121. Cornwallis.
122. Lafayette.
123. Cups and saucers, lustre decoration.
124. Castleford teapot.

## CHAPTER IX.

125. Cream ware, teapot.
126. Basaltes medallion.
127. Basaltes tea-set.
128. Basaltes vase.
129. Jasper flower-holder.

130. Jasper vase, blue and white.
131. Jasper vase, lilac and white.
132. Flower-pot.
133. Lustre candlesticks.
134. Wedgwood's patterns.

## CHAPTER X.

135. Toby, etc.
136. Lavender porcelain jug.
137. Davenport jug.
138. Newburg jug, Clews.
139. Minster jug.
140. Ariadne jug.
141. Alcock jugs.
142. Eagle and Silenus jugs.
143. Toby jugs.
144. Group of teapots, printed wares.
145. Groups of teapots, lustre decorations.
146. Group of teapots, painted wares.
147. "Lion Slayer."
148. Pepper-pot.
149. Nottingham Bear.
150. Cow and Calf.

# CONTENTS.

CHAPTER.                                                        PAGE.

PREFACE . . . . . . . v

LIST OF ILLUSTRATIONS . . . . . vii

I. EARLY POTTERY . . . . . . I

II. STAFFORDSHIRE WARES . . . . . 12

III. STAFFORDSHIRE WARES, CONTINUED . . 38

IV. STAFFORDSHIRE WARES, CONTINUED . . 61

V. PORTRAIT PIECES . . . . . . 86

VI. LIVERPOOL AND OTHER PRINTED WARES . 100

VII. ENGLISH PORCELAIN AND POTTERY . . 124

VIII. BASALTES, LUSTRES, WHITE WARE, ETC., . 166

IX. WEDGWOOD AND HIS WARES . . . . 185

X. JUGS, TEAPOTS AND ANIMALS . . . 234

LIST OF VIEWS . . . . . . 254

WORKS ON POTTERY AND PORCELAIN CON-
SULTED . . . . . . 284

INDEX . . . . . . . 285

# THE OLD CHINA BOOK.

## CHAPTER I.

### EARLY POTTERY.

TO-DAY, when our watchword seems to be " rush," when people who would like to pause and bide awhile are swept along with the multitude, the thoughtful person is likely to ask " How can I best withstand the pressure? "

The device which is of the greatest use is the cultivation of a hobby, an intense interest in some particular subject, let it be birds, butterflies or beetles, old laces, engravings, or china.

To be able to throw your mind into the contemplation of a subject which is of such interest to you that workaday worries are crowded out is not only a rest but a pleasure, and though you may have started on your gatherings without either thought or desire for improvement, insensibly you will find yourself drawn into new fields, into by-paths leading off from the main road, where you will find much to surprise and interest you.

It is not necessary to mention the shining lights of past and present times who have found pleasure in the gathering of china. I am sometimes asked if it is not a very costly pleasure. It may be, yet within my

own experience have come the following ardent collectors of " old blue " : a busy doctor, a woman who is
a cook in a restaurant, an editor, a butcher, an actor,
a school teacher, and dozens of women of leisure, some
with wealth and some with none, some owning
dozens, even hundreds, of pieces, some less than a
score, yet all rejoicing in the cultivation of an interest,
" a new interest in life," as many of them say, which
provides agreeable food for reflection, and which
stimulates as well as rests.

The making of pottery is one of the oldest arts,
practised even by prehistoric races, with the exception
of the cave dwellers of the Drift period. The sepul-
chral barrows of Great Britain have yielded many
specimens of this work, and to-day the attention of
most collectors centers on the pottery of England,
particularly that made in the eighteenth and the first
quarter of the nineteenth centuries.

During the reign of Queen Elizabeth there were
imported from Germany numbers of stoneware jugs,
generally called Bellarmines, which superseded for
drinking purposes home-made vessels. Not only these
German vessels but Delft ware and occasional pieces
of Oriental ware and Italian faïence also crept into
England, were eagerly sought, and brought good
prices. This stimulated the potters of England, who
had at their command, right at hand, the necessary
materials in great variety and abundance.

From this period, about 1560, may be dated the use
of the potter's art in England, and many utensils were
made which were not lacking in artistic feeling and
suitability for the purposes for which they were used.
Fifty years later the mugs and jugs with many handles,

the posset-pots and flagons were turned in a superior style of material, design and workmanship. During the second half of the seventeenth century many potteries started up all over England, most of them being content to imitate German stoneware or the Dutch Delft. There were a few potters who were progressive enough to try and improve their old-fashioned earthenware, and of all these early wares dated specimens are still to be found in England. Such as are in this country are museum specimens, so we need not go into further description.

As early as 1680 glazing by means of salt (a process which had been known in Germany for many years) became common, and superseded the coarse glaze hitherto known, which was called "lead glaze" and was opaque. Eventually this salt glazing was improved upon, and the ware to which it was applied was called "Crouch-Ware" (FIG. 1). Even at its best all this pottery was but rude ware, and the nobility and gentry still clung to plate and pewter, and even to wooden trenchers.

The chartering of the East India Trading Company in 1600, for carrying on business in the East Indies, is one of the chapters in English history that makes interesting reading. It was, perhaps, the first great trust or "combine" of which we have record, and its rapacities became so great that, finally, about the middle of the nineteenth century, the Crown was obliged to step in and take away its charter. It was, however, to this company that England was indebted for the introduction of porcelain from the Orient. To be sure a few pieces had been brought in prior to 1600, but even Queen Bess regarded highly her two cups. One was a porringer of "white porselyn," garnished with gold, a gift from Lord Burleigh, and the other a cup of " grene pursselyn," given by Robert Cecil. We may be very sure that the canny queen would have gathered in more specimens if her loyal subjects had possessed much of this " pursselyn," for at New Year's time she had the habit of demanding gifts from rich and poor alike, even ginger from the crossing-sweeper was not too small an offering for her gracious acceptance, and she " sware right lustily " if the gifts were not forthcoming on time. By 1631 the trading company had thrown out several tentacles, and with other spoils from the East began to bring in porcelain. The company suffered greatly because its officers engaged in smuggling " certain wares and merchandise." A long list of articles was drawn up which the officers were forbidden to bring in, but they were allowed to bring home as much china and " purslanes " as they desired.

On September 25, 1660, Pepys (whose sprightly diary is a record of all that was doing about town in those days), says, " I did send for a cup of tee (a China drink), of which I never drank before." So it seems as if some cups and bowls came in before the beverage for which they were ultimately used. Tea was then so scarce in England that the infusion of it in water was taxed by the gallon in common with chocolate and sherbet. Two pounds and two ounces were, in the same year, 1659, formally presented to the king by the East India Company as a most valuable oblation.

Now at this time the vessel known as a teapot had not been invented. Even in the land of the tea plant

Fig. 1.  SALT GLAZE PLATE.

Fig. 2.  TORTOISE-SHELL MUG.

Fig. 3.  QUEEN'S WARE PITCHER.

Fig. 4.  WILLOW PATTERN PLATTER.

the almond-eyed celestial brewed his tea by pouring hot water over the leaves in a bowl. It was left to more recent times and more civilized nations to use such a utensil as we call teapot, and to boil out all the injurious qualities from this cheering plant. With these facts in mind a letter which lies before me seems a little startling. It says " This teapot has been in our family two hundred and fifty years. It is red and yellow, and is decorated with the coat of arms of England. Can you tell me who made it?" This has happened scores of times to me. People of upright and sterling character, many of them possessed of New England consciences, write me such letters. They have no scruple in adding a hundred or more years to the age of a bit of china, while they might fairly hesitate in taking off ten or twenty years of their own age in the presence of the census-taker. It is well to fix in your mind the date, 1660, as the approximate time when porcelain from the Orient, in plates, cups and bowls, first began to appear in England. There were few teapots until nearly half a hundred years later.

Although, during recent years, England may well be proud of her porcelain products, she has equal reason to uphold the fame of her pioneer potters, when among them may be found such names as Adams, Elers, Mason, Mayer, Meigh, Ridgway, Wedgwood and Wood.

The term " pottery," in its widest sense, includes all objects made of clay, moulded into shape while in a moist state, and then hardened by fire. In ordinary wares, pottery and semi-china, clay was used which had impurities, while the paste of porcelain is of a purer silicate of alumina.   The essential difference in appearance between pottery and porcelain is that the latter is whiter, harder and slightly translucent.   The use of pounded flint was the cause of great improvements in earthenware.   The material was mixed with sand and pipeclay, and coloured with oxide of copper and manganese, making the agate, or combed, or tortoise-shell ware which became very popular. (FIG. 2.)   This particular tortoise-shell mug, with its graceful cover, is in the Concord Museum of Antiquities.   It is very light in weight, rich in colour, and absolutely perfect.   Pasted in the cover is the following legend—" Jonas Potter, born Feby 6, 1740.   Married Dec. 30, 1766, died, March 7, 1821."   It is the record of a whole life, and the monument to this unknown Jonas, one frail mug, has outlived him more than three-quarters of a century.   It is undoubtedly made by Wheildon, who never identified his pieces by any mark or name ; but their workmanship is so superior that they cannot be mistaken, for no imitator ever approached their perfection.   The choicest pieces of these wares were probably made between 1752 and 1759.

The cream-coloured wares followed the tortoise-shell, and were named in honour of Queen Anne, who admired them.   They were usually decorated with ornaments in low relief, copied from the forms of silverware of the period (FIG. 3).   After the plain coloured wares came those printed and painted, and this pottery was by no means lacking in beauty of form or design.   To the collector the " feel " of a piece of china is almost as great a guide as its looks.   The old china had a lightness, you almost may say a softness (which modern wares lack), particularly that old English ware known as semi-china.

The word porcelain comes from the Italian word *porcellana*, meaning cowry-shell, and we commonly call porcelain ware china, because it was first made by the Chinese. Porcelain is made of a certain kind of clay, which is purified and then baked, producing a hard, translucent material, the transparency of which is regulated by its thickness.

*Paste* is the body or substance of which the article is made, and may be either hard or soft. *Hard paste* is made of the natural clay, and appears, when broken, sparkling, fine grained and vitreous. *Soft paste* is more porous and dull, and is made of artificial clays. You may only distinguish the hardness or softness of the paste where there is a clean chip, but it is well to remember that all modern china is hard paste.

*Glaze* is the shiny material which covers the paste. *Hard glaze* is colourless and thin, making the object cold to the hands. *Soft glaze* is somewhat gummy to the touch, without the hard cold feeling which distinguishes hard glaze, and may be scratched with a knife. The rims or little rings on which pieces of hard paste porcelain rest are left unglazed. This is an easy method of distinguishing hard from soft paste porcelain.

All Oriental china is hard paste. Hard-glaze porcelain was made at Plymouth, Bristol and Liverpool. Soft glaze manufactories were at Bow, Chelsea, Derby, Worcester, and also at Liverpool and Rockingham. The Staffordshire porcelain was soft glaze, but had feldspar added.

*Biscuit* is the technical term applied to both pottery

and porcelain before they are enamelled or glazed. It is a dead white, and does not receive well colours which need a glaze to bring out their beauty.

*Faïence* is a French word which is applied to every kind of glazed earthenware, but does not include porcelain. *Majolica*, as the term is commonly used, means about the same thing as faïence, but formerly it meant exclusively Italian decorated pottery of the fifteenth, sixteenth, seventeenth and eighteenth centuries, made in the old Italian style.

*Stoneware* is seldom glazed by a " dip," the glazing and firing usually being done at one time by the introduction of salt in the kiln.

*Semi-china* is made with a large admixture of feldspar, and is almost as translucent as porcelain. The main differences in the manufacture of earthenware, stoneware and porcelain are due to a few minor ingredients, to the way they are prepared, and to the degree of heat to which they are subjected.

There is one mark which appears on new, old and middle-aged china that causes much perturbation of spirit. As many correspondents say it " is not in the books." This mark is somewhat diamond-shaped, with a capital R in the middle, and figures in the angles. It simply means "registered," showing that the pattern is registered.

On almost every piece of this old china ware, particularly " flat " or table ware, you will find on the face of the piece three rough marks in the glaze. On the back of each piece will also be found rough marks, three in a group, and three groups at equal distances. These are caused by the "stilts," or little tripods which were put between the pieces to keep them

separate when they were fired in the kiln.  They are
a very good test that the china is old.  When it is
said that a piece is in "proof condition," it means
that it is without crack or chip, fine in colour and printing, and not greased or scratched.  A piece may be
called perfect, and yet have some tiny surface crack, or
may show signs of wear, like knife scratches, but otherwise be in perfect condition.  A crack detracts from
the value more than a chip or nick, even if the latter
be on the face of the china.  The term "greased" is
applied, when, by much use, grease has penetrated
the glaze, and spoiled the colour.

The making of pottery took rapid strides after the
opening of the eighteenth century, and in the period
between 1722 and 1749 no less than nine patents were
taken out.  Among the earliest pieces made for domes-
tic uses were the Bellarmines, already spoken of,
copied from the German stoneware, ale jugs and
various drinking vessels, mugs and posset-pots.

The name "mug" was singularly derived from the
fact that these drinking cups were generally decorated
with a rude, or grotesque face, or "mug."  Posset-
pots were in popular use for supper on Chrismas eve.
In the tasty drink, with its spices and sippets of toast,
were dropped the wedding ring of the hostess and a
bit of silver money.  Each guest fished in turn after
taking a drink.  The one who succeeded in rescuing
the ring was assured a speedy and happy marriage,
while the one who got the coin was equally certain to
have good luck for the year.  These pots, seldom used
during the year but on this single occasion, were
handed down in families, and may still be found in
Great Britain.

The taste for collecting china began very early in England, but it was Oriental china that filled the cabinets, with sometimes a few pieces of Delft, decorated in Chinese fashion.  Before 1694 Queen Mary had quite a number of vases in which she delighted, and " on which houses, trees, bridges and mandarins were depicted in outrageous defiance of all laws of perspective."  It is a matter of speculation if the vases thus described had on them designs similar to what we now know as the " willow-pattern," and which every English potter turned his attention to at one time or another.  They are to be found all over this country, in every shade of blue and every degree of workmanship.  FIG. 4 shows a very fine example of this pattern.

The china mania in England reached its greatest height in the eighteenth century, and all who could filled their houses with jars and vases, cups and saucers, and "loves of monsters," without use or beauty.

Of all collectors Horace Walpole was the prince, and of him it was written :

" China's the passion of his soul ;
A cup, a plate, a dish, a bowl,
Can kindle wishes in his breast,
Inflame with joy or break his rest.'

He was so fond of his brittle treasures that he even washed them himself, though his poor hands were swollen and knotted with gout.  His collection was, perhaps, the largest ever made by an individual. It was all gathered between 1753 and 1776, and was kept at his Gothic villa at Strawberry Hill.

This priceless collection was sold in 1842 by Lord Waldegrave who inherited the property, and it took twenty-seven days to dispose of all the treasures at auction. It is a pity that it could not have been left to the nation, like the unrivalled Wallace collection of pictures, which was begun by the third Marquis of Hertford at about the end of the eighteenth century.

# CHAPTER II.

## STAFFORDSHIRE WARES.

ENGLAND is not a very large section of the globe, but the history of the villages and hamlets which comprise that district in Staffordshire known as the "potteries" would fill a large volume. The potting district was over ten miles long and comprised Stoke-on-Trent, Hanley, Cobridge, Etruria, Burslem, Fenton, Tunstall, Longport, Shelton, Lane End, and some lesser known works.

Ralph Shaw, in 1733, patented a salt-glazed ware, brown and white outside and white within. The patent did not hold, however, and his rivals copied and improved on his ware with great rapidity. Wedgwood has always been a famous name among potters, and as early as the seventeenth century there was a Wedgwood potting at Burslem. The Staffordshire potters who are of chief interest to us, may be said to begin with Enoch Wood, generally referred to as "The Father of the Pottery," who went into business in 1784, and who made all kinds of table ware, pitchers, punch bowls, and even statuettes. By this time, just after the Revolution, we were recovering from our struggles, and anxious for more comforts than we had hitherto demanded. Enoch Wood was practical enough to seize upon the occasion, and turned out from his pottery quantities of ware, serviceable, attractive and cheap. He did more than this, he made ware particularly for the American market, and used incidents and scenes which appealed in a peculiar way to the growing nation. The art of printing on pottery had now become well known. Richard Sadler had been practising it as early as 1752, and though, for many years, only black was used yet blue was found to run equally as well. The designs were engraved on copper, and impressions made on tissue paper, with prepared paints mixed with oil, and transferred to the pottery. The deep, rich blue we admire so much recommended itself on account of its cheapness and durability, for although to-day we pay, with the greatest eagerness, twenty-three dollars for a tiny cup-plate, three and one half inches wide, it was made to sell for three pence or even less. Although we cannot say with assurance just why blue was chosen, the fact remains that all the Staffordshire potters used it, and to great advantage.

There is a certain style of design known as " flow blue," which has nondescript patterns, flowers, geometric designs, and occasionally landscapes, and which has nothing whatever of beauty or interest to recommend it, but which was sent over here in quantities, and of which there is still much to be found.

Of all discouragements which a china collector has to meet, the very worst is flowing blue, next comes the inevitable willow pattern, which every English potter made at one time or another, and which is as plentiful as blades of grass. It varies in colour from the fine old blue, to a tint so reddish as to be almost purple, and is shown in every degree of clearness. It is worth next to nothing, but owners of it hold it at the very highest market price.

After the rage for old blue had somewhat subsided, say between 1835 and 1850, some of the potters took to printing scenes from all over the world, in various colours, red, green, etc. This second period lacked the interest of the first, for the pieces were less meritorious and decidedly inartistic. Many of them are held in this country, and I am in receipt of scores of letters asking if they are not as valuable as old blue. Perhaps I should say instead that the owners think they are as valuable as old blue, and ask if this is not the case.

## *Enoch Wood.*

The list of Staffordshire potters should begin (after we except Wedgwood, who will be treated in a separate chapter), with the name of Wood. Ralph Wood was succeeded by his son Aaron, a clever cutter of moulds for salt-glazed stoneware with perforated and raised borders. About 1783 Enoch, youngest son of Ralph, started in the potting business for himself. He had been a sculptor and had modelled busts of many celebrated persons. Enoch, as before mentioned, is the one who is of the most interest to us, as the bulk of his work was made for, and sent to, this country. Although a prosperous and prolific potter, English writers on pottery give him scant mention, and know little about his work for the American market. In their own country the Woods, Ralph, Aaron and Enoch, are known principally for their successful figure work and busts. rather than for their flat ware.

There are two of these busts in the Boston Museum of Fine Arts, made about 1781, of the Rev. John Wesley and of John Whitfield.

They also made blue and white jasper and black ware. They marked few of these pieces, admirable though they were, and this practice they carried out in much of the china sent to this country. The pieces they did mark were sometimes impressed, the mark being circular and an inch in diameter. In the center is an eagle with a shield and below him " Semi-china." Surrounding this are the words " E. Wood & Sons, Burslem, Warranted." In addition to the impressed mark is frequently found a mark in blue, consisting of the name of the scene, an eagle with a branch in his claws, and a scroll flowing from his mouth with the words " E Pluribus Unum."

It is perhaps well for us that it seems to have been a custom among these potters to design certain borders, which grew to be as distinctive a mark of the firm employing them as the stamped name. Enoch Wood chose sea-shells, and of this border there were two arrangements :

*First.*  The central view is shown in a circle, and a cockle shell is conspicuous in the border. Name of scene on the back (See FIG. 5).

*Second.*  The central view in irregular opening. Shell border but without cockles. Name of scene generally on face (See FIG. 6).

In this same series are three views of the ship *Cadmus,* which brought Lafayette to this country, as a guest, in 1824. It was fitted up by a patriotic American merchant, who placed it at the General's disposal. This was only one incident of the many that showed

to our guest that for once, at least, a republic was not
ungrateful (FIG. 7).

As will be seen by reference to the index, there
were very many more examples of the first pattern
than of the second, though the latter makes rather
the prettier plate.   The firm name changed in 1790 to
Wood & Caldwell, when James Caldwell was taken
into the business.   This partnership lasted but two
years, and the name was changed to Enoch Wood &
Co., and then, in 1818, to Enoch Wood & Sons.

In FIG. 8 we show a sample of the work turned out
during the brief period when Caldwell was in the firm,
that is from 1790 to 1792.   It makes this jug over
one hundred and ten years old.   The body is a light
shade of blue, highly glazed, and the figures and
ornaments are in white.   It is a charming piece, and
must have been well made, for that it has been put to
severe usage is most evident; the inside is a perfect
net-work of fine cracks.   It was picked up in London
half a dozen years since in a curiosity shop, and was
a part of odds and ends which came from the sale of
the effects of Lord Chief Justice Coleridge, the eminent English jurist, who received great honours during
a visit to America some years previous.

I have seen in similar ware, also marked Wood
& Caldwell, a charming eight-inch-high flower-pot and
saucer.   It stands on the mantelshelf in a quaint old
house, on the same spot where it has stood for fifty
years, a receptacle for neatly rolled bits of string.   It
has passed down through many generations, and the
present owner never remembers it put to any other
use or in any other spot than where it now stands.

There is one other piece of Wood & Caldwell's work

Fig. 5.  CITY OF ALBANY.  *Wood.*

Fig. 6.  "CHIEF JUSTICE MARSHALL."  (Troy Line.)  *Wood.*

Fig. 7. SHIP "CADMUS." *Wood.*

Fig. 8. WOOD AND CALDWELL JUG

which I have seen, and which is so unique and beautiful that it deserves mention. It is also a pitcher, in size and shape like the one in the figure, except that the blue background is a somewhat handsomer shade. It was made for a Miss Caldwell, sister of James, and in this case the figures of children playing were coloured according to nature, with gowns of the prettiest pale shades of pink, straw-colour and green. The grouping is very lovely, and nearly identical with some of the designs made by Lady Templeton for Wedgwood. Miss Caldwell came to this country many years ago, and died here, and the jug has remained in the possession of her descendants. Unfortunately the condition of the jug is poor, though handle and lip are still perfect. Some of the figures have peeled off, showing that they were cast in moulds and then stuck on while the clay was wet, and before glazing. The name Wood & Caldwell is printed in capital letters, impressed in a straight line.

"Wood" alone is sometimes found impressed, and stands for the period before the sons were admitted to the firm. E. W. & S. is also found on many pieces printed in black, or in the colour of the design on the face. These are all of a later period.

The great bulk of the china made by the Woods has the name Enoch, or E. Wood & Sons, either impressed or stamped in blue on the back. An impressed stamp is made in the moist clay before glazing, and sometimes is almost filled up by the glaze, so that it is hard to distinguish. The blue marks may be put on either under or over glaze, and consist of the firm name sometimes the name of the pattern, and occasionally a wreath, scroll, or an eagle with the words " E Pluribus Unum." The words "stone," "stone china," or "semi-china," are also sometimes used.

The Woods made forty or more views of our scenery from sketches and prints, and most of them are valuable historical documents in the story of our country's progress. They not only made flat ware, as plates, platters, low vegetable dishes, etc., were called, but toilet sets and pitchers as well. FIG. 9 shows a fine dish, probably a platter for a soup tureen, seventeen inches long, and perfect. Besides the words "Catskill, N. Y.," it has on the back, in blue, "E Pluribus Unum," and an eagle. The border on this piece is unusually handsome and clear. FIG. 10 is another piece which belongs, like FIG. 9, to class one. It is a view of Lake George, N. Y., and has markings similar to FIG. 9 on the back.

There are curious details to be noted in collecting this old china. You never seem to find a piece pertaining to a particular locality in the place it celebrates. If you want a view of Albany you might begin your search in Buffalo, and *vice versa*. The city of Rochester, so far as is known, has but two plates bearing the Rochester aqueduct, and both were found out of the state.

FIG. 11 shows one of Wood's most celebrated pieces, Castle Garden and the Battery, N. Y. I am repeatedly asked by owners how much their pieces are worth, and have invented an answer to suit all cases. "Whatever you can get for it." If you can find a collector who is very anxious to have the particular piece you hold, you rather command the market, for the china collector is ever haunted by the fear that if he hesitates some other "fiend" will rush in and get his treasure. Sup-

Fig. 9. CATSKILL, N. Y. *Wood*.

Fig. 10. LAKE GEORGE, N. Y. *Wood*.

Fig. 11.  CASTLE GARDEN AND BATTERY.  *Wood*.

Fig. 12.  THREE HUDSON RIVER PLATES.  *Wood*.

WEST POINT.                    NEWBURG.                    CATSKILL MT. HOUSE.

pose that you sell to a dealer, you will get the very lowest price he can induce you to take, and if you sell at auction,—well, it depends much upon the weather and the auctioneer.   The mate to the platter which is shown brought at auction in New York City, at the Gilbert Sale, November 8, 1901, one hundred and seven dollars and fifty cents.   It is eighteen inches long and in proof condition.   The price certainly is exorbitant, but though it may never be reached again, it is matter of record that it has been given once. The platter, though interesting, as a mere pictorial piece is less attractive than many others, less rich in colour, as, though deep, it is dull,   One is glad to note many little curious details such as the footbridge between Castle Garden and the mainland.   It gives an idea of the beauty of the old Battery Walk where the " Four Hundred " of those days came forth of an afternoon to walk up and down in the shade and enjoy the sea-breeze.   This Battery, which is now given over to the immigrant, elevated road and the aquarium, was built as early as 1692.   It retains nothing of what it was originally except its name, for it was constructed " to make a platform upon the outmost point of rocks under the fort to command both rivers."   For many years the Battery was the City's parade ground.   Here the Pulaski Cadets, the Light Guard, the red-coated City Guards, and the Tompkins Blues went through countless evolutions before the eyes of the admiring townsfolk.   Here, also, was played between the Red Stockings and the Blue Stockings the national game. Innumerable pleasure boats sailed up and down, and the land faintly seen in the distance is Governor's Island, which was owned by the War Department even before 1812, and on which was a fort to guard the Narrows.

The old fort on the Battery was first called "Fort Manhattan." This was as early as 1614. It soon was too small for the thriving Dutch colony, and a new one was built called Fort Amsterdam. In 1664 the English captured the city and fort, and re-named the latter, in honour of the Duke of York, Fort James. It did not hold this name long, for in 1684 the Dutch recaptured it and re-christened it Fort William Henry. This was its briefest experience with any name, for in a few months the English got it back, and once more it was Fort James. After this it was successively Fort William, Fort Anne in 1702, and Fort George in 1714, and so it continued until, in the year 1789, it was demolished as useless.

Picturesque views of the Hudson River and of some of the thriving towns on the banks are frequently found in the blue, as well as in other colours. Wood made some charming ones. In FIG. 12 there are three such, each of the pieces being six-inch plates and having come together in one collection from different parts of the United States. The shell border shows us that they are by Wood, and the name of each view is on the back. The central view is the Hudson River near Newburg. The plate on the right shows the Catskill Mountain House, and on the left we have West Point. The scenes look decidedly unfamiliar to our modern eyes.

The year 1820 was distinguished as completing the second century since New England's shores were "first impressed by the footsteps of those who gave an empire birth." This event was celebrated in Boston by a banquet, at which Daniel Webster delivered the commemorative address which has become a classic in our literature. The entire dinner service was made in England by Enoch Wood & Sons and appropriately decorated with a representation of the " Landing of the Pilgrims." It is some of the handsomest china put out by this conscientious firm, and has a central view of a boat coming ashore and the astonished Indians regarding it (FIG. 13). The border is very handsome, of scrolls and four medallions, two of them showing ships and two of them inscriptions. The top one says "America Independent, July 4, 1776," and the lower one "Washington, born 1732, died 1792." On a rock in the picture are the names of some of the pilgrims.

Besides the dinner service itself a small surplus was made, which was sold as souvenirs. We give, in FIG. 14, one of the pitchers, on which the arrangement was a little different from that on the flat ware. The pieces are always in demand, and a ten-inch plate, in proof condition, should bring about fifteen dollars, though three were sold at the Haigh sale in Boston, for fourteen dollars and a half, eleven dollars, and eight dollars, respectively.

Rarest of all Wood's plates are two that are shown in FIG. 15. They are in the rich blue, with very handsome borders of large flowers, and commemorate the opening of the Erie Canal, that great event in the history of New York State, which took place October 26, 1825. There are three of these plates, the aqueducts at Rochester and Little Falls, and the entrance of the canal into the Hudson at Albany. We give the Rochester plate on the left, size seven and a half inches, and the Little Falls in the center. This latter plate has been found of two sizes, ten-inch soup-plate and eight-inch plate. These plates are not marked except on the face with the name of the view, but a washbowl is on record with the Albany view and the floral border and with the impressed mark of E. Wood & Sons. As late as 1806 the town of Little Falls, two hundred miles from New York, was regarded as very much in the backwoods, and an English traveller relates with wonder that at an "inn there they had a tablecloth on the table, with plates, knives and forks. That the breakfast was very good, consisting of tea, bread and butter, steak, eggs and cheese, potatoes, beets and salt." All this profusion was furnished for twenty-five cents. This was nearly twenty years before the plate was made. The Table Rock, Niagara, plates are also much esteemed and sell for good prices. FIG. 16 shows one.

There is also china of a much less artistic value made by this firm, sometimes in one colour and some-times in two, such as the Washington vase, which is marked on the back " Pearl Stoneware, Washington Vase," and below " E. W. & Co." There is also the Washington memorial, blue and black, or red and green, with border of urns and willows, marked on the back " E. W. & S. " The shapes of the plates are pretty but the printing is badly done, the design is almost grotesque, and the colour feeble.

There were many American designs made about the same time, signed " E. W. & S.," and given the name of "Celtic China." They were printed in various colours, including light blue and green, and command a very small sum to-day, their only value being as heir-looms. The Woods made a few views of Canadian

Fig. 13. LANDING OF THE
PILGRIMS. *Wood.*

Fig. 14. LANDING OF THE
PILGRIMS PITCHER. *Wood.*

Fig. 15. ROCHESTER, LITTLE FALLS, UTICA. *Wood.*
( Erie Canal Plates.

Fig. 16. TABLE ROCK, NIAGARA.
*Wood.*

Fig. 17. FALLS OF MONTMORENCY,
NEAR QUEBEC. *Wood.*

Fig. 18. WOMAN OF SAMARIA. *Wood.*

Fig. 19. MARINE HOSPITAL,
LOUISVILLE, KY. *Wood.*

scenes also, one of which, the "Falls of Montmorency near Quebec," is given in FIG. 17. It has the shell border and is a very handsome plate.

There were also made by this same firm, in dark blue, a set of scriptural pictures on china, with a border of flowers and scrolls, with scriptural devices. In FIG. 18 we give one of these called "Christ and the Woman of Samaria." These designs seem to have been held in greater respect than the pieces which we call historical, probably on account of the significance of the decoration. There were also some few designs made by this firm in other colours than blue, called the "Sun of Righteousness" series, on account of the border which shows a rising sun as a feature of the decoration.

During the last two years much interest has been aroused in the gathering together of English views, made by the same potters, and at about the same period as the American scenes. As recently as eighteen or twenty months ago the pieces could have been picked up for the proverbial song; but every day sees them soar in price, and new collections are being started in every direction. Attics and closets are being ransacked, and these pieces, which were neglected by collectors of Anglo-American scenes, are coming to the fore in a rapid manner. In all this desire for these pieces it is hard to know of cupboards and bureaus, closets and presses being filled to overflowing with specimens of this precious china. I know such a place in a lumberman's office in New York State. All his treasures are hidden away; he seldom looks at them; few people know that he has them. If you attempt to buy, even offering very tempting prices, he will shuffle about, giving one excuse after another until the final one comes, " Mother would not like it if I sold that one," the truth being that " mother " neither knows nor cares about them. I doubt if she is aware of their number or value. This same hoarder has the curious fancy of collecting old clocks, not the "grand-father" pattern, but a large mantel clock, with carved side pillars and top and with painted glass pictures in the door. He does not care for them as clocks, and immediately removes the works, substituting one or two pine shelves, and using them as cupboards. Some of them are of great rarity and beauty and it would drive a collector wild to see the uses to which they are put. Old papers, bottles, and occasionally china are tucked away in them, their narrowness precluding their being used for storage of articles of any size.

For actual beauty of design the English views excel the American for the reason that the subjects that they depict are of greater beauty. Old and famous castles, manor houses and cathedrals possess more picturesque lines than our early buildings, and besides the glamour of antiquity, most of them have been made famous by their owners or builders, and by the history which has clustered about them. The Woods made perhaps a hundred of such views, over eighty have already been recorded, and more are constantly coming to hand. On one set they used a shell border of a different arrangement from those with which we are familiar on American ware, and this is rather handsomer and more carefully worked out. The opening is irregular, and the name of the view is introduced on the face. There are twelve or fifteen

Fig. 20. THE LIMEHOUSE DOCK, REGENT'S CANAL. *Wood.*

Fig. 21. WARWICK CASTLE. *Wood.*

Fig. 22. ELY. *Wood*.

Fig. 23. MILL AT CHARENTON. *Wood*.

views in this set, of places generallv. like Yarmouth, Isle of Wight, Dublin, Cowes, etc.

A second set, called "London Views," has the scene in an oblong medallion, with a frame-like margin, and the entire border of the plate or platter is covered with large bunches of grapes. This border is completely in accord with the laws of design, for it fills agreeably the space for which it is intended, is decorative, and the pattern of it is pleasing to the eye. The scenes in this set are chiefly from Regent's Park. One of them is the Limehouse Dock, Regent's Canal, with which we are more familiar to-day from Whistler's etching, made about forty years ago (FIG. 20). The names of these places are in a scroll with leaves, the words "London Views" being at the top, and below it the name of the particular object, and below that, "Regent's Park."

The third series is of country seats and castles, many of them well known to us, like Warwick and Windsor castles, Kenilworth and Guy's Cliff. The border to this set is flowers and grapes, with vines,— morning glories probably,—and on the edge is a twisted margin. The name of each place is on the back, in a sort of ribbon scroll with a few leaves.

The fourth set, "English Cities", is marked on the back "E. W. & S.," has the name of the series, and of the particular city on two scrolls, which are surrounded by a bishop's mitre and staff. The border is very unlike what we are familiar with as coming from this firm, and is not unlike the borders made by Jackson. It has six medallions, and a very rich arrangement of flowers and scrolls, and the central view is set in a regular circle or oval, separated from the border by an ornamental little pattern. These pieces are printed in different colours, including light blue, and, on account of the beauty of the scenes, and the careful workmanship are very handsome. There are in the neighbourhood of twenty of these views so far identified. (FIG. 22 shows Ely.)

Foreign designs made by this firm are not hard to find in this country, particularly a set of French views connected in one way or another with Lafayette. The border is very pretty and not so stiff as the shell ones which have been shown, and is composed of fleurs-de-lys, hollyhocks and bunches of grapes, pendant across the top. (FIG. 23, " Mill at Charenton.")

In addition to the views already enumerated, E. Wood & Sons produced many views of scenery characteristic of other countries, India, Africa, Italy, etc. They are to be found in considerable numbers, among them being such well-known places as Calcutta and " Cape Coast Castle on the Gold Coast, Africa." "A Ship of the Line in the Downs," is made to appeal to our national pride by bearing a large American flag.

## Andrew Stevenson.
## Ralph and James Clews.

Next in importance to the Woods, as having produced valuable and beautiful pottery, comes the name of Clews. In this case, as in those of several other potters, there were two brothers, and Ralph and James

Clews have left their name on much highly desirable pottery and semi-china.   Before taking up properly the product of the Clews pottery we must speak of the potter who immediately preceded them at the Cobridge works, Andrew Stevenson.   As early in the last century as 1808 pottery works were established at Cobridge, Staffordshire, England, by the firm of Bucknall & Stevenson.   They seem to have made the ordinary English wares, but after a few years Bucknall withdrew, and Stevenson carried on the works alone.   It was not long before he began to work largely to please the American market, and though he turned out only about twenty odd American designs, every one of them is good in colour and workmanship. He also had an advantage over many of his contemporaries in getting some better sketches to work from than the crude prints which were sent over from here.   An artist from Dublin, W. G. Wall, Esq., came to this country in 1818, and made quite a number of sketches of our prominent buildings.   (FIGS 24 and 25 are of the Almshouse, New York, and Columbia College.) It must have been arranged beforehand that he should furnish these to the Stevenson works, for he began to send them back to England very soon after his arrival here.   A number of designs were issued with his name in blue on the back of each piece, and yet these pottery works were sold by Stevenson to the Clews brothers late in that year, or early in 1819. In FIG. 26 is one of the views on a ten-inch plate.   It is a rare piece, New York from Brooklyn Heights. This view is shown upon plates and platters, the view being different on the two pieces.   See FIG. 27.   It is marked very plainly on the back in blue, underglaze, and bears Wall's name as well. He chose some curious subjects for his brush, among them a view of "Weehawk" as he calls it. The smaller plate in FIG. 26 is one of a dozen or more with similar border, which come at present under the heading "Maker Unknown." It is a view on the Hudson River near Fishkill. A plate has recently been found bearing the name of Stevenson, but having a shell border like Wood's.

Ralph Stevenson, who also potted at Cobridge, but some years later, is considered in another chapter. They both used as a mark the name "Stevenson" impressed. A circular stamp, impressed, of a crown, surrounded by the words "Stevenson, Warranted Staffordshire," comes on many pieces, which also bear the name of the view in blue, with an eagle. Sometimes an urn is found, with a bit of drapery about it and the name of the scene. This is not common on American pieces.

Andrew Stevenson made a series of very beautiful English views with floral borders, and is supposed to be the maker of FIG. 82, which is shown among the portrait pieces and spoken of there. All the English views were made about the same time as the American views, say from 1820 to 1840, and many of them seem of quite a superior degree of workmanship. The border in the English series is large flowers, roses with leaves, etc., the same border in fact as is found on the four-medallion plate with Niagara view (FIG. 82). The series consists of about twenty views, and all form very decorative pieces for shelf or wall. They are marked with an urn, and plates and platters are the pieces usually found.

It was Andrew Stevenson who was succeeded by
James and Ralph Clews. These potters worked at
Cobridge from 1818 to 1834, or possibly a year later,
and James came to this country in 1836 and endeavored to start a pottery at Troy, Indiana. The
story of his failure is told in E. A. Barber's "Pottery
and Porcelain of the United States," and was brought
about by the difficulty of obtaining competent workmen and clay for working. Since that time large beds
of kaolin have been found within a few miles of his
factory, one of the disagreeable freaks of fate to which
we are often subjected.

Undoubtedly the most celebrated china which Clews
put forth were the two patterns known as "Landing
of Lafayette," made to celebrate that hero's visit to
this country in 1824, and what is known as the
"States" pattern, bearing a border of festoons containing the names of the fifteen states. Both of the
views are great favourites among collectors, and are
generally among the first pieces sought. There is a
large quantity of the Lafayette china in this country,
and it has a beautiful border of leaves and flowers.
All the pieces, from three and a half-inch cup-plates,
to those of largest size are desirable, and they maintain
a stiff price, even if repaired. Ten-inch plates in
good condition bring ten dollars easily, and the platters
proportionately larger sums (FIG. 28).

The platter shown is what the owner calls "turkey
size," eighteen inches, and is in a splendid state of
preservation, having only a few scratches on its face.
It shows another view of Castle Garden, its footbridge
being a conspicuous object. All the shipping is
gathered in the foreground to make a brave showing.

This pattern shows several inaccuracies with regard to these boats which have been discovered recently. The two boats with the three masts were intended for the *Fulton* and the *Chancellor Livingston*, but as the *Fulton* had but one mast, it is evident that the English potter used his fancy to embellish his designs. The small boat in the foreground, without any masts, is quite as bad as the *Fulton*, for up to this time no steamers were made without masts, in this country at least. Steam was too unknown a quantity to be pressed too hard, and sails were used in case of accident, or to help along.

The States pattern presents many pleasing varieties. The border is always the same but the center varies according to the space to be filled, and the fancy of the potter. The border is composed of festoons, bearing the names of the fifteen states, and between the festoons are stars with five or eight points. There are at least a dozen different views in the center pictures. FIG. 29 is the White House at Washington. Besides the White House, Mount Vernon and the Custom House, there is one view of an English castle. There is a three-story building, also, which often appears, the foreground being varied by sheep or cows, or women walking. However, it is always extremely simple to name this platter under any conditions, for America and Independence are ever in full view, and the medallion of Washington is always the same. This platter brought at auction last year, at the Haigh sale in Boston, forty-six dollars.

The Clewses did not confine themselves to one or two borders as closely as did the Woods. The flowers and scroll is one of their best-known ones. On the

Fig. 26.   FISHKILL.
*Maker unknown.*

NEW YORK FROM BROOKLYN
*A. Stevenson.*

Fig. 27.   PLATTER OF NEW YORK FROM BROOKLYN HEIGHTS.
*A. Stevenson.*

Fig. 28.   LANDING OF LAFAYETTE.
*Clews.*

Fig. 30.   PITTSFIELD ELM.   *Clews*

Fig. 29.   STATES PLATTER.   *Clews.*

Pittsfield Elm plate is found a very handsome border of passion flowers and medallions.

The piece in FIG. 30 is a ten-inch soup-plate in perfect condition. It brought twenty dollars at private sale, but inferior copies, not perfect, may be picked up for less. The Puritan character of this design is well in keeping with the scene it was meant to perpetuate. In Revolutionary days the minister at this meeting-house was an ardent patriot, and one Sunday, so the story goes, he entered the pulpit wearing a long cloak. He began his sermon with moderation, but before long his patriotism grew too much for him, and throwing the cloak aside he showed himself in the Continental uniform. Calling on the men in the congregation he led them forth under the elm shown on the plate, and organized them into a company. The fence was put around the tree in 1825, showing the plates to be of later date, for up to that time the neighbouring farmers had used it for a hitching-post, as many iron staples driven into the tree testified. It was too late to save it, and, in the early sixties, it fell, the wood from it being made into cups and bowls.

The Clewses also issued a set of designs in various colours,—red, brown, black, light blue, etc. They were taken from sketches, by W. G. Wall, in water colour, comprising what he called his " Hudson River Portfolio." They are handsome pieces with a very rich and graceful border of flowers and birds, and they command fair prices. Clews also made three sets of dark blue designs, which are eagerly snapped up by collectors and fetch larger prices. They are the Syntax, Wilkie, and Don Quixote designs. The first series contains the largest number of pieces, and is taken from those quaint books illustrated by Rowlandson, and for which William Comb, for forty-three years an inmate of the King's Bench debtor's prison, wrote the verses. The first volume was printed by Ackerman in book form, as early as 1815, and was called "Doctor Syntax in search of the Picturesque." The success of this book was so great that it was followed by the "Second Tour of Doctor Syntax in search of Consolation," published in 1820, and in 1821 by the third tour, "In Search of a Wife." About thirty of these designs have come to hand.

In FIG. 31 is shown a small tray, supposedly the tray of a fruit dish (though I have heard of a soup tureen which stands in a similar tray, but larger), and is in perfect condition. This picture is from the third tour, and is called "The Advertisement for a Wife."

FIG. 32 shows a scene from the second tour, "Doctor Syntax and the Blue-Stocking Beauty." Only two pieces of this pattern have come under my notice, both six-inch plates, and for one of them, which is held in Boston, the price asked is forty dollars.

There must have been a great demand for this china, which was made to sell for about seven or eight cents apiece, and Clews took advantage of the growing market.

Sir David Wilkie, an English artist who lived and worked during the first half of the nineteenth century, made a set of comic pictures which were very popular, and from which plates were made by Clews. The borders are beautiful, a passion flower is conspicuous, and there are other flowers and scrolls. The colour is deep and rich, and they are very decorative.  In FIG. 33 is shown "The Valentine."  The precious missive seems to have been snatched away from its owner, and she is trying to get possession of it again.  The other views are similarly coarse in sentiment, but they are certainly very ornamental on the wall and a beautiful piece of colour.

Not content with catering to the popular taste with these Syntax and Wilkie patterns, Clews made the third set, scenes from the life of Don Quixote.  The border is less pleasing than in the other patterns, as it is irregular points and flowers.  The colour of the pieces is good, however, and they command fair prices, not as high as either of the other sets, a nine and three quarters-inch plate of "Sancho Panza at the Boar Hunt," bringing eleven dollars at auction.

There are two variations which have recently come to light in the Syntax plates, which present two of those china puzzles that are constantly arising to con-fuse the china collector.  One of these puzzles is a plate, "Doctor Syntax returned from his Tour," in a medium shade of blue with a raised border.  The mark of Clews is on the back, the stilt marks are all right, and the piece is light in weight, as all this ware is.  I have also been informed by a china collector that he has in his possession a Syntax plate with the oak leaf and acorn border, which has always been ascribed to R. Stevenson and Williams.

Then comes the series of English views, consisting chiefly of castles, abbeys and cathedrals.  About twenty-five of these have come to hand, but all are not yet identified.  The borders vary, some being much more beautiful than others.  One of them, enclosing such views as Fountains Abbey, Ripon, etc., is large flowers, too large in fact for the space they occupy. The series is called "Select Views," and bears this name on the back enclosed in a little wreath of leaves tied with a ribbon, and below, on a ribbon scroll, the name of the view. Bluebells and aster-like flowers make up the border of a second set, and just here another puzzle comes to the front. Although this bluebell border is used by Clews on at least eight or ten views of such famous places as Wells Cathedral, and Dulwich Castle, it is as a border of Adams that we know it best. Lumley Castle (FIG. 34) is an example. Occasionally the pieces, in addition to the frame with flowers which enclosed the name of the view on the back, bear the name of Clews, but not always.

There is another border also used by Clews, composed of trees meeting in foliage at the top and with growing plants at the base. This is entirely surrounded by scroll work, consisting of circles with a little leaf in the middle. Adams and Clews both used this border also, and it can only be explained by presuming that Adams bought some of Clews' patterns when the latter's works were closed. The exact dates, that is within a year or two, when various potters began or stopped potting, are quite uncertain. The authorities to be relied on are town histories and chronicles, and these are not so accurate as one could wish. In the American views we have come to depend quite implicitly on the certainty with which we can allot a certain border to a certain potter, so that these vagaries on English views are quite confusing. However, on these foliage border views the name of

Fig. 31. "THE ADVERTISEMENT FOR A WIFE."
SYNTAX TRAY. *Clews.*

Fig. 32. "BLUE-STOCKING BEAUTY."
SYNTAX PLATE. *Clews.*

Fig. 33. "THE VALENTINE." *Clews.*

Fig. 34. LUMLEY CASTLE, DURHAM. *Clews.*

Adams or Clews is always stamped, but while they make that matter clear, they never mark the name of the view, which can only be identified from engravings or views on other china.

Clews' mark, like most of the others, is subject to variations. One of them is circles, impressed with a crown in the center, and "Clews Warranted Stafford-shire," in a circle about it. The "Picturesque Views" set had a mark of its own, which, in addition to the crown, and "Clews Warranted Staffordshire," impressed, was put on all the pieces. It is a little view with trees and a lake with a small boat. It has through it a bar with the name of the view. These were probably some of the last work done at the Co-bridge works by James Clews, before he closed them in 1829 or 1830.

## *Joseph Stubbs.*

For a potter who did not make any great number of pieces for the American market, the name of Joseph Stubbs is held in unusually high estimation. Nor, after you have become acquainted with his work, will this seem strange. Every piece which bears his name, and even those which bear only his well-known border, are admirable pieces of work in every way—colour, design and finish. FIG. 35 and FIG. 36 are a platter and a plate by this maker, who made table services decorated with American designs. He owned the Dale Hall works at Burslem, from about 1790 to 1829 or 1830. The series he sent to this country is deco-rated with what is called the eagle and scroll border, and is generally arranged on plates with three eagles at equal distances between flowers and scrolls, and on platters with four eagles. FIG. 35 is always eagerly sought. It is the Boston State House platter, and on the left is John Hancock's house, and in the foreground his cows, or so it is supposed. On this platter there are but three eagles in the border, though it is a sixteen-inch size, and there are no gravy wells.

The question of these same gravy wells is a much mooted one among collectors. Many prefer their pieces without these depressions, which are found on many of the choicest platters. It is always to be remembered, however, that, originally, the platters with wells were those which brought the highest price. The Boston State House platter sold in Boston, in 1901, for fifty-five dollars.

This lovely old platter always furnishes so much food for thought that it seems slighting it to pass it by with a mere mention. It shows those delightfully sylvan days when the Common was common, a pasture for cows. John Hancock's were not the only ones pastured there, and the practice was continued till so late as 1830, when it was discontinued owing to the protests of indignant citizens who objected to being " tossed and gored " while pursuing their peaceful way across the public grounds. The story goes, that once upon a time many guests descended upon Mr. Hancock, and the servants were put to it for supplies ; so that several went out and milked all the cows on the Common to provide, at least, enough milk.

It was also from this same house we see through the trees that the china was thrown from the dining-room window. Mr. Hancock was, in his later years, a sufferer from gout, and during his attacks the clatter

Fig. 35. PLATTER—BOSTON STATE HOUSE AND COMMON. *Stubbs.*

Fig. 36. NAHANT. *Stubbs.*

Fig. 37. CAPITOL AT WASHINGTON. *Ridgway.*

Fig. 38. ALMS HOUSE, NEW YORK. *Ridgway.*

of china on the mahogany made him very angry
One day, finally, it irritated him so much that he
ordered his negro butler to throw it all out of the window and substitute pewter ; so the Lowestoft—fortunately it was not "old blue"—was thrown carefully
on the grass, so as not to damage it, and became loot
for the butler.   Negroes are true lovers of china ; they
hoard it away, and are always loth to part with it.   I
know of much which has come out of cabins within
the last few years, where it has lain since war times,
when it was given away, or was rescued from deserted
houses and safely stowed away.

The Nahant plate is interesting also, showing life at
the beach and a curious vehicle in the middle distance.
Was it that fashionable equipage known as the Italian
chaise ?

The mark was Stubbs, impressed, in capital letters, and, sometimes, " Joseph Stubbs, Longport,"
in a circle around a star.   Apparently he took into
partnership later a man named Kent, for the name
" Stubbs & Kent, Longport," is found on many pieces.
He made the milk-maid designs found on tea and
toilet sets, and I have seen parts of tea-sets with decorations of flowers, the pieces of exactly the same shape
and size as the milk-maid pattern, and having the
same curious, raised ornament in place of handles.
Prime does not mention either Stubbs, or Stubbs &
Kent, neither does Chaffers, and it is strange that
more is known about many of these potters and their
products in this country than in their own homes.   In
addition to the fifteen or twenty American patterns
by which we know Stubbs, he made some beautiful
English views.

# CHAPTER III.

## STAFFORDSHIRE WARES, CONTINUED.

MANY collectors who began to gather these beautiful wares years ago have been able to weed out their
poor specimens, and to settle down, either on one particular colour, like old blue, or on the different coloured
printed wares, or some one class of specimens like teapots, pitchers or cup-plates, which latter class is, perhaps, the most difficult to collect, and certainly, in
proportion to the size of the objects, the most costly.
For my own part it seems as if the greater pleasure lay
in a certain catholicity of taste, that a corner cupboard
—the most charming place to display old china—is a
greater mine of wealth and enjoyment if a jug has for
a background a platter or plate, and if a rare old
pepper-pot stands contentedly beside a cup and
saucer.

If you "specialize," as seems the tendency now-a-
days in everything, what a collection the china connected with New York State alone makes, and if you
include the coloured printed ware, as well as old blue,
your collection will number considerably over one
hundred pieces. Plates and platters are comparatively easy to obtain. If you have the "gift," which
must be born with you, like the knack of spelling, or
good looks, china collecting will come easy. Pieces
will drop down before you, fairly "blow in," as one
collector has it, and you will gather treasures from

most unexpected places, and for small sums. That the ways of the collector are devious every one knows. The simon-pure collector has got rid of every rag of conscience, and in return has his collection, a fair exchange many of us think.

If you live in a small city or town you may add to your stores by sitting down and letting it be known that you buy old china. You will be surprised at the result, for though good, bad and indifferent will be presented to you, careful culling will give much that is good. Odd and unpromising bundles often yield rare and curious pieces. Not long since a collector was heard to remark that a ragged newspaper bundle made his heart beat and his wallet throb in his pocket. He never knew what would be drawn forth. I saw three plates recently, all by Clews, ten-inch, dark blue, and perfect, one from the Syntax, one from the Wilkie, and one from the Don Quixote set, which came in this unexpected way. A man, who showed that he held close communion with the soil, appeared at the front door with a negligently wrapped newspaper parcel one summer morning. He announced that he had come to "dicker," and then ensued a most amusing scene, he falling and the collector rising, till at last they met, and the bargain was struck. One's feelings are apt to get the better of one under such circumstances. The seller would not tell how he came in possession of the plates, the only statement that could be extracted from him was a nonchalant "Oh, I got them in our town." What the town lost no doubt it never knew, what the collector gained he feels tingling through his veins every time he regards his plates.

Embarked on the hunt yourself, you never approach your quarry with the direct question. " Have you old china to sell?" If you did your quest would be in vain. After selecting your house, which will probably be well weather-beaten, with straggling lilac bushes beside the door, and will perhaps boast a well-sweep, you modestly knock, and when the door is opened a crack, ask, " Does Mrs. Preston live here?" Of course you know she does not, and are not disappointed in the reply, which you follow up by asking, " Do you know where she does live?" You are not amazed that they do not, and then proceed to step three in your pre-arranged schedule, and say, " I am sorry, for I thought she might have some old china she would part with." Observe, you entirely eschew the word "sell," it is "part with." No doubt the party of the second part behind the door will, by this time, have opened it a little wider, and if she has the truly hospitable spirit of the country, will say, "Come right in, perhaps I have got some." If she does not, you must get along as well as you can by asking if she knows of anybody in the neighbourhood who has. When once inside the door the task is comparatively easy, but every collector has his own little methods. I know of one who has successfully worked a portion of New Jersey, and who located many choice specimens but could not get even within the houses which contained them. He had in his employ a young man of insignificant appearance, who had a " way with him," who followed after the collector, at a decent interval of a day or two, and gathered in easily and at small prices the specimens which the collector himself had not even been able to see.

The true collector, who gathers his wares for the pleasure of it, and who is content to let his collection grow by degrees, here a plate and there a platter, now a pepper-pot and next month a pitcher, will have each piece stand to him for joyful memories and difficulties overborne. You may make mistakes, but what of that ? Tuck the ware away when you have found out your error ; you will know better next time.

## *J. & W. Ridgway.*

Of course with the series of the well-known potters one cannot make mistakes, and in following down the Staffordshire potteries we come next to consider the Ridgways, one of the best-known names, in America anyway, in connection with the much-sought-after "old blue."

The pottery built at Hanley, Staffordshire, England, in 1794, by Job Ridgway, the father of the Ridgway brothers, produced much beautiful table service and toilet sets as well, and a quantity of it was sent to America. After some years the sons, John and William, were admitted to partnership, and the firm was known as Ridgway & Sons. Still later, about 1814, after the death of Job Ridgway, the father, the firm name became J. & W. Ridgway, and it is through the work of the sons that we become most familiar with the output of these potteries.

The chief contribution which J. & W. Ridgway made to the dark blue American china was what was known as the "Beauties of America" series. There are twenty or more views on the various pieces which

comprised the table services, and in FIG. 37 we give
the "Capitol at Washington," FIG. 38 "Almshouse,
New York," and FIG. 39 "Boston Hospital." In
FIG. 40 is repeated the view shown in FIG. 37 the
"Capitol at Washington," as it is the only drainer for
a fish plate that I have come across. The dish to
which it belongs has, long since, been broken, or at
least parted company, and it is a decorative piece,
even with the numerous holes that pierce it. The
border of this series of "American Beauties" is a conventional rose with a few leaves set in medallions,
while around the central view is a small pointed edge
with dots. The colour is not so dark a blue as is seen
in many of Wood's pieces, is clearer and more shaded,
giving in this way a greater variety to each design.
In fact some of Wood's ware, for instance some of the
French views, are so dark that it is hard to distinguish
the pattern, showing that in many cases the designs
were used after they had become too worn to do good
work.

As is usual with this early china, the "beauties"
were chiefly alms and court houses, insane asylums
and churches, but the workmanship is so fine, the
colour so rich, and the medallion border so pleasing,
that every specimen of this china is truly a beauty,
and worth getting for its decorative value, if for
no other reason. The "Octagon Church, Boston"
(FIG. 41), is a notably handsome plate. It is really
the "New South Church," and came to be called "Octagon" from the shape of the body of the building,
which was eight-sided. The original church was dedi-
cated in January, 1717. The pulpit was filled at first
by candidates who were paid the moderate sum of

STAFFORDSHIRE WARES, *Continued.* 43

twenty shillings per sermon. The picture on the china is not of the old church, but as it appeared when rebuilt in 1814. The church was beautifully situated at the corner of Bedford and Summer streets. The octagonal body was built in a square of seventy-six feet diameter, and the steeple, "sky scrapers" being unknown then, was deemed very lofty. This church was demolished in 1868, to give way to business buildings, and our "American Beauty" gains new value as showing a New England landmark now swept away. The quaint vehicle, a travelling chaise no doubt, with post-boy, is as curious to our eyes as the famous "one hoss shay," and we can hardly imagine a modish Boston belle, with her sprigged India muslin and Leghorn bonnet with ostrich plumes, getting about in such a conveyance.

From 1814 to 1830, the brothers Ridgway worked together; but at the latter date they separated, John, the elder, carrying on the works at Cauldon Place, built by his father in 1802, while William established half a dozen works in Staffordshire, and turned out much ware for the American market. Indeed so highly did he think of this country as a market for his goods that he placed them on sale in several cities, and came to this country with a view to establishing a pottery here. A site was selected in Kentucky, but the plans got little further, and William Ridgway returned to England.

After the separation of the brothers the making of the "Beauties of America" series was stopped. John Ridgway made several patterns for the Harrison campaign of 1840, of variations of the Log Cabin, which were printed in black, brown, red and pale blue. The border was large stars, the space between them being filled with scattered stars of a much smaller size. Flatware, teapots and pitchers are found with these designs. The marks found on Ridgway's " Beauties of America " series are all in blue. First come the words " Beauties of America," below that the name of the particular view, and below that " J. & W. Ridgway."

William Ridgway made about fifteen patterns from American views, but they are printed in other colours than dark blue. There is a small series of views, printed in light blue, marked "Catskill Moss," and " C. C.," which have only recently been identified as being originated by William Ridgway. The borders are irregular scales overlapped by sprays of moss. The most interesting view in the series—there are but six or seven so far identified—is a well-wooded scene with a railroad showing one of the very early engines, more of an English than an American type. However, the first locomotive used in this country was of English make, and was called the " Stourbridge Lion." The cars are of the stage-coach pattern, but the view is plainly marked " Albany and Schenectady R. R." This road, sixteen miles long, was opened in 1830, and for the first year the cars were drawn by horses, so the view was probably made a year or two later.

In fact, the foundations on which the name of Ridgway must rest are the " Beauties of America " series and their English views, and they are broad enough to stand for many a long year yet.

John Ridgway made one dark blue design of the Capitol at Washington which is still made by his successors. There are also to be found pitchers of white ware, called the " Apostle " and " Tournament " pitch-

Fig. 39. BOSTON HOSPITAL. *Ridgway.*

Fig. 40. FISH PLATTER SHOWING THE CAPITOL AT WASHINGTON. *Ridgway.*

Fig 41. OCTAGON CHURCH, BOSTON. *Ridgway.*

Fig. 42. LAFAYETTE
LANDING.
*Clews.*

MT. VERNON.
*Ridgway.*

BATTERY AND CASTLE
GARDEN.
*Wood.*

ers. They are interesting and I know of one particularly fine specimen with a cover, also of the ware.
These Apostle jugs are very quaint in their arrangement. They are octagonal in shape, which, of course,
gives room for only eight apostles. The other four are
accommodated as follows: one forms the handle, one is
below the lip, and one within and one on the outside
of the lip. Those in the niches are full length, dignified figures; the last four are rather crowded. In FIG.
42 is shown one other "Beauties of America" piece, a
preserve dish giving a view of Mt. Vernon. On
either side are grouped cup-plates, on the left a
"Landing of Lafayette," and on the right "Castle
Garden," the latter by Wood, the former by Clews.
They are three and a half inches across the face, and
both are remarkably clear impressions of the views
shown.

As we have said before, the collecting of cup-plates
is remarkably difficult, yet in South Framingham,
Massachusetts, there is a single collection numbering
over four hundred of these tiny pieces. That the
practice which we condemn as reprehensible to-day was
in good repute among our ancestors, these cup-plates
abundantly testify. Great-grandmama could not bear
to have her linen stained, or her mahogany marred
by the rims of teacups; so when the fragrant Bohea—
I doubt if they had Orange Pekoe in those days—was
poured into the saucer to cool, the cup was neatly
placed in the little plate provided for it.

All the pieces of the historic sets seem to survive
except these plates. The only "Beauties of America"
cup-plate I have heard of is in this Massachusetts collection, and has on it a picture of the Baltimore

Exchange.   Side by side with this choice piece are a
" Stoughton Church," Philadelphia, with the acorn border, a " Mendenhall Ferry," " Savannah Bank," and the
" Pittsfield Elm."   " Mendenhall Ferry" is unusual on
a cup-plate, yet two five and one-half inch plates with
this view have come to light recently in a negro cabin.
The " Savannah Bank" is more unusual still.   There
are also examples of the Syntax, Wilkie and Don
Quixote designs.

A year or two ago I wrote that " historic cup-plates
were worth their weight in gold," and some of my
correspondents took exception to my statement.
Within a few weeks I have heard of two four-inch
Lovejoy cup-plates which have come upon the market, and give the respective prices they brought.   The
first was sold at public auction in New York City,
and brought twenty-three dollars.   The second was
"traded" by a collector, with two dollars and fifty
cents added, for the four following pieces; one nine-
inch, dark-blue Wilkie plate " The Valentine," in
proof condition, by Clews; one ten-inch, pink " Catskill Mt. House, U. S.," by Adams, proof; one seven
and one-half-inch, dark-blue, "Southampton, Hampshire," proof; one ten-inch brown, Picturesque Views
plate, " Troy from Mt. Ida."   It seems as if my esti-
mate had hardly been high enough.

The Ridgways—to pass on from American pieces
—like all other potters of their time made many English views.   These are all distinguished, like the other
pieces from their potteries, by fine colour and good designs.   The borders are unusual, flowers alternating
with quaint medallions of children and goats.   The
central view is almost invariably set in an eight-sided

panel, but the views are all made from careful sketches and are handsome in colour and design (FIG. 43). It is quite noticeable that the English views are much better than the American ones, probably from the better class of drawings they had to work from. Mr. Prime mentions in his valuable work on " Pottery and Porcelain " that they sometimes used the same view under different names. He says that he has the " State House at Boston " on one plate and the "City Hall, New York," on another, both views being of the latter building. The Ridgways also started a series with a very elaborate border of twisted scrolls which they called the "Zoological Gardens." Two designs have come to light so far: the bird cages and bear cages. They are printed in various colours and were probably of late production.

## *Ralph Stevenson.*

In studying and gathering this Staffordshire ware, although it is all lovely and you cannot afford to miss a piece that you can possibly make your own, yet it is impossible to prevent preferences for particular makers, either from the colour, consistency of paste, or manner of printing their ware. Everybody strives after Ralph Stevenson's designs. There are identified, so far, about twenty-one or twenty-two, and when you secure one it is generally put in a commanding position in your collection (FIG. 44). All the designs with the vine-leaf border, which are so ornamental, are eagerly sought and bring high prices, and you may find these same central views with a raised border in white.　One collector has written that he has a Syntax plate with the acorn and oak leaf border, which is quite as well known as the vine leaf.　Perhaps it is the air of mystery that surrounds all that is known of this potter and his work, either when he potted alone or in company with Williams, which makes his pieces so desirable.　No date can be given, with any degree of accuracy, as to just when this firm worked, or whether it was before or after the partnership that Stevenson alone put forth his handsome pieces.　It is curious that in less than one hundred years the history of this man and his pottery should be completely lost.　His works were at Cobridge in Staffordshire, and no doubt he potted at the same time that the other Staffordshire works were sending their wares here.

Carlyle says: "From a small window one may see the infinite."　We would paraphrase it to read: "On a small plate one may read the history of a nation."　In FIG. 45 is given a view of the Battle of Bunker Hill, that event in our history which has made a hundred thousand men to fight more bravely, and caused the arrogance of other nations to meet with an unexpected check.　It is a lovely old tray, part of a fruit dish; for there was, no doubt, a basket to stand it in when it was first sent over.　The round spots in the border are holes which pierce it, a very curious style of ornamentation.　As we see it on the china the battle seems almost a toy affair, the proverbial "thin red line" broken by two little prancing horses in the center.　But in reality the very élite of the British army were in this action, Percy's Northumbrians, the Royal Irish, the Fourth Corps, or the Kings Own, and the Royal Welsh Fusileers, bearing on their colours the

Fig. 43. ALL SOULS' COLLEGE AND ST. MARY'S CHURCH, OXFORD. *Ridgway*

Fig. 44. BATTERY AND CASTLE GARDEN, NEW YORK. *R. Stevenson.*

Fig. 45. BATTLE OF BUNKER HILL. *R. Stevenson.*

Fig. 46. LAWRENCE MANSION, BOSTON. *Stevenson.*

badges of Edward the Black Prince, consisting of a rising sun, red dragon and plumed hat, and the motto " Ich dien."

In the fulfilment of an ancient and honourable custom these Welsh Fusileers were preceded in review by a goat with gilded horns and adorned with garlands of flowers. Every first of March, on the anniversary of their tutelary saint, David, the officers of the Fusileers gave a splendid entertainment to all their Welsh brethren. After the removal of the cloth, a bumper was filled to his Royal Highness, the Prince of Wales, whose health was always the first toast on that day. The goat, gilded and loaded with flowers, was brought in, a pretty little drummer-boy mounted on his back, and the drum major was to lead him three times around the top of the table. But on March first, 1775, at Boston, the goat had other views, and giving a vicious spring, threw off the drummer-boy, leaped over the officers' heads, and ran back to the barracks, to the unconcealed joy of such of the Americans as had gathered to see the festivities.

Opposed to all the trained soldiers of old England were our twelve companies, each mustering fifty-six effective rank and file. They were largely composed of "raw lads and old men, half armed, with no practice or discipline, commanded without order, and God knows by whom." Who can look on the quaint old plate without a quicker beating pulse, and what is the intrinsic value compared to the lesson of patriotism it teaches us all ? The English potter was not sensitive when he made us this design, and in any form it is a welcome addition and an ornament to a collection.

In FIG. 46 is given another New England view. It

has the well-known vine-leaf border, and is as beauti-fully coloured and printed as was all the output of these works. It is the Lawrence Mansion, Boston, situated on Park street, a very elegant residence which saw much hospitality. It would hardly be guessed that the illustration shows a wash bowl—the pitcher, alas, did not survive—which measures twelve inches across, the usual size of these articles in the early part of the nineteenth century. However, we read in Col-onial records that our ancestors' habits were not as primitive as might be inferred from the size of this bowl. The whole family was " rounded up " Saturday night for the weekly scrubbing, down to the unwilling pickaninnies, who took their turn in the great tubs of wood bound with brass, which stood before the kitchen fire. This process was superintended by mammy, the cook. This custom prevailed not only in the South but in New England as well, and is mentioned in Smith's " Colonial Days and Ways," a delightful record of a dozen generations of sterling Connecticut stock.

In FIG. 47 is presented a platter, beautiful in colour and pleasing in design, which has been a subject of much discussion among collectors. For years it has been known as the Lawrence Mansion, but it has at last been decided that it is not an American view at all. Prominent collectors who have it, still keep it in their collections, and hope scmetime that it will be identified. We give it in order that the two pieces may be easily compared. The view shown in FIG. 48 is a pretty rendering of the Capitol at Wash-ington with which the other potters have made us familiar.

Fig. 47. SO-CALLED LAWRENCE MANSION.

Fig. 48. CAPITOL AT WASHINGTON. *R. Stevenson.*

Fig. 49.  CITY HOTEL, NEW YORK.  *R. S. & W.*

Fig. 50.  SCUDDER'S AMERICAN MUSEUM, NEW YORK.  *R. S. & W.*

The designs made by Ralph Stevenson & Williams are quite as choice and interesting as those bearing the imprint of Ralph Stevenson alone. The borders are acorn and oak leaf, a pretty and artistic pattern covering the edge of the plate, and separated from the central design by a small beading. All the central views are good and generally of interest, almshouses being rather conspicuous by their absence.

In FIG. 49 is shown one of those early landmarks of old New York that invite one to tarry awhile and study it. It is the City Hotel, New York, which once filled the entire front of the block on Broadway, between Thomas and Cedar streets. The building itself was plain enough, architecturally, as one may see, but it was comfortable without and within, and very well furnished. The dining-room was large and famed for its neatness, and it accommodated many guests and numerous waiters. There was a second dining-room devoted to ladies, and this was used, as occasion demanded, for lectures, a favourite form of entertainment, and more rarely for concerts. The proprietors were two old bachelors, Jennings and Willard, famed far and wide for their jovial manners and attention to business. They performed all the duties incident to their business, that haughty creation of modern times, the hotel clerk, being then unknown. Jennings did all the purchasing of supplies, while Willard presided over the inside of the hotel; and both men had that happy faculty of remembering both names and faces that is such a necessary factor in successful hotel-keeping. Trinity Church steeple is visible in the distance, and the woodpile in the foreground tells a tale of leisure that is completely jarred out of mind by the ceaseless clang of the trolley which usurps its place to-day.

Buckhorn Tavern stood at Broadway and Twenty-second street, and was another famous inn at about the same time; but it was very much out of town, quite a day's drive from the City Hotel.

Scudder's American Museum, which is shown in FIG. 50, was where P. T. Barnum first started as a showman and laid the foundation for the fortune he subsequently made.

Quite as interesting as the old buildings which have long since given way to many-storied business struc-tures are the pictures of colleges which Stevenson made. They are found on plates and platters and are eagerly snapped up at high prices. I know of one Harvard College plate, the one shown in FIG. 51, which travelled for some years between town and country as the cover for a butter-pot. The farmer's wife brought it into the house one day, instead of removing it beforehand as usual, and thought that she had been more than well paid when she took two dollars for it. It is a ten-inch, dark-blue plate, in perfect condition, and is quoted now at fifty dol-lars. It shows Hollis Hall, built 1763, Harvard Hall, 1766, Holworthy and Stoughton. There is another view on smaller plates, showing University Hall. It has in the foreground a figure on horseback. Six-inch plates (all these have the acorn border) show a third view by Stevenson, also of University Hall. So far as is known he made no views of Yale Col-lege, which is odd, as after Harvard it was the oldest college. In fact there are no views of it by any maker in dark blue, but Columbia is shown in three views by Stevenson.

FIG. 52 shows a seven and one-half inch dark-blue plate, with acorn border by Stevenson, showing Columbia College as it was after 1820, when a belfry and two wings were added. Starting out in 1756 as King's College, after the Revolution the name was changed to Columbia. The college buildings stood in a twenty-acre tract presented by the legislature, between Fifth and Sixth avenues and Forty-seventh and Forty-ninth streets. One of the views has the vine-leaf border, and is marked R. S. FIG. 52 is marked R. S. W., and the third view, with flowers and scrolls on the border, is marked A. Stevenson.

There has always been such a feeling of uncertainty in the minds of the more conservative collectors as to whether " R. S. W." really stood for R. Stevenson & Williams, for it might belong to Ridgway, Son & Wear, that the discovery by a well-known collector of Pennsylvania of two Stoughton Church cup-plates with the usual blue stamp, the R. S. W. mark, and also the impressed mark Stevenson, is welcome assurance. It has been known for some time that medallion plates, with portraits of Lafayette and Washington, are in existence, which bear in full the name of R. Stevenson & Williams. But then again these have other borders than the vine leaf or acorn.

There are portraits also by Stevenson which will be spoken of in the chapter devoted to those designs. There are also two designs in other colours than blue, signed " R. S.," having a lace border with six bunches of flowers, and enclosing as central view Erie Canal at Buffalo, showing packet boat, the second view being of the city of New Orleans.

Of course Stevenson made " English Views." and

as might be expected, they are as admirable as the work with American designs. The oak leaf and acorn decorate one series, the lace border, which we have just mentioned in connection with two American scenes, surrounds a fine view of Eaton Hall. Fonthill Abbey, with a graceful foliage border, is plainly marked on the scroll on the back, " R. S." and " Panoramic Scenery." The name of the view is not given, but the same building is shown on pieces by other makers which are stamped, and is in this way easily identified. He probably began a series of views of the English lake scenery, for one such view is found with a very ornate flower and scroll border. It is marked " British Lakes, R. S. & S.," and is identified as Lake Windermere. The design of Harewood House is very handsome, the view being well composed and decorative, and, as is so invariable with this potter, the colour is very fine (FIG. 53).

# E. J. Phillips & Co.

This firm, like so many others whose work we seek and cherish, has its history wrapped in obscurity. It has been ascertained that they had potteries at Longport, Staffordshire, at least as late as 1830, and two pieces are in evidence as coming from their works. The first and most interesting to us is a cup and saucer (FIG. 54), showing Franklin's tomb. The name of Franklin is on the urn which surmounts the tomb. This design was a favourite one with potters. The Woods made three tomb designs, and there has always been much discussion as to the figures standing in

Fig. 51. HARVARD COLLEGE. *R. S. & W.*

Fig. 52. COLUMBIA COLLEGE. *R. S. & W.*

Fig. 53. HAREWOOD HOUSE, ENGLAND. *R. Stevenson.*

Fig. 54. CUP AND SAUCER SHOWING FRANKLIN'S TOMB. *Phillips.*

contemplation near them. One collector by years of patience has got together six cups and saucers, all with tomb designs, five of them by Wood and the sixth being the rare one by Phillips, given in FIG. 54.

Next to cup-plates, cups and saucers seem to be the most difficult pieces to come across, though why, as they are large and stout, one can hardly say. They do not boast any handles, and were fashioned to hold a generous measure of the infusion. Robert Morris had one of the finest houses in Philadelphia filled with beautiful furniture and luxuries of every description. The Prince de Broglie visited Philadelphia some few years after the Revolution and called upon Mrs. Morris. He says, writing of the visit, "I got some excellent tea, and I think I should be drinking it yet if the Ambassador had not charitably warned me when I had taken the twelfth cup, that I must put my spoon across my cup whenever I wanted this species of torture by hot water to stop, since, said he to me, 'it is almost as bad manners to refuse a cup of tea when it is offered to you, as it would be indiscreet for the mistress of the house to offer you more when the ceremony of the spoon has shown what your wishes are in the matter.'" If Mrs. Morris's cups approximated the size of this one we do not wonder the Prince called it "torture by hot water." Probably, though, her cups were porcelain ones and these large ones came in when tea was a less expensive beverage.

Washington and Franklin both liked blue china for every-day use, and the father of his country, plain citizen though he called himself, liked his household appointments abundant and suitable. His "every-day ν se" was blue and white Canton, and there is a letter by him ordering a set : " Not less than six or eight dozen, however, and proportionable number of deep and other plates, butter-boats, dishes and tureens will suffice."

Franklin liked blue and white also, and among some barrelfuls which he sent over to his wife, was a certain little squat blue and white pitcher, which he particularly commended to his wife's notice, for he says, " I bought it because it reminded me of you know who ! " No doubt this preference for blue and white was largely instrumental in influencing the English potters to use the colour blue when they were starting to make their wares attractive to our market.

In the Phillips tomb scene the figure of the man has on long trousers. In one of Wood's designs the figure wears small clothes, is standing by the tomb, and carries in his hand a scroll. For years this has been known as " Lafayette at Franklin's Tomb," and the reason why collectors have decided that it is Washington is curious. When Lafayette visited this country in 1824 he was sixty-seven years old. Knee breeches had begun to be discarded shortly after eighteen hundred by young men, but were retained by some of their elders till as late as 1820, or thereabouts. Trousers had become an established fashion by 1824, and it was unusual to see small clothes except on the limbs of some conservative member of the old régime. Top boots with the yellow lining falling over, and cordovans or half boots, made of elastic leather and fitting itself to the shape of the leg, also belonged to this time.

To the mind's eye the vision of Lafayette is always that of an heroic figure, with a queue, brocade coat, silk stockings, and with a sword by his side, as he, no doubt, was when, at twenty, he came to prop our feeble fortunes. But these pieces were made after his visit in 1824, when he was comparatively an old man, weakened by years of exile and imprisonment and by cares of state in his own perturbed country. He wore the prevailing trousers, a coat with skirts, his own hair, and no sword. It is the running down of these small details which has resulted in settling the design to be some other figure than Lafayette's, presumably Washington's or Jefferson's, though the lace ruffles on the shirt front are hardly consistent with what we are instructed to regard as Jeffersonian simplicity.

The second piece, marked with the firm name of E. J. Phillips & Co., is an English view of Eton College, with a very ornate border of flowers and scrolls. It comes on the tiny toilet sets we have mentioned, and is a handsome building with many little pointed turrets. This college was founded by Henry VI in 1440, very near to Windsor, and the habit worn by the boys, the short coat and beaver, makes them almost as marked figures in the streets of London as the Blue-coat Boys, with their indigo robes and bare heads.

No English works on pottery make any mention of Phillips, and it would seem as if the time had come for a comprehensive and well-written work on the pottery and porcelain of Great Britain. Amid the number of voluminous works so far issued there is no mention of the vast quantity of semi-china or pottery made for this market, or even of the numerous and elaborate sets of English views, with which we are becoming more familiar. There are pieces of this " semi " ware to be found bearing the words " British

Flowers " on the back, the words being surrounded by a pretty floral wreath. There are also the impressed initials " E. & G. P.," which seem to stand for E. & G. Phillips plainly enough. The designs on the face of the china are graceful bunches of fruits and flowers, distinguished by the same careful printing and true blue which we notice on the other Phillips designs. These pictures are, of course, of trifling value, as are all pieces with merely floral embellishment, and such designs as were issued by the Halls. These series are named respectively " Oriental," " Italian," and " Indian " scenery, and are marked with the firm name of I. Hall & Sons, the scenes on the front being indicative of the countries represented. On the Indian views elephants and pagodas abound, and the oriental views are equally striking. These latter views were taken from " Travels in Mesopotamia," printed about 1828. (See list of English Views.)

There are thousands of pieces of Staffordshire ware in this country, literally of no value except as family heirlooms, printed in all colours and diversified by fancy titles, such as " Ivy," " Myrtle," etc. Even Wedgwood made a little fine pattern which he called " Jassamine," and which I have found in a whole tea-set. It is clearly and beautifully printed in brown, the pattern fulfilling the laws of design, and even to the lettering on the back showing that attention to detail for which this potter was remarkable. These latter pieces are not useful even for decoration, and would better occupy a back shelf in a pantry closet. From about 1830 to 1850, a potter named Clementson had the Sydenham potteries. He made " iron-stone " and signed it " Sydenham, J. Clementson." The colour was often a pale blue; the subjects are what our grandmothers would have called in " classical style," and they have little beauty and small merit.

Riley is another name which the china hunter often runs across, and comes to connect with a splendid shade of blue, decorated with fruits and flowers. Many eighteen-inch platters have come to my notice signed by this firm, " J. & R. Riley," all of which make a fine spot of colour, but lack the historic interest which we are apt to demand. They made the universal willow-pattern in their ware, and at least contrive to give it an artistic touch and some approach to grace. The name Riley is impressed, or the lettering is " Riley semi-china." (See list of English Views.)

This " willow.pattern," which most china collectors devoutly wish had never been invented, was first introduced on English wares at the Caughley Pottery, which became known as the Salopian works. It was first put on porcelain ware about 1780, and became so popular that it was freely copied at almost all other works and was put on stone-ware, pottery and porcelain indiscriminately. That all people do not feel an antipathy to the willow-pattern is shown from a letter which lies before me. In it a gentleman tells me that he has a country place called " The Willows," and in it are three thousand pieces of willow-pattern china, some of which, in peculiar shapes, he had made in England! Besides all these reproductions he had carpets made in the same design, " wall-papers, bedspreads, furniture covering, and draperies, in cotton, silk and linen." Surely there may be too much of a good thing.

Why the really handsome " blue dragon " pattern

did not suceed in winning popularity and the willow did, will forever remain a mystery to the china collector. Pieces of this dragon pattern may be found occasionally tucked away in dusty " butteries," and it may have an edge showing traces of having been richly gilded. The specimens are not always marked, but the letter " S " in blue under glaze, sometimes having a small cross in addition, a butterfly, or a pair of crossed swords, like the familiar Dresden mark, were all used at Caughley. Such pieces are desirable and should be secured if possible. The oblong platters with circular centers are worthy a place in any collection.

# CHAPTER IV.

## STAFFORDSHIRE WARES, CONTINUED.

ABOUT the year 1829 the Dale Hall works at Burslem again changed hands. They were bought from Joseph Stubbs by the Mayer brothers, who became successful potters. Just at what time Thomas made his ornamental set of the Arms of the States is not known, but they are merely marked with the name T. Mayer. His mark is very conspicuous, and is found on the plates and platters on which these seals are usually found. There is an impressed mark of " T. Mayer, Warranted," and " Stone Staffordshire," with an eagle. In addition there is also an impressed eagle in blue, with a ribbon in his mouth, with the well-known words " E Pluribus Unum " on it. He bears a branch in one talon, and bolts in another, and has, as a background, thirteen stars. The border is alike on all the pieces, vine leaves and trumpet flowers. The marginal borders are overlapping scales broken at equal distances by wheels. Inside there is a lace like border surrounding the arms themselves. These are by no means easy pieces to find. Pennsylvania (shown in FIG 56), is taken from an eighteen-inch platter, which is valued at over one hundred dollars. At a recent sale in New York City only two were offered, both badly cracked, one an eight-and-three-quarters-inch plate and one a ten-inch plate, and yet each brought in the neighbourhood of fifteen dollars. A perfect plate, with the Rhode Island Arms, eight and three quarters inches in size, cannot be had for less than twenty-five dollars. Just why these Arms should command more than the New York Seal it is hard to say. Perhaps less were made. At any rate the fact remains that it is so.

Recently an artist wrote to ask if the New York Arms had any value. He was gratified to be assured that it was worth a round sum. In the early days of " rummage sales," three or four years ago, there were great opportunities to pick up old china, which had lain neglected scores of years, and which house-keepers were glad to clear out. It was in such circumstances that the Queen's ware pitcher (shown in FIG. 3), was secured for six cents. But these Arms plates and platters, when one does find them, are usually in very fine condition, not scratched or greased. Perhaps it was their unfamiliar look which saved them, as a feeling of reverence seems to have saved the scriptural pieces.

In FIG. 58 is shown Delaware, one of the handsomest of the series, though that of South Carolina, with its palmetto tree, comes next to Pennsylvania, which is undoubtedly the most ornamental and best coloured of them all. The whole thirteen would be a noble decoration for a hall or dining-room and an interesting study as well, for some changes have been made from the original designs. For instance in the Arms of New York the figures now stand beside the shield instead of being seated. Delaware preserves hers quite as it was originally. Rhode Island still uses an anchor and the word Hope. but in different

Fig. 55. RHODE ISLAND. *T. Mayer.*

Fig. 56. PENNSYLVANIA. *T. Mayer.*

Fig. 57. NEW YORK. *T. Mayer.*

Fig. 58. DELAWARE. *T. Mayer.*

arrangement, while South Carolina has abandoned. her characteristic tree and uses two ovals in a circle, less agreeable in every way.

I made an interesting discovery the other day in looking over some sugar bowls and teapots of old blue, all decorated with the tomb design. One had the design showing Washington's Tomb (so marked). The design was exactly like the one on Wood's pieces; but the border, which was somewhat indistinct, was of other flowers than those which Wood uses. But the seated figure, the setting sun, the temple in the distance were identical. Yet the piece was plainly marked with the impressed stamp "T. Mayer, Stone, Staffordshire, Warranted," all in the familiar circle with eagle in the center. Of course Mayer did not make sugar bowls alone. There must have been other pieces to go with the sugar bowls, and the former may very easily have been overlooked, or classed as belonging to other makers, as the sugar bowl is usually the only piece marked in these tea sets. All these years Mayer has been credited with making the Arms only, and now the tomb piece has appeared, and there may be other patterns yet awaiting identification (FIG. 59).

Lowell says, "I stand by the old thought, the old thing, the old place and the old friend." We do not give anything time to grow old, to get that dignity which a hundred years bestows. We are too anxious to renew, rebuild, pull down and put up something larger. I think that one of the reasons why this old china is so eagerly sought is because it stands for a measure of antiquity; it has the hall mark of age, and we love to have it to sober down our newness of yesterday. There are some people who are harbouring these angels unawares. I have a letter from one enthusiast in the West, who discovered that she had in the attic a perfect vegetable dish of the "Landing of Lafayette." She says, "I read your description carefully, and then flew up to the attic and got down that old blue dish which had lain there ever since I could remember. When it was dusted and I saw the pattern and lettering, a weird, holy, sentimental thrill crept down my spine, and I had to write and let you know I had it."

## William Adams & Sons.

The Adams family, first the father, William, then the two sons whom he associated with himself, had potteries in seven different places. The original works were at Stoke, were opened early in 1800, and were operated until the sons were taken into business, about 1830. Some years later works were built at Tunstall and Greenfield, where much printed ware was made, the old blue being superseded by other colours.

The only American design in dark blue which the elder Adams produced was a picture of the old china warehouse of Mitchell and Freeman, which stood on the corner of Chatham street, Boston (FIG. 60). It has the handsome foliage border with which we are familiar on the English views, with the ever-present pine tree on the left side, to distinguish it from the foliage borders by the other makers. On some of the small-sized plates this tree is omitted. When the firm removed to Tunstall they made a number of American designs, all of them interesting from the careful manner in which they were printed and from their choice and artistic borders.

The Columbus series consists of eight views of highly imaginary scenes in the adventures of Columbus after landing on our shores. FIG. 61 gives one of them from a private collection in New Jersey. The borders are irregular medallions, with different animals, and in the spaces between are pretty bunches of roses. These views are printed in red, mulberry, black, etc., and while not held at high prices—a perfect ten-inch plate brings about five dollars,—are both ornamental and interesting. Adams had a predilection for medallion borders, for there is a single view of New York City, most humourous in design, with three large medallions of a sailor boy and a ship, filling almost the whole border.

Another series, with roses and scroll-work border, has ten or fifteen designs, printed in red, black, etc., of such scenes as Conway, N. H., Harper's Ferry, etc. As in the other series all the designs are very pictorial and pleasing, the printing is good and clear, and the shape of the plate pretty.

But our chief interest in Adams's ware lies in the notably fine English views, of which they issued such a number, presumably before the sets dealing with American subjects, as the use of different colours for printing succeeded the use of the dark blue. In the foliage series which was mentioned before, is shown a splendid fifteen-inch platter, with the picture of St.

George's chapel, Regent Street London, on it (FIG. 62). The mark on the back is a printed blue eagle with extended wings, and grasping a twig in one claw, and four arrows or darts in the other. Below him is a ribbon festooned, and on it is printed the name of the view. There are many views in Regent's Park, London, almost as many as in the Wood's series. In the series with the border of bluebells and other flowers, which has been used by Clews as well as Adams (see FIG. 34), the stamp, with the name of the view in a scroll, with flowers, is identical with the mark used by Clews, except that Adams's name appears also. There are eighteen or twenty of these views already identified, and Branxholm Castle, Roxburghshire, one of them, is shown in FIG. 63.

It is so unusual to find any mention of the Staffordshire potters in English works, that the scrap of information contained in Downman's "English Pottery and Porcelain" is welcome. It says that William Adams was Wedgwood's favourite pupil, and that he was initiated into all the mysteries of Etruria. That it was his experiments which led to improvements in the blue jasper body by adding gold filings to its chief ingredient, the sulphate of baryta. "After Josiah's death Adams settled at Tunstall and produced many fine specimens of ornamental jasper and basalt ware." It goes on to say, what has already been mentioned, that most of Adams's manufacture was marked with his name, impressed, or "by a peculiar border ornament of interlaced circles." Of course there is no mention of either the American or English printed blue ware.

Fig. 59. WASHINGTON'S TOMB. *T. Mayer.*

Fig. 60. CHINA WAREHOUSE, BOSTON. *Adams.*

Fig. 61. COLUMBUS AND INDIANS. *Adams.*

Fig. 62. ST. GEORGE'S CHAPEL, REGENT STREET, LONDON.
*Adams.*

Fig. 63. BRANXHOLM CASTLE.
*Adams.*

Fig. 64. JOHN HANCOCK HOUSE.
*Jackson.*

## *J. & J. Jackson.*

The firm of J. & J. Jackson, which occupied a position of importance among the minor Staffordshire potters, made many designs particularly for our market, in various shades of red, mulberry and brown, and also in light blue and black. They had works at Burslem, England, and, as they made no dark blue ware, it is probable that they came on the scene rather late. No record is found of them after 1845, so that the numerous specimens of their ware which abound over here, were made prior to that time. The best known piece by them is the Hancock House, Boston (shown in FIG. 64). I have seen it in eight-inch plates alone. It is most often found in red or brown, and makes an ornamental piece of colour, particularly in the red, which is a rich shade. Although these plates are not in the much-desired blue, they command very high prices, a perfect one, even in its small size, bringing between fifteen and twenty dollars, and one with a crack holding its own for twelve dollars. It is pleasant to think that it is the historic interest that makes it valuable.

Before John Hancock came into the possession of this stately house he passed through many stirring times. In ante-Revolutionary days living was strenuous, and many and secret were the meetings in out-of-the-way taverns in the suburbs of Boston, when companies of rangers and minute men were organized. Mr. Hancock was a brilliant figure in these days, six-feet tall, broad-shouldered and dressed in the tip of the mode. He appeared one night at one of these secret meetings dressed in an apple-green cloth coat, with knee breeches of silver net tied at the knees with pea-green ribbon.   He wore white silk stockings and pumps with large silver buckles, and displayed much fine lace at wrist and throat.   His hair was rolled and pow-dered and tied in a queue.   No wonder such a figure took the fancy of Dorothy Q., when, in 1775, Hancock and Adams, who were excepted from a general pardon, were taking refuge in the house of the Rev. Mr. Clarke at Lexington.   She was staying in the same house under the care of an aunt, and Dorothy and her gallant lover whiled away the tedious hours in court-ship, while the graver Mr. Adams discussed theology and politics with their reverend host.

The Hancock mansion was built in 1737 by Thomas Hancock, and came by inheritance to his nephew, John Hancock.   The site of the new State House was Hancock's pasture, and orchards surrounded this princely mansion.   The building was of stone, a low stone wall protected the grounds from the street, and a paved walk and a dozen steps conducted to the mansion.   A wooden hall, sixty feet long, was at-tached to the north wing, and here Hancock received D'Estaing in 1778, Lafayette in 1781, Washington in 1789, and in later times Lords Stanley and Wortley, Labouchere and Bougainville.   Governor Hancock was a generous host, and during the stay of D'Estaing forty of his officers dined every day at the governor's table.   It is a pity that the efforts to retain this nota-ble mansion were not successful.   As late as 1863 it remained intact and filled with the original relics, pictures and furniture.   But it was pulled down, and with it disappeared the only monument to a notable figure, until one was recently erected in the Granary burying ground.

## *Rogers.*

Between 1810 and 1836 or 1840, there were several firms of Staffordshire potters that made one, two, or half a dozen American designs, sometimes in dark blue, sometimes in various colours, and generally of some merit. The Rogers brothers, and afterwards the Rogerses, father and son, were such a firm, and they chose for their subject the Boston State House, of which they made three views. One of these, the one that has cows in the foreground, is almost identical with the view made by Stubbs, but the border of roses and forget-me-nots makes the identification simple. In Fig. 65 is presented a pitcher with this design. On the other side is a view of the City Hall, New York. The pitcher is five and one-half inches high, and sold at auction in Boston for twenty-eight dollars, in November, 1901. It was in proof condition and of a very rich shade of blue. Doctor Holmes says, in his " Autocrat at the Breakfast Table : " " Boston State House is the hub of the solar system, you couldn't pry that out of a Boston man if you had the tire of all creation straightened out for a crowbar." While Rogers made his views many years before this was written, he seems to have appreciated the feeling. He also made a series of designs of no particular interest or merit, not in dark blue, of such subjects as " The Adopted Child," " Love in a Village," etc.

## Thomas Godwin.

It would be a matter of interest to know why
Thomas Godwin, in marking his pottery, did not put
the word "Wharf" below his name, or separate the two
in some way.   It has caused collectors much annoy-
ance to find no mention of T. Godwin Wharf in any
book, while they owned interesting American views
marked in this way.   Thomas Godwin had his works
at Burslem Wharf, but left out Burslem and added
Wharf to his name.

The views are in the usual colours, other than dark
blue, some of them being printed in a fine shade of
green.   The border is a stiff arrangement of morning
glories and nasturtiums.

Godwin confined himself chiefly to views of cities,
Baltimore, Utica, etc.   His eighteen-inch platters are
eight-sided and quite decorative, being well and clearly
printed.   They bring from fifteen to twenty dollars
each, which seems a very high price for ware which
can never be esteemed as highly as the dark blue.

## S. Tams & Co.

## Tams & Anderson.

## Tams, Anderson & Tams.

The view of the United States Hotel, Philadelphia,
with the impressed mark, S. Tams & Co., has long
been known to collectors.   Fig. 66 shows it.   The
piece is handsome, fine in colour, with one of the foliage borders which are so soft and ornamental, and

Fig. 65. STATE HOUSE, BOSTON.
*Rogers.*

Fig. 66. U. S. HOTEL, PHILA-
DELPHIA. *S. Tams & Co.*

Fig. 67 RICHARD JORDAN'S RESIDENCE. *Heath*

Fig. 68. LOUISVILLE, KY. *Maker unknown.*

Fig. 69. SANDUSKY, OHIO. *Maker unknown.*

variations of which were used by Wood, and also by Adams on some of their Staffordshire ware. It is only within a short time that new pieces have come to light with the same border as is shown in FIG. 66, and marked variously S. Tams & Co. ; Tams ; Tams & Anderson ; Tams, Anderson & Tams, proving that these designs issued from the same works under different firm names. None of these names is found in books on English potters, but this is the rule with regard to the Staffordshire men, rather than the exception. There are two American views which have been identified, and five, possibly six, English scenes, with which is included the post office at Dublin, Ireland. The American pieces have the mark " S. Tams & Co.," impressed. The English views have a blue stamp, very large and heavy, bearing in it the name of the view and the words " semi-china."

The Crown works, London, belonged to the Tamses, and about 1840, John Tams, who had probably succeeded to the Crown works, as it is known that he potted in London, made for a wealthy Philadelphia merchant two sets of plates in a medium blue, decorated with portraits of General Harrison on one set and of Henry Clay on the other. The borders were undecorated save by two lines of blue. At the same time, and in honour of the same campaign, were struck off many pieces of glass, bottles, cup-plates, etc., bearing portraits and various devices. Some of these relics are still in the possession of descendants of General W. H. Harrison, as well as much interesting furniture, brass, silver and pewter which have belonged to the family in various generations since early colonial days.

## Joseph Heath & Co.
## (J. H. & Co.)

(See FIG. 67)

Joseph Heath & Co. must have run a large and prosperous pottery at Tunstall. The mark "J. H. & Co." is abundantly familiar to china collectors on many pieces of the ever-present willow-pattern and the more tiresome "flow blue." There are also pieces which have a moderate interest, the Ontario Lake view for instance, which must have been left to the fancy of the English potter, who made the lake a river and ornamented its shores with towers and castles and gaily dressed ladies.

The most interesting design made by this firm is the one which shows the residence of Richard Jordan, an eminent Quaker preacher. The border is very handsome, with flowers and scrolls, and the view is printed in half-a-dozen different colours, the best being a fine shade of red and mulberry. The plates have the wavy margin found in many plates of this period, and the ware has more than the usual lightness that is characteristic of the semi-china.

## Charles Meigh.

The grandfather of Charles Meigh had pottery works at Hanley as early as 1770. These potteries have always been esteemed for the class of work put out by them, the high standard being kept up by the father of Charles, and afterwards by the latter himself.

When various colours had succeeded old blue, Charles Meigh made a small set of American views. He called them "American Cities and Scenery." The border is of small flowers and is known as the "chickweed" border, but is not very pretty or artistic. He made, however, the only view of Yale College which has yet appeared. Indeed he potted down to such very recent times (1861), and the output from the old Hall works was so varied and, in general, of so high character, that he is distinguished by quite extended notices in the works on pottery by Englishmen. Perhaps what gave him his greatest reputation were the pieces he made in Parian ware, like the beautiful Minster jug which is shown in FIG. 139.

His printed ware was good, but does not begin to show the artistic excellence of this beautifully modelled jug.

## *Thomas Green.*

Thomas Green had a pottery at Fenton in the middle of the nineteenth century, and worked until almost the beginning of our Civil War. His ware is not good; it is made in various colours; and the subject, William Penn's Treaty with the Indians, is set forth in grotesque fashion. There are half-a-dozen or more variations of this theme, in which Penn himself, Indians in oriental dress and surroundings, tropical fruit and other eccentricities are duly pictured. The border is very ornate, of geometric figures, giving a somewhat pointed effect.

## *J. & T. Edwards.*

Among the latest of these Staffordshire potters were the Edwards brothers, who had works at Burslem. They did not work here long, and one of the brothers, James, bought the Rogers works, also at Burslem, about 1842, and made some marine designs, called the " Boston Mails " series, showing the cabins of a steamboat. They were made in various colours, as all this later and less interesting ware was.

## *Mellor, Venables & Co.*

These potters, whose works were at Burslem, made, at about the same period as the Edwardses, some half dozen or more designs to please the American market. Although printed in light blue, red, mulberry, etc., the pieces are rather pleasing, and have strong enough colour to be decorative. The border is in medallion style with coats of arms, festooned with wreaths, and between them bunches of small flowers. The pieces are named, but it seems as if the designs were made by an English artist, and were totally imaginary.

## *" J. B." " F. M." and Thomas Ford.*

Each made a single design of small merit. "The Texan Campaign" is signed J. B. "The American Marine" is by F. M., and Thomas Ford made " America."

## " *Unknown Makers.*"

## *Designs in dark blue.*

### (See Fig. 68)

Under this heading is found some of the best pieces of old, dark-blue china known. Whether it was that some of the English potters preferred not to sign the ware intended for us, content to gain only the spoils, one cannot say. Yet much china was sent over with borders which render it easy of identification, and an occasional marked piece has been a guide to much more. The plan of grouping by borders, started by Mr. Barber, and of such use to all collectors, is absolutely necessary here.

There is a large number of pieces, chiefly views of cities, with similar borders, of large flowers and scrolls, one of which is given in FIG. 69. This is an eighteen-inch platter, with a view of the city of Sandusky, Ohio. This particular platter is now owned in the South. It was recently discovered in New Jersey in an attic, covered with dust, and treated with scant care by the lady to whom it belonged. She regarded it as such an "ugly old thing" that she was unwilling to have it about. However, as it had been in the family for many years, she offered it to some relatives. They agreed with her as to its lack of interest and beauty, and would not take it as a gift; so it returned to its resting place of a half a century, the attic. But old china, like murder, cannot remain hid, and somehow two collectors living in the same town got wind of the treasure and started out to secure it. One was so sure of his ability to bear away the prize that he took a basket to carry it home in.   He went away empty-handed.   The other, having better luck, got the plat-ter, the owner taking five dollars less than she was offered, she was so sure the platter was not worth it. Our collector's luck still stood by him, and he sold his platter for fifty dollars and a ten-inch States plate in proof condition.   I know of only five of these platters, and have recently received a letter from a lady who was born in Sandusky, and wishes a platter as a memento of her early home.   Often a small beginning will start a collection, and if she secures her platter it will not be long before a mate to it is wanted, and lo ! the madness is on.

FIG. 70 is another view in the same set, and shows a view of Albany, N. Y.  They were delightfully primitive in Albany in those days, and the ferry seems equally open to man or beast.

The small plate in FIG. 26 shows another one of this series.   It is a view near Fishkill-on-the-Hud-son.   In the teapot given in FIG. 71 is another piece which is also labelled "unknown."   It is a fine speci-men, of a splendid blue, and, as you see it, restored to its original proportions.   When it "blew in," on a third of July a year or two ago, it had no knob to the cover, and the spout was quite half gone.   The farmer who brought it wrapped in the usual bit of newspaper, thought "a dollar a'naf would be about right."   He went off with his money, well satisfied. Perhaps he enjoyed his Fourth as well as the collec-tor, but I doubt it.

There is another set of views which is always pro-vocative of much discussion among collectors.   Till recently the three views, one of the ship *Cadmus,* one of the Baltimore and Ohio Railroad, and the third of the " Fulton Steamboat," as it is called (FIG. 72), have always been classed among American views. Many collectors have been at much time and expense to get these pieces, and they are all handsome, of a rich blue colour, and with a clear and handsome border. The first view, the *Cadmus*, is unmarked in any way. It shows a ship dressed with flags, but in this view, as well as in FIG. 72, no American flag is shown.

The English potters, in making ware for our market, regarded our flag as particularly appealing to us, and inserted it in many scenes and on many ships that could not possibly have been American. So its absence on this occasion does not seem significant. The theory is advanced that the building on the shore is not all American ; but on the other hand, a small detail like this did not stand in the way of the English potter.

Very recently two cases of views wrongly marked were brought to my notice. The well-known view of Lake George, with shell border, by Wood, was marked "The Battery" on the back, and the view of " Newburg on Hudson," by Clews, has been found marked " Hudson City, on Hudson." Of course as the views were equally unfamiliar to the potters, we can see how easily they might be confused.

There is still another set of " Unknown Makers " views, which are quite as ornamental as those shown. The border is fine bunches of fruits and flowers, and so far there are but four pieces identified with it, two views in Baltimore and two in Philadelphia. In addition to these series there are quite a number of other views with various borders, which have, so far, not been identified with regard to the pottery from which they were issued. They are all good, some are hard to find, and most of them command quite as high prices as the pieces marked with maker's stamp. Then, too, there are a few pieces which come under the head of "Inscription Pieces."

The best known of these is commonly called the "Eulogy Plate." It was struck off to commemorate the opening of the "big ditch." It is given in FIG. 73. The inscription can easily be read on the plate itself, and it sometimes varies as to one word. Some of the plates read "Late Governor," and in some, ours among the number, the "late" is omitted and its place filled by a scroll. This plate is of ten-inch size, has two bad cracks which are even visible in the photograph, and yet sold for twenty-five dollars.

To us with our "flyers" and lightning expresses, to say nothing of motor cars, the canal seems a most poky and tame affair. Turning over the leaves of an old diary I came across this note: "Commended my soul to God, and asking his defence from danger, I stepped aboard the canal-boat and was soon flying toward Utica." No doubt one of the boats shown on the margin of the plate was the famous packet, "Redbird." The writer of the diary quoted, mentions the excitement when the "Redbird" raced with a rival boat. There were people who adhered to the stage coach rather than brave the perils of the raging canal, but for bridal trips this packet was "the thing."

In FIG. 74 we show the eight-inch Utica inscription plate, which reads as follows, "Utica, a village in the State of New York, thirty years since a wilderness, now (1824) inferior to none in the western section of

Fig. 70.  ALBANY, N Y.  *Maker unknown.*

Fig. 71.  BALTIMORE ALMSHOUSE.  *Maker unknown.*

Fig. 72. FULTON STEAMBOAT. *Maker unknown.*

Fig. 73. EULOGY PLATE
*Maker unknown*

Fig. 74. UTICA INSCRIPTION
PLATE. *Maker unknown.*

the state, in population, wealth, commercial enterprise, active industry and civil improvements."
These plates are made evidently by the same firm
that made the Eulogy ones, as the borders plainly
show. They are very rare, and are held at fifty dollars each, and over. Happy the collector who is able
to "pick one up."

These inscriptions are sometimes found on pitchers
as well as plates. The other two inscription plates are
not in dark blue, but are of a somewhat later period.
The next in point of interest is the Lovejoy plate, as
it is called (FIG. 75). This pattern is found on both
dinner-sets and tea-sets in medium blue, and also in
mulberry. The border is composed of four medallions
with inscriptions, alternating with eagles and shields.
The background of the border is dotted with stars.
In the center is the following: "Congress shall make
no laws respecting an establishment of religion, or
prohibiting the free exercise thereof ; or abridging
the free exercise of speech, or of the press, or the right
of people peaceably to assemble and to petition the
government for a redress of grievances. Constitution
United States."

On many pieces, ours among them, are found in the
top medallion the word, "Lovejoy, the first martyr to
American Liberty. Alton, November 7th, 1837."
This china is believed to be the gift of English anti-
slavery believers to the American Abolitionists. It is
unfortunate that this fine old piece was selected for
forgery. Any person who is used to handling this old
ware gets to detect differences by mere touch that
would escape the casual observer. Not only were the
forged plates heavier, but they were thicker, and colder

to the hand. This unprincipled act has reduced the price of these plates about one half, and collectors are warned to examine specimens carefully before buying them. The cup-plates of this pattern have escaped the general suspicion and are selling for as high prices as ever.

The fourth plate in this group is the one known as the "Millenium," by Meakin. It is very rarely found in a dark shade of medium blue, but the usual colour is pink, black or brown. It has on the top, in the border, an eye. In the center is a group, the lion and the lamb, etc., and the motto, " Peace on Earth." Fruits and flowers, with grain, make up the rest of the border. There are quantities of these plates all over the country. In fact such numbers of them were offered for sale last year, in several sizes of plates, that suspicion was aroused. The marks of the stilts used in firing should be carefully looked for, and the quality of the china tested, before purchase. These coloured pieces, or the medium blue, are easier to forge than the rich dark blue. The darkest pieces are practically safe.

The other inscription plates are all of less interest and value. Perhaps I should except a single example, that of a large square panel with the inscription " Thou God, see'st me," in the center, in a wreath. The border of this panel is quite ornate, and is covered by the handsome pink-spotted Sunderland lustre.

Half a dozen other Scriptural phrases and the Lord's Prayer may be found also. There is in addition a verse printed in black, with a border of raised figures, animals and children, which should be included here :—

" Jesus, my all, to Heaven is gone,
    He whom I fixed my hope upon;
    His track I see & I'll pursue
    The narrow way till him I view."

While the value of the various coloured crockery is
always less than that of the dark blue, whether by
known or unknown makers, there are quite numerous
designs which collectors are glad to secure, as they are
decorative and the prices comparatively low. The
borders are generally different; but, in FIG. 76, we
show one of three designs, with what is called the
" Phoenix and engine border." The mark on the back
of the plate is very showy and comprises a large eagle
with extended wings, and in front, concealing his legs,
a panel containing the words, " Exchange, New York."
Above the panel are the words " Stone Ware," and
over the eagle's head the letter " D." These pieces
were made after 1833, when the great fire occurred
which destroyed so many buildings. The " document " which this plate stands for is most interesting.
In the first place it shows the quaint fashions of the
times, and of deeper interest still the inadequate means
there were for battling with a great fire. The particular plate figured is a soup plate, printed in mulberry, and was found in a small village in New York
State. In its present aspect it is a triumph of the re-
storer's art. On its outer edge, the first time I saw it,
there were eighteen nicks, showing the hard service
to which it had been subjected, in the chicken house,
if I remember rightly, before it was rescued and restored. The other two designs in this series are
equally interesting. One is the ruins of the Exchange

after the fire, and the third piece is the " Burning of
Coenties Slip, New York."

Of all these plates the latter would appeal most
strongly to the relic hunter and antiquarian, for Coenties Slip is a name that has still survived, though the
arm of water it once stood for has been crowded back
into the river, and in its place is the one green spot in
all that busy neighbourhood.  At the head of what
was once Coenties Slip is still a tiny lane not much
more than fifty feet long, and on this lane (leading off
from Pearl street), was built, in 1642, the first City
Hall—" Stadt Huis," Governor William Kieft called
it.  The site of this old City Hall may still be found,
as a tablet to its memory has been fastened to the
business building which stands where it once did.

Any of this old crockery, " old dishes," as it is
sometimes contemptuously called by people who do
not care for it, is nice to own as heirlooms, or for
decoration.  But the ware of this secondary period
has not the value of the rich dark blue.  The English
potters were so anxious to capture our market that
every species of device which they thought would be
popular was eagerly seized upon.  Many of Franklin's
sayings were printed on cheap white ware with embossed borders, or the alphabet on the edge, chiefly
for the use of children, on small plates and cups.
The plates come not only circular but octagonal as
well, and the motto, or maxim, is often illustrated by
rude figures, printed in black and touched with colour.
No list is given of these pieces as they speak for themselves ; and the collector is averse to buying many of
them, as quite a number of the patterns have been reproduced in modern ware.  Their only interest is their

Fig. 75. LOVEJOY PLATE. *Maker unknown.*

Fig. 76. BURNING OF MERCHANTS' EXCHANGE, NEW YORK. *Maker unknown.*

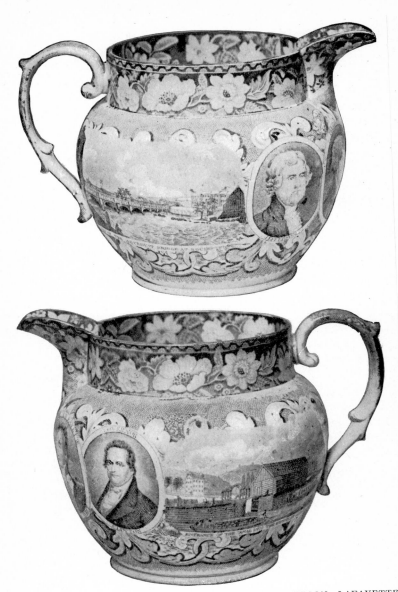

Fig. 77. MEDALLION PITCHER, WASHINGTON, JEFFERSON, LAFAYETTE
AND CLINTON. ROCHESTER AQUEDUCT BRIDGE, ENTRANCE
OF CANAL AT ALBANY. *R. S. & W.*

quaint character ; for they have absolutely no beauty, and a collection of them is decidedly monotonous.

Scriptural designs, besides those made by Wood, were also made by Stevenson, Mason, Jackson, Adams, Ridgway, Meakin and Dillon. They explain themselves so easily that we have not listed them. There are, perhaps, about fifty designs in all, by different makers, and occasionally a new one comes to light. Such a one is a nine-inch, flat red plate, by Adams, marked " Cyrene." It has a different border from the more common Palestine designs, and is better printed than those in two colours.

About the time of the Centennial Exposition in Philadelphia, numerous designs were made for our market by English potters which possess a certain degree of merit. They are not listed, however, for the time has not yet arrived when they possess any degree of interest or value. They are all very plainly marked with the views they are intended to represent, and he who runs may read their story.

Within the last few years there has been a very large number of American scenes made in England for our market, and printed in a shade of dark blue. The best ones are made by Wedgwood at Etruria, and by Minton. They can be purchased both in Boston and Philadelphia from the firms that have copyrighted and imported them. This winter I have also seen large quantities of blue china, with American views, for sale at department stores all over the country. They are not intended to deceive, but are frankly sold at small prices as modern ware. None of the old views or border patterns are copied, and no one who has any interest in old china can for a moment regard them as anything but the newest of the new.

Quite different, however, are a series of intentional forgeries which have been put out within the last year by one or more unscrupulous dealers to deceive purchasers. So secure were collectors that the rich old blue could not be copied that they bought freely of these forgeries, suspicion only arising at last from the large number of certain pieces, all of the same size, that appeared on the market. The Lovejoy plate, of which we have already spoken, was the first of these. Then appeared one of the rare Syntax plates, "Doctor Syntax painting a portrait," and so successful was the forger that many of these plates were sold. If you compare a forgery with an original old plate the differences are very marked. The colour is a little different, the ware is heavier, and there are no marks of spurs on either back or face, an almost unfailing test of an old piece.

I have seen several of Ridgway's New York City Hall plates, of ten-inch size, of which I am very doubt-ful. They are very suspiciously new looking, are without the spur marks, and were offered for sale this last year in such numbers, and sold for such small prices, comparatively, that suspicion was at first aroused.

The portraits of Lafayette and Washington, printed in other colours than blue, are supposed to have been counterfeited, and some collectors believe "The Landing of Lafayette" has been copied by some unscrupulous dealers. It will generally be the novice who will be deceived by these reproductions. A collector who studies his specimens learns to distinguish very easily,

and a buyer should always insist on seeing his purchase before closing his bargain. A seller who has
nothing to conceal will be willing to send his wares
on approbation. If any decline to do this it would
be just as well to have no further negotiations with
them. It is both difficult and unsafe to attempt to
buy by photograph, for defects do not often show,
and you are not able to handle the china, which is so
important in detecting frauds. Although many old
specimens come to hand in an almost perfect condition, without any mar or blemish, or even knife
scratches, they are easily told by the colour of the
crockery, the cockspur marks, and the remarkable
lightness of the pieces. A Richard Jordan eight-inch
plate will weigh just about one-half of what a modern
eight-inch stone china plate will tip the scales at.
There are few dealers who will imperil their reputations
by selling this spurious ware. If you buy from
people who have but a piece or two to dispose of the
risk is still further lessened, and it is generally easy to
trace the history of " farmhouse spoils." No collector would, presumably, pass off an imitation in trade
or exchange, and the open market seems to be the
place where the most caution must be displayed.

# CHAPTER V.

## PORTRAIT PIECES.

A VERY large proportion of the pieces of this interesting Staffordshire has on it portraits of patriots and heroes who laboured, and in many cases died, for the welfare of their country. Washington, Franklin, and that brave Frenchman, Lafayette, to whom we owe so much, lead in the number and variety of china made in their honour, and no collection is complete without at least one or two of these portraits.

It seems peculiarly fitting that Washington's memory should be perpetuated in this way, for he was a genuine china enthusiast himself, and was constantly adding to his stores of such goods by importation from England, and by purchase in this country. As early as 1759 he wrote to England for ornamental china, "images" and busts, though not for table ware, and after the Revolution was over and he could give his attention to his private affairs, he set about remodelling Mt. Vernon and adding to its household goods. There are letters still extant containing directions for goods to be purchased for him, dated 1785. But it was not till some years later that lavish orders were sent over. Virginian wealth was not to be counted till crops were harvested and got to market. The current price of tobacco might leave you with or without a balance to your credit in London—your

Fig. 78.  ST. PAUL'S CHAPEL.  *R. S. W.*

Fig. 79.  PORTRAIT PLATTER—WINDSOR CASTLE, ROCHESTER AQUEDUCT
AT BOTTOM.  PORTRAITS OF JEFFERSON, WASHINGTON,
LAFAYETTE, CLINTON.  *R. S. W.*

Fig. 80. JEFFERSON AND CLINTON. BOSTON HOSPITAL.
*R. S. & W*

Fig. 81. LAFAYETTE. *Clews.*

FAULKBOURN HALL. 4 medallions.
*A. Stevenson.*

only clearing house, as it chanced. Your purchases must be made through agents or factors, and both what you bought and what you sold must take the hazards of a sea voyage, was at the mercy of sea captains and the chances of a foreign market. At one time you must be farmer and merchant, and manage your own negroes and overseers as well. You must conduct a correspondence with your over-sea agents, know current prices, how rates of exchange varied, and how to meet these changes in markets and merchants, while an ocean rolled between you. All this required an alertness, an attention to detail, a sagacity in farming and a shrewdness in judging of your market which was impossible to idle or inefficient men.

But Washington took pains to succeed. He had a zest for business. The practical nature of his genius grew in him from boy to man. His factors in London, Messrs Cary & Co., must have known his letters at a glance from their bulky size. No details escaped him, and to keep his lucrative patronage they must be as punctilious as he was. It did not take him long to learn how to make the best tobacco in Virginia, and to get it recognized as such. Barrels of flour marked "George Washington, Mt. Vernon," were passed by the inspectors without examination. It is the face of this man which looks so gravely out from so many of these choice portrait plates, and makes one such piece the central ornament of a collection.

Not lacking interest are the curious advertisements which appeared in the papers at this time, setting forth the goods brought home from China, teas, porcelain, " best Nankin blue and white stone china ; with bowls, mugs, guglets and sneakers, basons and water jugs."

Then, too, at these public vendues were sold silks and painted gauzes, opium and arrack, rhubarb and gamboge. Umbrellas, or " umbrilloes " as they were then called, were first used in Boston in 1768, and in this same sale, 1785, are advertised silk umbrellas of all sizes, showing that they had now come into general use.

Of the pottery and porcelain that bears the name, and what is supposed to be the portrait, of Washington, by far the largest part is found in Liverpool ware, chiefly in pitchers. These are treated by themselves, as the portraits considered in this chapter are those in the blue Staffordshire.

The Metropolitan Museum of Art has a large collection of Washington portraits on every kind of ceramic ware, from copies of the well-known portraits by Stuart, Peale, Trumble and Savage, to the conception of the " father of his country " by the almond-eyed Celestial. The Staffordshire portrait pieces, many of which have come to light within the last few years only, are extremely valuable. They command such very high prices that we hesitate to give them here, and content ourselves with saying that all ten-inch plates with these portraits command fifty dollars each and over.

Of the pitcher shown in FIG. 77 too much cannot be said. Only two examples of it are known so far, the one shown measuring seven inches in height and twenty-three inches around the center. This pitcher is unmarked. The other one is six inches high and has the mark " R. Stevenson & Williams." The handsome border is not the one with which we are familiar on Stevenson's American views, but a special one, the flowers showing at the top of the pitcher, inside and out, and the scrolls at the base. Plates are found having the portraits of Washington and Lafayette in the center with this same border, and also having the name " R. Stevenson & Williams, Cobridge, Stafford. shire." Like the pitcher these plates are very hand. some, the printing being very clear and well defined and the colour rich. On the front of the pitcher are the four portraits, Jefferson, Washington, Lafayette and Clinton, with which we have become familiar on the various medallion plates and platters. On the sides are the Rochester Aqueduct, so popular with English potters, and used in connection with so many different views, both English and American. On the other side is a view called " Entrance of the canal into the Hudson at Albany," and shows a different view from that which we find on Wood's plates with this scene. It is, however, quite identical with the small views of this scene found on the acorn-bordered pieces which have long been such a topic of interested dis- cussion to collectors, now, as we have previously mentioned. happily set at rest by some pieces with this border, and the mark " R. S. & W.," and also " Stevenson " impressed.

In FIG. 78, " St. Paul's Chapel, New York City," many of the collectors agree that the handsomest one of these medallions is found. It comes on six-inch plates. and is a wonderfully fine bit of colour and printing. The portrait of Clinton is clear and good, the oak leaf and acorn border as ever admirable, and St. Paul's Chapel, one of the most interesting bits of old New York left standing. Every time I see this plate I wonder why just this combination of scenes and portraits was chosen, for in most cases the central view was selected on account of its shape or size being suited to the place it was necessary to fill, and St. Paul's steeple is shorn of half its glory. This church was built in 1776, far up Broadway, as it was then regarded, overlooking the "fields or old cow pastures." It faced the river, and the chancel was placed on the eastern side of the chapel in accordance with the ritual, and this caused much grave debate. Still the builders persisted, and the church has ever turned its back on busy, bustling Broadway. St. Paul stands in his niche over the portico, sword in hand, and rarely a passer-by turns to glance up at him, though thousands pass there every day. How many of these thousands know that George Washington used to attend services in this church, and that his pew has been preserved as he used it? Just above it on the walls is the coat-of-arms of New York. The chapel narrowly escaped burning in 1776, when the invading British fired the city. To this same quaint old church Washington came on the day he was inaugurated, and he sat in the pew which you may see to-day. In his diary, for all the time he was in the city, occurs this note for every Sunday, "Went to St. Paul's Chapel in the forenoon." Over the pulpit is an odd sounding-board, and on the top of it is the coat-of-arms of the Prince of Wales. This board escaped in some way the ardour of those patriots who, in Revolutionary days, rushed through the city and destroyed everything which in the least suggested our allegiance to England. So this old pre-Revolutionary relic stands in its original place.

This chapel and its graveyard are a volume of our

early history.  The Indian wars seem remote, yet here beside the western wall is the bust of John Wells, a well-known lawyer, who died in 1823.  He was the sole survivor of a large family, every member of which, except himself, was killed by the Indians at the massacre of Cherry Valley.  This is just the beginning of the history which may be found in a six-inch plate, provided the owner has an interest in it apart from its face value.

In a four-medallion platter, with portraits of Washington, Lafayette, Jefferson and Clinton, the central view is Windsor Castle, England, and the Rochester Aqueduct is depicted at the bottom (FIG. 79).  It is one of " R. S. W.'s " pieces, also with the acorn border, and while a very valuable and showy piece, has not a tithe of the real interest bound up in our little six-inch St. Paul's.  The view of Windsor Castle is fine, the Round Tower is standing up above the surrounding buildings, and the whole scene not markedly different from what it is to-day.

Faulkbourne Hall (spelled Faulkstone on the pottery) is another English view used, and Harewood House.  On these English views our Republican heroes are all kept in countenance by the Rochester Aqueduct at the bottom.  In our day, when the canal is a mere water-way for freight, we do not realize what it meant to the country in 1825.  DeWitt Clinton always had the honour of carrying this project through to a successful conclusion, as indeed he did ; but the name of the real conceiver of the enterprise, Christopher Colles, is almost forgotten.  For years he spoke and gave lectures on the subject, but he did not live to see his ideas carried out, for he died in 1821.  He

lies buried in St. Paul's churchyard, New York, and on
the little plate of FIG. 78 you can see the part of the
yard where he lies buried, and below this picture,
curiously enough, is a view of the canal, his pet
project.

There is always a chance for a discussion on old
blue, because the history of its potters and potteries
are wrapped in so much obscurity. After it had been
comfortably settled for years that A. Stevenson sold
his business to James Clews in 1819, the discovery of
these portrait plates with his stamp on them has set
the collector adrift once more. Of course, these plates,
made to celebrate an event which occurred in 1825
(opening of Erie Canal), must have been made after
that date. Indeed, the great bulk of this dark blue
was made between 1820 and 1840, and the English
views are as late as the American. It is thought by
some collectors that Ralph Stevenson used the stamp
" A. Stevenson " at his own works, which were operated
till 1834. From this date until 1840 they were worked
under the firm name of Ralph Stevenson & Sons. But
why should R. Stevenson have got possession of A.
Stevenson's stamps and designs when the works were
sold to James Clews, probably with the dies and
stamps? To my mind it seems more likely that Clews
used these properties, for Clews did not part with the
Cobridge works until 1829, and all the events com-
memorated by these pieces took place some years
before that.

FIG. 80 presents a two-portrait medallion plate, with
Jefferson and Clinton. The central view is Boston
Hospital, with chaise in the foreground, and the
Rochester Aqueduct at the base. The plate, like

most of these, has the name of the central view on the back in dark blue.

For a single-portrait piece I have chosen the Lafayette plate, with the bust in blue on a white ground, with a raised border, and the margin in blue. About the portrait is inscribed the words, " Welcome Lafayette, the Nation's Guest and our Country's Glory." This plate was made by Clews, and is extremely desirable. FIG. 81 gives it. This particular plate was picked up some years ago in ordinary fashion for a few dollars, but I know of another which fairly dropped like a ripe plum.

St. Justa and St. Rufina are, according to Mrs. Jameson, the patron saints of potters. She neglects to state what particular saints watch over the fortunes of china collectors. That some collectors have such genii assisting them I am very sure, else other poor mortals would have similar luck. For instance, one of these favoured individuals told me that within a few days she had received a lot of eighteen old-blue, historic plates from the " Cumberland Ridge." The sender had named his own price, five dollars. " He didn't care about the old stuff anyway." The second Lafayette plate came to hand as follows. An expert collector had penetrated to the buttery of an old-fashioned farmhouse, and the owner put before her a pile of four old plates, saying, " Take any or all of them, I sha'n't ever use the old things again." A glance at the top plate showed the collector it was worthless, and she was about turning away when some impulse decided her to lift it up. Below lay the Lafayette plate, greasy and dusty, but otherwise perfect. To use her own words, she " almost swooned."

but asked as calmly as possible, " How much do you want for this?" " Nothing; take it, I give it to you," the housewife persisted, but finally accepted twenty-five cents, saying to the departing collector, "You've given me just twenty-five cents more than it is worth." The market price for this plate is just forty dollars.

During Lafayette's triumphal tour through the United States, in 1824, there were many articles worn by men, women and children, that bore his portrait, or had welcoming or laudatory sentiments printed or worked on them. I have seen a kid glove, yellow with age, and of the single-button variety which was fashionable at the time, that was worn by a young woman when Rochester, N. Y., was visited by Lafayette in 1824. She was young and a beauty, and the gallant general not only pressed the little gloved hand, but, as the story goes, kissed the glove with his image upon it. The fair enthusiast tore off the glove, declaring she would keep it as long as she lived, and so she did and her descendants after her. The glove for the left hand was not so honoured and its fate is unknown.

In FIG. 82, one of the latest discoveries in the four portraits, the head of Lafayette is much better looking than on the single portrait plate. It is taken from a more youthful portrait, and though his uniform is the same as in the Clews platter, the presentment is more pleasing.

This plate with the handsome floral border is another piece which causes the dust of argument to fly. It bears on the back the impressed mark of Stevenson, and, in blue, an urn with the name " Niagara," the same view is found on nine-inch and ten-inch plates without the

Fig. 82. NIAGARA. 4 PORTRAITS. *A. Stevenson.*

Fig. 83. FRANKLIN.
MIRROR KNOB.

Fig. 84. COMMODORE
O. H. PERRY.

Fig. 85. BUTCHER'S ARMS PITCHER.

Fig. 86. BUTCHER'S ARMS PITCHER. REVERSE SIDE.

medallions. I have seen two of these plates with the medallions, both were ten inch, and in the one shown the medallions are just about half the size of those on the other plate. In FIG. 82 it is possible to see the Falls on the left of the picture beyond the house, while on the other plate the portrait of Jefferson completely obscures them. The house closely resembles one which stands on the Canadian side to-day, and the coloured man in the foreground, shearing sheep, is not at all un-American. The border is the same as that used on a series of English views, and not on any other American view. Yet these medallion plates were manufactured among the last of the dark blue pieces, were, no doubt, expensive, as they required so many printings, and few were made. It was probably the highest expression of old blue. This particular plate took the collector who now owns it many a long day to acquire. The woman who had it had some knowledge of old china, and had learned that she harboured something of value. Dollar by dollar the collector rose in her bids, always haunted by the fear that the plate would be snapped up by some "hunter," and she only secured it when she had offered one hundred times its original value. When the news of this sale got abroad, every other woman in the town where the Niagara plate was found hunted up her "old blue delft," as it is so often called, and hurried with it to our collector, eager to get a sum which would exceed the profits on butter money for a whole year.

While Franklin was not included in any of these medallion portraits he had more ceramic honours than even Washington himself. No doubt his long residence abroad was one reason for this, because very large numbers of these portraits were made by both English and French potters. The Metropolitan Museum of Art, New York, and the Trumble-Prime collection at Princeton, New Jersey, have many of these examples. They were made not only in crockery, but clay medallions were struck of various sizes, some even small enough to be set in rings, and others of the right size to be set in patch-boxes and snuff-boxes. Many of these had the fur cap with which we are familiar from engravings. Even Wedgwood tried his hand on these rugged features and made medallion portraits in basaltes as well as jasper. There were many statuettes, ranging from seven to thirteen inches in height, and varied busts, some even in Dresden china. Punch bowls and pitchers are also found, and the following inscription is taken from a bowl with the fur-cap portrait: " Benjn Franklin, Esq. LL.D. and F.R.S. the brave defender of the country against the oppression of taxation without representation—author of the greatest discovery in natural philosophy since those of Sir Isaac Newton, viz., that lightning is the same with electric fire."

The portrait of Franklin shown in FIG. 83 is on one of those choice and rare ceramic treasures, a mirror-knob. These are examples, in most cases, of transfer printing ; some are merely in outline ; and some have the outline, filled in with tint. They came into use before Revolutionary days—" looking-glass nobs " they called them then—and were often in rosette shape, mounted on the end of a spike, and screwed into the wall about two feet apart, leaving the knobs standing out from the wall about two inches. On these screws the lower edge of mirror or picture rested. The opal glass ones were also used to fasten back window curtains upon them, and a variety of them was used as knobs to bureau drawers. The one that is shown here is a delicate piece of printing mounted in a brass frame and on a long brass screw. In the same set are portraits of Washington, Franklin, Perry and Lafayette.

None of the portraits presents Franklin in any other aspect than that of old age. The rather short, stout figure, and the heavy features are those selected for reproduction. Curiously enough Franklin seems somewhat proud of the number and variety of portraits made of him. He writes from France to his daughter, Mrs Bache, in 1779, as follows: "A variety of others (clay medallions) have been made since of various sizes, and the number sold are incredible. These with the pictures and prints, upon which copies and copies are spread everywhere, have made your father's face as well known as that of the moon, so that he durst not do anything that would oblige him to run away as his phiz would discover him wherever he should venture to show it. It is said by learned etymologists that the name of doll, for the image children play with, is derived from the word idol. From the number of dolls now made of him he may be truly said, in that sense, to be idolized in that country."

In one collector's house a pair of these knobs, bearing the head of Lafayette, have been screwed into the wall, and on them rests a letter from him, written in a quaint copperplate hand and signed with a flourish, and one of the delicately tinted, old engraved portraits, framed together. In addition to all the portraits of those whom we may call our great heroes, there are many pieces devoted to the rank and file of minor heroes, who did good and often great service for their country. Such a portrait is shown in FIG. 84. It is also on a mirror-knob and is of Commodore O. H. Perry, who was sometimes called " Hero of the Lake." He had numerous plates and pitchers struck off in his honour, with not only busts but full-length portraits, and with mottoes in addition, such as, " We have met the enemy, and they are ours." Jackson and Bainbridge, with " Avast boys, she's struck," and Pike, with " Be always ready to die for your country," were also honoured in this way. All of these pieces, while of secondary interest and value, are good to have and add to the historic value of any collection, if not to its beauty. The list of these portraits on Staffordshire is constantly being added to, as these pieces are drawn from cupboards and closets and from beneath the attic eaves.

Of all these old English wares the printed blue Staffordshire is the most absorbing to an American. One cannot fail to get interested in the scenes it represents, even more than in the composition of the paste and the amount of feldspar, borax, flint or bone which enters into it. Still it is necessary to learn enough about the qualities and peculiarities of wares to be able to stand alone and not take the judgment of dealers. In many cases unmarked wares so closely resemble each other that even expert collectors classify them in a half a dozen different ways, and you have to make up your own mind by study, comparison, and handling. Staffordshire ware had a coarse body. and the stone ware was but little better. and all the early efforts of the Staffordshire potters were put forth to improve this table ware, and the deep rich blue assisted to cover imperfections.

The interest which led to the collecting of old blue stimulates further study, and with the china hunter every piece gathered leads farther along those flowery fields ridden over by every happy possessor of a hobby.

# CHAPTER VI.

## LIVERPOOL AND OTHER PRINTED WARES.

LIVERPOOL, city of docks and smoke, and the largest sea-port in the world, has had time to give to arts and crafts and the skilled workmen to invent printing on china and to carry on the peaceful art of potting. Some factories existed as early as 1600, and among the first wares made was what was known as Liverpool delft. This was an imitation of the Dutch ware, had a coarse body and was smeared on the face with a fine white clay, on which the design was drawn in blue. The collector in this country has small interest in this ware, as it is seldom found here except in tiles, which are occasionally taken from old houses. They are very crude in drawing, and have, usually, scriptural designs with chapter and verse placed below to help out the picture. I have seen a set which was taken from an old house at Sag Harbour, Long Island, and so ruthlessly treated that, of the twenty or thirty which framed the fireplace, I was able to rescue but two perfect ones.

The most interesting names connected with the Liverpool potteries are those of Sadler and Green, for to John Sadler, an engraver, the world is indebted for the invention of transfer-printing on pottery and porcelain and the subsequent cheapening of production. This discovery was due to an accident, as early as 1752, and for many years Sadler and his partner,

Guy Green, were able to keep the process a secret. The art of transfer-printing was first applied to tiles, but the process was soon found to be applicable to table ware and other goods. Sadler and Green laboured hard to perfect their work, and their black prints on a cream-coloured body have an unusually fine style of workmanship. In fact it was so superior to what other potters were able to do that Wedgwood himself was one of their customers and sent his goods by carrier and cart, or even in panniers on pack-horses while it was still in the biscuit state, and, after printing, had it returned by the same precarious method and fired in the home kilns.

The work was very cheaply done, the charge for printing a table and tea-service for the actor, David Garrick, in 1783, was £8 6s ½d, about $41.50. This was done on order from Wedgwood, and it would be interesting to know how much he charged Garrick for the set completed.

" Landskips " were always in demand, sometimes as many as thirty views going on a single service. The usual rule was a fresh design for every dozen plates of a dinner service, and distinct ones for each dish, tureen and center piece. Wedgwood furnished his own patterns, and his patrons and friends supplied him with charming prints, coloured and otherwise, of flowers, shells, fruit, birds, butterflies and country scenes.

At the close of August, 1768, Sadler, it appears, had dropped printing in all other colours than black and red. In May, 1770, Wedgwood wrote to Bently concerning Sadler's printing : " I have had a good deal of talk with Mr. Sadler and find him willing to do anything to improve his patterns. He has just completed a set of landskips for the inside of dishes, etc., with childish scrawling sprigs of flowers for the rims, all of which he thinks very clever, but they will not do for us. He is trying the purple and thinks he will manage it, and is willing to have a sett of the red chalk stile, or mezotint flowers, but thinks they can do them at Liverpool best. I am afraid of trusting too much to their taste, but they have promised to off-trace and coppy any prints I shall send them. I have promised to send him the red chalk plates and a few prints of flowers immediately, and beg you will send him the plates, and pick out some prints of different size flowers to send along with them to Liverpool."

About 1772, John Sadler retired from business, and Guy Green, who was a much younger man, became head of the firm. From this time on improvement became manifest, the patterns were better and more colours were used ; so that, by the end of 1776, many of the patterns hitherto enameled were printed in outline and then filled in by hand. Young girls did this latter work, and one of the favourite patterns was shells and sea-weeds. After a little more time crests and coats of arms were attempted and were most successful, and this was a great saving of expense to Wedgwood, who had long complained at the great cost of enamelling these. Even after Wedgwood began to print his own wares—and it is curious how long it was before he did this (1784)—Green still printed many of the old patterns, such as the green shell, green flower and red landscape. After 1787 the very finest borders were made by printing ; even tendrils and tiny leaves and all such parts as were outlined were filled in either in Liverpool or Etruria, as the case might be.

Dinner and dessert services, which had come into fashion as early as 1769, increased in favour still more, and in one cargo sent to Amsterdam were fifty "splendid dinner and dessert services chiefly pierced and gilt."

For the benefit of collectors we give the following list of borders popular in 1774, printed by Green, by Wedgwood's order. Some were printed only ; others combined the two processes of printing and painting ; and some were exquisitely enamelled :

| | |
|---|---|
| Printed bird pattern, feather edge. | Marine pattern, purple edge. |
| Oat border. | Calico pattern and spriggs. |
| Arrow pattern. | Laurel border. |
| Green flowers. | Green feather-edge and flower. |
| Green husks. | Super purple flowers. |
| Strawberry leaf. | Green oat-leaf border. |
| Black flowers. | Brown antique border. |
| Blue shell-edge. | Black antique border. |
| Green shell-edge. | Shaded figures, purple grounds. |
| Ivy border with spriggs. | Queen's pencilled. |
| Purple arrow heads. | Calico pattern. |
| Purple antique. | Parsley leaf. |
| | Grape leaf. |

By 1787 Wedgwood was doing a part of his own printing, and the list of patterns popular then are given among Wedgwood's own wares.

The printed pieces made for Wedgwood and marked with his name, with pieces made by and marked Sadler and Green, are now so rare as practically to be confined to museum specimens. Sadler and Green's marked tiles are sometimes found in England and are remarkable for the beauty and clearness of the printing.

Richard Chaffers was another Liverpool potter who went to work as early as 1752 and did much to improve the character of his ware. He is credited with sending wares to America; but I have never seen a marked piece, and the pepper-pots, which are supposed to be thick as blackberries among us, seem to have lived only in the mind of an enthusiastic china collector. Chaffers made not only earthenware but hard paste porcelain as well. His punch-bowls had a great reputation and were large affairs, often twenty and one half inches in diameter and nine inches high. Among other small pieces made as early as this were labels for different liquors, lettered " Cyder" and " Brandy" or " Rum," as well as " Peppermint " and " Wormwood." They do not often turn up ; they are made of the coarse clay body, faced with finer clay and glazed, exactly like the tiles. They have a hole in the upper portion through which a string may be passed to tie the label about the bottle's neck. Chaffers died about 1770.

What grew to be the largest and most successful pottery at Liverpool was founded in the year 1790 by Richard Abbey. He had been employed by John Sadler, had learned his secrets, and produced many effective groups for mugs, jugs and bowls, the most usual utensils found in the cream-coloured Liverpool ware. Tea-sets there are and an occasional plate, but the former pieces are the most common.

It was while in the employ of Sadler that Abbey made his most famous productions, the various " Arms " jugs. The designs of these arms are both pretty and

Fig. 87. BLACK-PRINTED LIVERPOOL WARE.

Fig. 88. APOTHEOSIS JUG.

Fig. 89. WASHINGTON MAP JUG.

Fig. 90. WASHINGTON **JUG.**

**Fig. 91.** MONUMENT JUG.

Fig. 92. WASHINGTON JUG.

Fig. 93. MASONIC JUG.

witty. Jewitt describes the Farmer's Arms at some length and says there is a teapot with this design in the Museum of Practical Geology in London. On the reverse side are the verses which speak of the joys of a farmer's life :

" May the mighty and great
Roll in splendour and state ,
I envy them not, I declare it ;
I eat my own lamb
My chicken and ham
I shear my own sheep and I wear it.
I have lawns, I have bowers,
I have fruits, I have flowers,
The lark is my morning alarmer ;
So you jolly dogs now
Here's to ' God bless the Plow '
Long Life and Content to the Farmer."

In addition to the Farmer's Arms, which is the only one mentioned by Jewitt, there is the Blacksmith's Arms, with the motto, " By Hammer and Hand all Arts do stand," and the Buck's Arms with stags and hunting emblems and the motto, " Freedom with Innocence "; the Baker's Arms, which has for motto " Praise God for all," and the Hatter's Arms with the legend, " We assist Each other in Time of Need." The only one I have seen in this country is given in FIG. 85. It is the Butcher's Arms and is a very handsome jug, clearly and beautifully printed and with a pretty English scene on the reverse side. The initials " W. W." are under the lip, and it was sold by the grandson of the man for whom it was made in England. I have heard of, but never seen, another, the " Ironworker's Arms," which bears the motto, " Benevolence and Union go hand in hand."

These " arms " jugs were made for the members of the various guilds, which have always played a more or less important part in London's history, their greatest strength dating from the time of Edward III, when enactments were passed which made membership in a guild necessary to the privilege of freedom of the city. At one time the guilds numbered over one hundred. At present there are but seventy-six, and some of these which are left represent trades which are extinct, a delightful instance of England's conservatism. The twelve so called " Great Guilds" claim precedence over the others, and though the Fishmongers' and Grocers', as well as the Salters' and Vintners' are among the twelve, the Butchers' is found in the less privileged classes.

Nobody seems to have made these jugs but this Richard Abbey while with Sadler and Green, so they were all made prior to 1790, when he went into business for himself, taking as a partner a man named Graham. In 1796 Worthington, Humble and Holland bought the pottery from Abbey and Graham, and called it the Herculaneum Pottery. The works were kept up, under one firm and another, until 1841, when they were dismantled and the site used for the Herculaneum Dock. Richard Abbey died in 1801 while leading the singing in a church choir. He was eighty-one years of age at the time.

The period between 1796 and 1800 at the Herculaneum Pottery does not seem to have been distinguished by any particular marks, but after that time, that is from 1800 to 1841, there are three periods easily distinguishable by the different marks. From 1800 to 1822 the word Herculaneum was printed in a half circle around a crown, or printed on a strap which entirely surrounded a crown. The second period, from 1822 to 1833, had the words " Herculaneum Pottery " in a straight line, and the third period had the figure of a bird, the liver or lever, which was the crest of the Arms of Liverpool. Some pieces found over here, and apparently made for the American market, have, in addition, an eagle. An example of the porcelain is shown in another chapter.

In FIG. 87 is shown a part of a tea-set, which we will place under the general head of Liverpool. The ware is beautifully creamy, the printing fine and clear and the twisted edge prettily gilded. The oblong plate shows its irregularity even in the photograph, but the cup has a handle which the earliest ones were without.

Nearly all the great potteries which we have already considered made printed ware of varying degrees of beauty and clearness; but it was generally unmarked, and, after this lapse of time, has all come to be classed under the generic head of Liverpool. The most interesting pieces of this ware are found in pitchers, cream coloured and black, printed, and capable of holding a gallon each. Such a one is shown in FIG. 88 and, as is the case with so many of these Liverpool jugs, is in honour of Washington. This particular one is called the " Apotheosis " jug, as you may see on its face. There is a tomb in the oval picture with Liberty and an Indian (strange companions in view of later day developments), seated side by side. Father Time is raising Washington. clothed in a shroud, from the tomb.

while an angel holds Washington's hand and points upward. On the tomb is the inscription, "Sacred to the memory of Washington ob. 17 Dec. A. D. 1799 Ae. 68." A semicircle of cherubs' heads forms a border to the medallion, and in the midst are various insignia which belonged to Washington. This pitcher bears under its lip the name of the man for whom it was made; but many copies of it, instead of the name, have a motto, something like this, "A man without example, a patriot without reproach." On the reverse side is a ship in full sail. This pitcher is ten inches high and was bought within the year for the unusually small sum of $12.50.

In FIG. 89 is shown another of these Washington jugs, which, on account of its rarity, brought $56, though it is but eight inches high. The side shown in the picture is a medallion of Washington with the figure of Liberty seated beside it. An eagle, with branch and bolts, fills the upper part of the oval, which is surrounded by a chain of fifteen links, each link bearing the name of a state, and in the center of it a star. Below the portrait is an inscription which reads "Washington crowned with laurels by Liberty."

The reverse side of this pitcher is quite as interesting. It shows Washington and Franklin inspecting a map of the United States, which is almost as much of a curiosity as the famous old "Mappa Mundi." Liberty has Washington in charge while History takes care of Franklin, and in the upper part of the picture a very frisky Fame blows a trumpet. Louisiana goes under the name of the Country of Mines and extends as far north as Lake Superior. This pitcher, while classed as Liverpool, is really Staffordshire, as it is

Fig. 94.  DEATH OF WOLFE.          Fig. 95.  COMMODORE PREBLE.

Fig. 96.  SUNDERLAND JUGS.

Fig. 97.   PRINTED TEA-SET.

Fig. 98.   BOW PICKLE–LEAF AND CREAMER.
Boston Museum of Fine Arts.

marked " F. Morris, Shelton." I have seen one with these designs on it marked 1796 on the front, showing that they were made before the death of Washington.

While FIG. 89 is unusually small for this style of pitcher, the common size runs from ten to twelve inches, making a pitcher capable of holding several quarts. No such innocent beverage as milk or water filled those generous jugs; but cider, which almost might be called the national drink, and some of the varieties of spiced decoctions then so popular were liquids which poured from these fine large lips.

It is quite remarkable to run back and see how early apple orchards were planted and began to bear freely. New England led off in the quantity of cider made, and in the potency and manufacture of rum, which was known throughout the colonies as " Killdevil." As early as 1721 one Massachusetts village, boasting but forty families, made from its own apples three thousand barrels of cider. At Oyster Bay, one of the oldest settlements on Long Island, in 1726, Henry Townson leaves by will to his father, " one hundred bushels of good, sound apples out of my orchard yearly, and also a load of hay during his life." By 1740 so many orchards had matured that cider was the common drink among the people. At three shillings the barrel even the poorest need hardly be without their winter supply, and so general was its use that members of the clergy often stored forty barrels or more for winter use. In summer, diluted with water, sweetened, and spiced with nutmeg, it made a refreshing drink, when it had been cooled in a spring or cellar.

FIG. 90 is a twelve-inch Washington jug with a more than usually swelling shape. There is a small portrait on the pedestal, and the words " First in War, First in Peace, First in Fame and First in Victory." A naval officer and Fame stand on either side of the shaft, and the picture is surrounded with scallops showing the names of thirteen states. Notwithstanding the pedestal or obelisk, I should place this jug as made prior to 1800, from the use of but thirteen states in the border. On the reverse side is a full-rigged ship with the American flag in colours, and on the front in a wreath the inscription " A present to Capt. Nath'l Gunnison." It is in perfect condition and sold for sixty dollars. Ten years ago fifteen dollars was thought a good price to pay for such a pitcher. Recently I saw four of these Liverpool pitchers with Washington designs on them, and varying in size from nine to twelve inches, which were bought in a lot two or three years ago at seven dollars each. They have been sold within the last few months at forty dollars apiece. In the Rooms of the Antiquarian Society at Concord, Mass., there are several of these jugs, of large size and in good condition. FIG. 91 shows one such with unusual lustre decoration about the top. It is ten inches high, and is generally known as the " Monument Pitcher." It comes in twelve-inch pitchers also. On the top of the picture is the legend, " Washington in Glory," and below it on a band, " America in tears." An eagle and a female figure, both very drooping, are on either side of the monument, and on the reverse side are Liberty and two negro boys with portraits.

The English potters amused themselves, or, perhaps, suited the tastes of their patrons by varying the patterns on different pitchers. I have seen this monument pitcher with the map of America, previously spoken of, on the reverse side, and also with a full-rigged ship. Sometimes these pitchers are known as Masonic pitchers, and every Mason liked to own one with the picture of the greatest Mason of all on it. If the purchaser was a seafaring man, of course he chose a ship for the second side, to take home to an appreciative family. These pitchers were turned by hand, as may be seen by the slight variations in shape and by the wavy lines in the bottom. Another stout one is figured in FIG. 92.

A fairly good portrait of Washington within a laurel wreath occupies the center of the medallion, with Justice and Liberty at right and left and Cupid above holding a glory of stars. A very singular combination truly. The oval is surrounded by an entwined scalloped border with the names of fifteen states and fifteen stars, making a more decorative picture than is usual with this class of pitchers. This design I have seen on two sizes of pitchers only, nine inches and seven and one half inches, and it is extremely rare. On the other side is a four-line verse, with liberty cap and other emblems. On two seven and a half-inch pitchers, which have passed under my notice, were, on the reverse side, two different designs. On the first were Peace, Plenty and Independence in an oval, surmounted by cannon, American flags and a screaming eagle. On the second one was this inscription, " By virtue and valour we have freed our country, extended our commerce and laid the foundation of a great empire." Washington stands with one foot on the neck of the British lion, and there are grouped about four soldiers and a ship in full sail, with flags, cannon, etc., and below " Success to America." It seems almost incredible that these sentiments and devices were made by Englishmen for the very country which had asserted its independence.

Fig. 93 shows a Masonic jug which was long in the possession of Mr. John Haigh of Somerville, Mass., a Mason of the thirty-third degree. It has many Masonic devices, as may be seen, and in front has square and compass with "G" in a triangle. It also has the inscription "Samuel Fowler, Salisbury, 1795," which, of course, adds to its value. It is in perfect condition, nine inches high, and worth between twenty-five and thirty dollars.

The verses on these jugs are generally doggerel of the worst order. A very common verse ran as follows:

> "The world is in pain
> Our secret to gain,
> But still let them wonder and gaze on,
> For they ne'er can divine
> The word nor the sign
> Of a free and accepted Mason."

Even rarer than the Masonic pitchers are a few that one occasionally runs across, like that shown in Fig. 94. It is the death of General Wolfe. On the reverse is a picture of a naval battle. This pitcher is always beautifully printed and seems to come in but one size, ten and one half inches. The pitcher made in commemoration of Commodore Preble is given in Fig. 95. His portrait is in the oval, and above is a figure of Fame with wreath and trumpet. An Indian maiden with a scroll and a flag and shield fills the base of the picture. On the reverse side is shown the Commodore's squadron attacking the City of Tripoli, August 3, 1804. This pitcher is but nine inches high, while the pitcher made to celebrate Perry's victory comes as small as seven and one half inches.

The Herculaneum Pottery contributed pitchers depicting the death of Montgomery and the death of Warren. There is also one with a print called " The gallant defence of Stonington, August 9, 1814," showing the famous scene when, with one gun, the inhabitants successfully resisted an attack of the British and drove off her ships, sinking one. Under this picture is the legend " Stonington is free whilst her heroes have one gun left." On the reverse side are a ship and a ribbon wreath enclosing some patriotic verses.

More generally interesting than the Masonic jugs were the sailor pitchers. I have seen numbers of them in the interior towns as well as on the sea-coast. They are generally classed as Liverpool ware, though I believe most of them were made elsewhere. For instance J. Phillips at North Hylton made many of these printed sailor jugs, of the same creamy ware, and similar in shape. His pieces also are seldom marked, but he has certain verses which are almost as distinctive as the Staffordshire borders. They occur over and over again, and when you find a pitcher with the following verse on it you may set it down to North Hylton :

‘ REST IN HEAVEN."

" There is an hour of peaceful rest
To mourning wanderers given ;
There's a tear for souls distrest,
A balm for every wounded breast—
'Tis found above, in Heaven."

Jack Tar is nothing if not sentimental when about to set sail on a cruise, and on the opposite side to that

showing the pious verse above quoted is a ship in full
sail, a sailor and his lass in the agonies of parting and
the words, " Jack on a cruise. Avast there. Back
your maintopsail."

On another Hylton ship pitcher I find this verse:

> "Glide on, my bark, the summer's tide
> Is gently flowing by the side ;
> Around thy prow the waters bright,
> In circling rounds of broken light
> Are glittering as if ocean gave
> Her countless gems to deck the wave."

In FIG. 96 is shown an unusually interesting group
of Sunderland pitchers, all of them of that rare and
interesting pink-spotted lustre characteristic of these
potteries. The largest one of all, gallon size, was
found in Maine within the year, and bought for six
dollars—simply nothing for such a jug in perfect condition. On the side shown is a view of Twymouth
Haven with ships in the distance. It is printed in
black and touched by hand in colours. On the reverse
side is a ship, flanked on either side by a sailor and a
female figure, also touched in colours, and the verse:—

> " The sailor tossed on stormy seas,
> Though far his bark may roam,
> Still hears a voice in every breeze
> That wakens thoughts of home ;
> He thinks upon his distant friends,
> His wife, his humble cot ;
> And from his inmost heart ascends
> The prayer, 'Forget me not.'"

The next smaller pitcher has the picture showing
the parting between a sailor and his wife and child,
and a verse called the "Sailor's Farewell." It runs:

"Sweet, oh, sweet, is that sensation,
Where two hearts in union meet,
But the pain of separation
Mingles bitter with the sweet."

This pathetic verse seems exclusively the property of the Sunderland potteries. Punch-bowls of this ware have it as well as pitchers.

The little jug in the center is one of those interesting pieces which were cast in an old silver mould and then lustred. It is made of coarse pottery, as a chip on one foot shows, and came into the present owner's possession for the small amount of twenty-five cents.

Sunderland and Newcastle are always classed together in descriptions of their pot works, of which the earliest were established between 1730 and 1740. At Sunderland, beside the jugs pictured with the joys and sorrows of maritime life, favourite patterns were Nelson's victories and the famous bridge over the Wear, commenced in 1793 and finished in 1796. Newcastle made the same style of ware as Sunderland, earthenware, and what was called "cream-coloured fayence." It was crudely printed and painted, and some was made like the Leeds ware, pierced and embossed. The well-known "frog mugs" were made at Newcastle, and in them a frog is represented as climbing up the side of the mug, gradually being revealed as the drinker sups the liquor. The outside of the mugs are ornamented with the verses of the day. None of these pieces is marked, and I have never seen one that was; but the marks of these potteries, when used, were impressed in the clay, or stamped in transfer.

It was not alone the jugs which bore inscriptions,

but even teapots were used for showing popular sentiments.    For instance a black printed one has this
motto :

> " Let love abide
> Till death divide."

It almost seems as if such a piece must have been
used as a love token or a marriage gift.

Even as early as 1742 these inscriptions began to be
popular, and it pictures a very unusual state of subjec-
tion when we read on a plate :

> " But if his wife do frown
> All merriment goes down."

Punch-bowls bore inscriptions which their size and
the potency of the liquid they carried did not seem to
bear out :

> " With gratitude receive ;
> With temperance enjoy."

When one reflects that the ingredients that went to
make up punch were arrack, tea, sugar, water and
lemons, with personal touches, by individual mixers, of
rum, French brandy, cider royal, etc., and that the
bowls held many gallons, one does not wonder that
such words as " cocky, fuddled, groggy, jagged,
screwed and hazed " were necessary to express the
condition of convivial souls after meetings at club or
tavern.

It is on a small jug that the sentiment,

> " A heart that conceals,
> But a tongue that never reveals "

is found.

> " From rocks and sands and barren lands,
> Good fortune set me free,
> And from great guns and women's tongues
> Good Lord deliver me "

is on one side of a mug, with ship and nautical emblems on the other.

Many hunting pieces also have mottoes on them. One has a brown decoration on a cream body, and a picture of a hare in full flight.

> " The fearful Hare does run apace
> Because the hounds are on their chace
> The country he is forst to fly
> Whilst they are out with Hue and Cry
> Nature hath taught him in this strife
> To seek for to preserve his life
> Which he by running doth obtain
> And the Hounds returne againe
> The Huntsman seeing that doth cry
> Let him goe his meat is dry
> I'll to my landlady with speed
> For I of her have greater need."

One is allowed to punctuate this at pleasure, and the date on the jug is 1804.

Occasionally we may come across one of those curious jugs or mugs dealing with English royalty and containing verses eulogistic or very much otherwise. Perhaps the Georges came in for most of the " otherwise " verse, and here is one :

> " George the First was always reckon'd
> Vile, but viler George the second ;
> And what mortal ever heard
> Any good of George the Third ?
> When from earth the fourth descended
> Praise the Lord, the Georges ended."

This was made after 1830, when George IV died. It was his action with regard to Caroline, his queen, which divided all England, and the strong feeling which raged both for and against her found its way even on crockery :

> " Long live Caroline, Queen of England,
>     As for the green bag crew
>     Justice will have its due,
>     God save the Queen !
>
>     Confound their politicks,
>     Frustrate their knavish tricks,
>     On her our hopes we fix
>     God save the Queen ! "

A recent book on the melancholy life of this un-crowned queen does much to throw light on a career which is quite unexampled for the cruelty of treat-ment and humiliation undergone by a woman of royal blood.

On a very handsome gallon jug, which must have taken a very steady hand to manage, I find this verse :

> " Come, my old friend, and take a pot,
>     But mark me what I say ;
>     Whilst thou drink'st thy neighbour's health,
>     Drink not thy own away.
>
>     For it too often is the case,
>     Whilst we sit o'er a pot,
>     And while we drink our neighbour's health,
>     Our own is quite forgot."

This one on a mug goes right to the point :

> " Call freely,
>     Drink merrily,
>     Pay honestly,
>     Part quietly. "

The New Hall works at Shelton, Staffordshire, began about 1810 to make the paste with a large admixture of bone, giving up the porcelain body which they had manufactured from 1777 to 1810. They made quantities of printed ware of excellent quality. The earliest mark was the letter " N " in script, the later mark the words " New Hall " enclosed in a double circle, the whole mark in red. The works ceased to operate in 1825; so all china with this mark is previous to that date.

In addition to all this printed ware, which is called Liverpool, though made at several different places, there is a large amount belonging to what may be called the " debased period " in china. That is to say, between 1840 and 1850. Even while it is not comparable to the dark blue, with either English or American views, to my mind there is much of it deserving a place in a collector's cabinet and of both ornamental and intrinsic value. In this class I put many pieces printed in red, green, or brown, or in combinations of these colours. I know of a tea-set which has been got together after years of patient waiting that is a cheering sight every time it appears on the table. The teapot is one of those graceful and quaint shapes copied from old silver ware, and the paste is a lovely creamy tint. On it are printed in red and green really charming scenes, which come under the head of " Continental Views," with spires and towers, water in the foreground, and boats, etc. These are pretty compositions which engender delightful speculation, every time that one of them is seen, as to just what part of which continent was in the potter's mind when this teapot was made. Accompanying it, but not mated with it, is a squatty little creamer, printed in red, on four sturdy legs, and decorated with a view illustrative of Thompson's " Seasons." There is a haying-field with loaded wain in the foreground, and peace and plenty in rich orchards and fertile fields compose the background. A female figure raking hay gives human interest to complete the scene, and, although illustrating an English scene, yet it might well stand for the fair Virginia landscape, whence this little creamer wandered north.

No doubt the lady in the picture is that Sophronisba, the iteration of whose name caused so much ridicule to be heaped on poor " Jemmy Thompson," as he was called by friend and foe alike. The scene on this creamer illustrates those four lines which smack so strongly of the sentiment no poet of the eighteenth century was without :

> " An elegant sufficiency, content,
> Retirement, rural quiet, friendship, books,
> Ease and alternate labour, useful life,
> Progressive virtue, and approving Heaven ! "

The cups which go with this set stimulate reflection as well as the larger pieces. The first one is in brown, and is from a scene by Turner, that singular man with the fingers and faculties of an ideal artist, and with the degraded appetite of a tramp. It is a scene from one of his Italian sketches, and I fancy it was one of those he made during the second tour in 1828, when Ruskin had so advanced his reputation by judicious puffing that his work was in demand on every side, and for many purposes. The scene on this cup is very lovely, and clearly and beautifully printed. Like all the other pieces in this little group, it is unmarked.

The Japanese have a proverb that " Even the worst tea is sweet when first made from the new leaf," which could be paraphrased to read, " Even the worst tea is sweet when sipped from so dainty a cup," for surely half the delight of a meal is derived from its pretty appointments. In FIG. 97 is shown a little set of various kinds of printed wares. One of the charms of such a set is these variations. It is like sets of books. How much greater individuality they have when each one is differently bound, than when clothed all alike in dull uniformity, the only means of identification being numbers.

In inventories of estates, in notices of auction and other sales in newspapers, and in old wills do we come across the lists of the household goods of our ancestors, and learn their scant number and the value placed upon them. The care with which minor household articles are specified forms one of the curious features of these family bequests, and the lack of articles of pottery and earthenware is extremely noticeable, particularly in those documents dating from 1700 to 1776.

Feather beds and slaves were the objects that seemed to be in the greatest abundance. In fact, hardly a will is without a specific mention of the former, and after the slaves, either Indian or African, comes the family Bible. Silver cups, some with "two ears," are mentioned, and in one family of wealth the four daughters each got one silver spoon, which was an uncommonly large supply for those days.

The earliest mention of earthenware to be found among old wills is in 1711. Evert Van Hoole specifies that his wife shall have " a new cupboard and three great and twelve small earthen cups that stand on top of said cupboard, and six varnished chairs, her looking-glass, Dutch Bible, and a brass kettle and a tea-kettle and a bed, with all thereunto belonging." As the earthen cups come first in the list, we may judge of the estimation in which they were held. Apparently they were more for show than for use, and as they belonged to a Dutchman we can guess they must have been delft. Some years later a Hempstead, Long Island, farmer leaves to his daughter " one feather bed, an iron pot, six plates, three platters, two basons, one drinking pot, one cupboard worth three pounds, six chairs and six sheep." While the good man was writing this list we could wish that he had specified as to the material of said plates, platters and "basons." I fancy they were pewter.

The little set shown in FIG. 97 is printed ware, showing one of these same cups and saucers with Turner's designs. One can see what a dainty picture it makes. The teapot is black printed Liverpool, quite uncommonly charming, with pretty scenes on the sides, of a garden with ladies in it, and of a very populous beehive. The border around the top of the pot and also on the cover is scrolls and a wreath of flowers. On the scrolls are such moral maxims as " Flee the vicious," " Be industrious," and "Sorrow's best antidote is employment." There is a motto for every day of the week and several extra for Sundays and holidays. The shape of this pot is very agreeable, with its four stout legs, its fluted sides, and a nicely turned spout.

The creamer is also a waif and stray, with black printed view and a little leafy decoration in pink lustre. When in use the set stands upon one of those fine old trays of inlaid satin wood which Wedgwood kept on sale, and on which he showed off his dainty boudoir and breakfast sets. He knew well how attractively the china was reflected in the polished wood, and how conveniently all the necessary articles could be carried from pantry to dining parlour. The old George III silver spoon, with its straight handle and little bowl, seems to fit better with such a set than the more modern and more weighty curved handled spoon.

If one can come across anywhere a spoon with a "rat-tail," that is a slender rib of silver running down the back from handle to bowl, it may be chosen as a fitting companion to this old china, particularly as you will probably be able to find, impressed on it somewhere, a letter showing the date of its manufacture, and a design showing its nationality.

# CHAPTER VII.

IN studying the beginnings of most of the porcelain and pottery works of England, it is found that generally all of them began with imitating Delft decoration in deep blue. A chapter might well be written headed " The Colour Blue " and dealing exclusively with its use on china. This colour, least common of all the colours given by nature to bird, insect or blossom, has been selected by the Oriental potter for many of his most exquisite achievements and copied from him by other nations to whom a brush-stroke or a colour does not have the significance that it has for the Chinese worker. In the sixteenth century cobalt was introduced, either by Jesuits or Mohammedans, into China and used more or less freely under the name of " Moslem Blue." This shade was brighter and more vivid than the restful grayish shade used for centuries previously and on china made for palace use only, the colour of which was known as " blue seen through a rift in the clouds after rain."

The shade of blue is subject to infinite variations. due to the presence of certain ores—manganese, iron, etc.—and may become almost a violet tone, or take a reddish shade, or vary again from the delicate tint of the robin's egg, through mazarine and sapphire, to peacock blue. To the original users of this colour, blue meant much ; it had a religious and mythological, as well as an historical significance, which was lost in its transit across seas, and blue was chosen in the Occident for its durability and cheapness, and because the Chinese models were the best obtainable.

Hard glaze porcelain was made at Plymouth, Bristol and Liverpool. Soft glaze porcelain was made at Bow, Chelsea, Derby, Pinxton, Rockingham, Swansea, Nantgarw, Liverpool and Worcester.

The very early Staffordshire potters commenced with what must be called "English Delft," though properly that term should only be given to such ware as was made in England in direct imitation of the Dutch ware and covered with tin glaze. However the term "Delft" was applied long after tin glaze had been superseded by translucent glaze, and was broad enough to cover the painting of birds and flowers in the Chinese style which was so popular with the Dutch china painters and imitated from them by the English.

"Old Delft," properly speaking, is that faïence made in Holland during the seventeenth and eighteenth centuries, covered with a heavy opaque glaze of tin, which, like salt glaze, has many tiny holes in its surface. It is very friable, and chips and scales easily, as nearly all pieces of genuine old Delft will testify. English Delft with tin glaze was made in Bristol and Liverpool, as well as in Staffordshire and Lambeth.

The approximate dates for porcelain manufactures in England were Bow, about 1730, Chelsea, 1745, Derby, 1756, Worcester, 1751, Caughley, 1751, and Lowestoft, 1756, Plymouth, 1760, Bristol, 1768.

## *Bow.*

Bow, or Stratford-le-Bow, is the "Stratford atte Bowe" which Chaucer writes of in the "Canterbury Tales":

> "Ful wel she sange the service devine,
> Entuned in hire nose ful swetely,
> And French she spake ful fayre and fetisly,
> After the scole of Stratford atte bowe,
> For French of Paris was to hire unknowe."

It has long since been absorbed in London town. It is, or rather was, a little town on the bank of the river Lea, and is in Middlesex, the smallest county in England, but with the largest population, since the City of London is in it and overflows into four or five other counties beside.

Bow is not far from the famous Tower of London, and you may ride out there on the top of a 'bus, but you will not find any china there, and but rarely a bit among the London second-hand shops. It is all snapped up by eager collectors or their agents.

As early as 1730, at Stratford-le-Bow, was made the first soft paste porcelain known in England. In 1744, Thomas Frye and Edward Heylin took out a patent for making ware "equal to imported china or porcelain." It is not usually suggested that Bow sent out any but painted wares; yet in a curious old account book of the goods furnished during a part of the year 1756, are, among many others, these three entries:

> "One pint printed mug."
> "One half pint do."
> "One sett compleat of the second printed teas."

Many pieces of china classed as Chelsea belong to Bow. Among the most notable of these is a pair of china figures of Kitty Clive the actress and Woodward the actor, exquisitely modelled and finished and bearing, stamped in the clay, the date 1758. A pair is known which came direct from the factory to the family whose descendants still own them. These figures have now become the rarest specimens of Bow manufacture. The lovely Kitty Clive, that famous English actress who took the town by storm early in 1700, created as one of her most famous parts that of Lady Riot in " Lethe." So popular were both actress and part that these exquisite little figures were issued. Kitty is shown in a monstrous petticoat with laces and furbelows. The companion figure, Woodward, who plays the fine gentleman, struts gaily in cocked hat and ruffles, both figures being most delicately modelled. Good specimens easily bring $150 each. In FIG. 98 are given two charming examples of Bow. What could be more dainty than the pickle leaf laid across the basket work, and coloured to nature with veining and stems? The butterflies and bees are brilliant in colouring also, and are repeated again and again on the little creamer, which shows a pretty ribbed effect, with three plain medallions which have bunches of flowers, birds and insects. This same ribbed effect is also seen on other wares than Bow, and was popular no doubt, for everything that met the fancy of the day was seized upon and copied. The pickle dish has a tiny anchor in red, one of the numerous Bow marks.

The goat jugs, with or without the modelled bee were always attributed to Bow; but they were made

at Chelsea as well and are found marked with the
Chelsea triangle. In the same old account book previously spoken of, and which makes such interesting
reading, we learn of many articles made at the factories of which the collector would otherwise be unaware.
For instance, in this year, 1756, there is the record of
the making of "two dozen crimson buttons." They
made also many harlequin figures and swans. Among
many other articles there were sent to a Mr. Fogg
"twelve dragon breakfast cups and saucers of a good
deep colour, a milk pot, same pattern, and a vine-leaf
milk pot."

In May the Duchess of Leeds ordered a " blue
dolphin pickle stand." An order reads, " Goats, swans,
and every other sort of toys to be sent in Baxter's
order." There were also knife-handles, candlesticks,
animals of every description, salt-cellars on shell, coral
or rock-work stands, pastoral, garden and hunting
scenes, and exquisite vases and jars with raised decorations, coloured like nature.

The paste of Bow porcelain varies much in hardness,
the earlier specimens, made with American clay as
early as 1744, being harder than the subsequent productions, which were soft paste. These latter are
heavy, with a firm compact paste. The glaze is thick
and somewhat milky in colour and blots out the finer
lines in relief work. The decorations are in delicate
colours, cleverly arranged, and consist of birds, butterflies, insects, etc. The flowers on dresses of the figures were generally in yellow or crimson, with gold
leaves. Embossed wares in pure white were made in
large quantities, with the flat surfaces decorated
with paintings of insects and flowers. The hawthorn

sprig was a favourite at this factory. The ware was first finished in a biscuit state and the blue decorations laid on before being glazed. After being dipped in the glaze, which consisted of half a dozen ingredients, the articles were put in cases and burned with wood until the surface was clear and shining. The decorations in colour and the gilding were done over glaze and fired in a muffle kiln.

The marks employed at this factory are open to much discussion. There was no regular factory mark, and daggers, arrow-heads and anchors were scratched and painted on different pieces, while the triangle, formerly assigned to Chelsea, is now assigned to both factories. Mrs Bury Palliser and Prime, who follows largely in her wake, give nineteen possible marks for this factory. An authentic Bow creamer, with the goats and bee in relief, has sold at auction in London for £25 10s, another for £3 5s, and for various intermediate sums. They are sometimes found in this country for much smaller prices, and, whether Bow or Chelsea, are much esteemed in all collections. In 1776 Mr. Duesbury of Derby bought the works and moved them to Derby, as he had previously bought the works at Chelsea.

## Chelsea.

Chelsea town, like Stratford-le-Bow, has become an integral part of the great city of London. It had, nevertheless, an interesting history of its own, and its manor was given by the much-married Henry VIII to Catherine Parr.

During the eighteenth century, and while the china works were in operation, "the village of Chelsea," as it was called, was the home of many famous men. Swift, Steele, Smollett and Sir Horace Walpole were among them. The gay Ranelagh was frequented by the " smart set " of those days, and these grounds were in Chelsea. So were the Cremorne Gardens which still flourish as a place of popular entertainment. More in our day was Cheyne Walk, where the Carlyles dragged out an embittered existence, he distraught over his neighbours' roosters and she waging warfare over the " blacks," as those huge roaches are called in London.

Greatest of all Chelsea's monuments is the famous old hospital for invalid soldiers, begun in 1682 by Sir Christopher Wren. Even as late as 1801 Chelsea was thought very suburban—a quiet country retreat.

The beginnings of Chelsea china are meagrely told and obscure. Large quantities of ware were brought into England from Holland, and the best workmen in this branch of the art, Dutch workmen, were induced to come to England and settle there, and Chelsea was one of the towns where they worked. By 1745 the Chelsea works had been several years in existence and had gained celebrity both at home and abroad for the wares made and decorated there. From 1750 to 1765 were the years of Chelsea's greatest popularity, and enough ware could not be made to supply the demand.

George II did much to encourage these works and also procured material and workmen, so that this factory might successfully compete with those of Saxony and France. Horace Walpole wrote in 1763

Fig. 99. CHELSEA. THE MUSIC LESSON.
Boston Museum of Fine Arts.

Fig. 100. CROWN–DERBY. FALSTAFF.
Boston Museum of Fine Arts.

that he had seen a magnificent service of Chelsea
china "which the King and Queen are sending to the
Duke of Mecklenberg. There are dishes and plates
without number, in short, it is complete, and cost
£1200." The varieties of products turned out from
the Chelsea factory were immense. Vases, flat ware
and tea services, candelabra, statuettes and groups, as
well as quantities of pieces which come under the head
of "toys," consisting of snuff-boxes, patch-boxes, trin-
kets for watch-charms, smelling-bottles, etc. As early
as 1754 auction sales were begun as a good and quick
method of disposing of the wares. Some of the smelling-bottles, seen now only in collections, are charming, being modelled in the forms of children and birds.

From about 1760 to 1763 the famous coloured
grounds of Sevres were copied very successfully, the
most popular being the claret colour, and next in
favour coming turquoise, apple-green, deep blue and
crimson.

The body of Chelsea is very uneven, as if poorly
mixed, and so soft and susceptible to heat that it
would bear but one firing ; so all decoration was done
at one time. By holding a specimen, like a plate, up
to the light it will be found to contain spots "the
unmistakable Chelsea spots,—moonlike discs scattered about the piece irregularly and more translucent than the rest of the material." Most pieces of
Chelsea china have the stilt marks with which we are
so familiar in Staffordshire wares. The earliest specimens are blue and white, as was to be expected, and
the glaze was thick and unevenly laid on.

After the Dutch style came copies of Oriental
patterns, chiefly on cups and saucers, and after that

Sevres and Dresden were used as models and successfully rivalled both in colour, form and execution.  The
charming groups of figures which are the highest
exponents of Chelsea work were now produced in the
greatest perfection, the most eminent workmen in
these lines being employed to make them.  FIG. 99
shows a dainty one of these, called the "Music
Lesson" and dated 1770.  The perfection of this
group, one hundred and thirty-two years old, is quite
remarkable, since, as may be seen, the apple blossoms
which form the background are quite unbroken and
look fresh enough to smell.  The shepherdess with
her lambs and the shepherd with dog and pipe are
just as gay and debonair as when they left the potter's hand so long ago.  Not even a finger is missing
or the strap by which she holds her lamb.  After
seeing such a group as this the term " as dainty as
Chelsea china " seems not to come amiss. · The beauty
of the dresses should be noted and the careful modelling of all the parts.  The most important figures
made by this factory are well known, and among
them are Britannia seated on a lion and holding a
medallion portrait of George II.

Shakespeare and Milton are a companion pair, and
on the former is the inscription :

> " The cloud cap't towers and gorgeous palaces,
>   The solemn temples, the great globe itself,
>   Yea, all which it inherit, shall dissolve,
>   And like the baseless fabrick of a vision,
>   Leave not a wreck behind."

This figure of Shakespeare is modelled from the
monument in Westminster Abbey.  This same figure
has been reproduced in porcelain or pottery by nearly

all the noted English potteries. There were also figures of Falstaff, Minerva, Neptune, Diana, Fame, Justice, etc. An exceedingly rare piece is a dove-cote, richly decorated with raised flowers, and at the base a pointer and partridges.

On the flat ware were painted the daintiest little sprigs, dropped on as it seems, so realistic are they, and attracting by their true colour and beauty, gay insects, butterflies, bees and moths. The birds, also, which formed little groups, were carefully modelled and well painted. At the famous Strawberry Hill sale of Horace Walpole's china, a pair of cups of the famous claret colour brought twenty-five guineas. In the British Museum are specimens of this ware, presented in 1763.

## *Derby.*

With the travelling about of workmen from one pottery to another yes—even their travelling from one country to another—with set styles of workmanship and decoration at their command, most of these early unmarked pieces may often belong to one factory and yet be classed with another. It seems a pity that so beautiful a product as came from the Chelsea works should have been so soon merged with another and finally absorbed, and that the absorber, by overproduction of inferior goods, should decline and at last cease production.

The Mr. Duesbury who bought the Chelsea works in 1770 was one of the original firm who started the works at Derby in 1756. Their chief china maker was a Frenchman, named Planche, who had learned the secret of china making in Saxony, where, on the death of his father, a French refugee, he had lived. Mr. Duesbury was the business manager of the firm and built up a profitable business, selling many cases of his china in London as early as 1763.

The finest work sent out, however, is generally credited as belonging to the Chelsea-Derby period, from 1770-1775. As was common at the time, the work from the factories was disposed of at auction, but from 1773 there was a London warehouse where the porcelains were put on sale and a large business was done. The example of Derby shown in FIG. 100 is the famous little image of Falstaff, which was so popular at this date. The mock heroic figure is most amusing and shows the careful modelling which was seen in nearly all the wares of this period. The colouring is brilliant, and the marks are very clear, showing the number of the pattern which was incised thus: "No. 291." The period is made clear as Crown-Derby, 1785-1796, as the letter "D" is painted below a crown, all in red. There is also the number "34," probably the decorator's number.

From 1785 till 1796, the date of Mr. Duesbury's death, his son was associated with him, and both father and son applied themselves to the improvement of their designs and to the spreading of their popularity among the nobility and those who could afford to pay well for superior work. To this period belong those services distinguished for the medallion decoration of landscapes, and for many of the portrait pieces, which were painted by a man named Kean, sometime a partner in the firm. This is the Crown-Derby period, but the get-rich-quick-policy did not permit the keeping up of a high standard of merit, and the works declined.

The porcelain of Derby was a beautiful shade of pure white soft paste, and the decorations were in great variety and good taste. Vases of a wide-mouthed pattern were a favourite product of these works, decorated with birds, flowers, landscapes and figures in medallions, with a background of deep rich blue and much gold decoration. They made a specialty also of beautifully decorated porcelain thimbles. Their best flower painter, named Billingsley, worked at this factory twenty years and more, and he was only one of many who were equally successful in painting flowers, birds, or Oriental subjects and figures. Ribbed or fluted cups and saucers handsomely gilded were made before the Chelsea works were finally closed.

In the Crown-Derby period were made many beautiful patterns, and the porcelain of the highest class was always costly. Dr. Johnson, in 1777, complained that the porcelain cost as much as silver, and to-day one of the choice patterns is worth almost its weight in gold.

The marks varied with the successive periods, the first being a capital " D " or the word " Derby." Then there were " Derby " surmounted by a crown, the word " Derby " with an anchor on printed ware, and of the last period, " Bloor-Derby " on an oval or round strap. There is little difficulty in making out these marks, for " D " or " Derby " is included in them all and belongs exclusively to these works. These works did not exist for quite an entire century, and the whole time

may be covered by six periods, as follows: **Duesbury,**
1751–1769; Chelsea-Derby, 1769–1775; Bow-Chelsea-
Derby, 1775–1786; Crown-Derby, 1786–1796; Duesbury and Kean, 1796–1815; Bloor-Derby, 1815–1848;
Towards the end of 1700 white Derby china was sold
to be painted by amateurs, which explains the care-
lessly decorated pieces sometimes met with, and
which present such a problem to the collector.

## *Bristol.*

Whether one turns to pottery or porcelain, that
made at Bristol seems especially desirable, but elusive.
Bristol was one of the centres where hard paste
porcelain was regularly made, and a book has been
written, called " Two Centuries of Ceramic Art in
Bristol," which covers both the pottery and porcelain
products.    It was not until 1735 that flat ware, bowls,
etc., were made here, and the most interesting period
dates only from 1768–1778, when Champion made
hard paste porcelain.

Specimens of Bristol pottery are to be found as
early as 1703.    Queen Charlotte had a pair of high-
heeled shoes or choppines, very dainty affairs with a
big buckle, made at this pottery and dated 1705.
Just here it may not be amiss to say that about 1800
there was a pottery at Burton-upon-Trent, where the
only product made was the ordinary Staffordshire
ware, and the only designs used were boots, shoes and
slippers, and the celebrated Wellington boots.    The
works potted only four years and belonged to a Dr.
Nadin.    This Staffordshire foot-wear is occasionally
found, but is not so valuable or interesting as that

Fig. 101. BRISTOL. FLORA.

Fig. 102. BRISTOL POTTERY.

Fig. 103. LEEDS WARE.

made at Bristol. Some of these Bristol shoes are found dated as late as 1722. Of course this early "delft" was blue and white, and there are blue and white specimens, in flat ware chiefly, as late as 1760. The later Bristol colours are generally a grayish blue, with small quantities of green and yellow, and the enamel is hard and durable, not chipping off as is usual with pottery.

While Bristol was prominent early in the manufacture of pottery, she was later than several other cities in making porcelain. The first mention of it was 1766, when it was made by Champion, who, in 1773, bought Cookworthy's patent and works. Champion made his goods from models from Dresden, following in the wake of other English makers and copying freely popular subjects. He also imitated Chinese ware in colour and design, and in general such pieces have no mark, or only the cross on them.

In 1778 the works at Bristol were closed, and the patent right was sold, in 1781, by Champion to a company of Staffordshire potters who had works at New Hall. Every piece of true Bristol ware, owing to the short time the works were in operation, is rare and of value. Everybody has heard of the Smith set, presented by Edmund Burke to his friends Mr. and Mrs. Smith of Bristol, which is extolled as the "best the manufactory could produce." Many extremely beautiful vases were made, brilliantly painted, as well as plaques of crests, flowers, wreaths, etc., in biscuit. Figures were made also, some of the best known being the " Four Seasons " and the " Four Elements" (also made at Derby), and many shepherds, milkmaids and other figures. See FIG. 101.

The paste is not fine but is disfigured by fire-cracks and warpings ; the glaze is marred by bubbles and pin-holes. The frequent practice of baking paste and glaze at one firing is, no doubt, responsible for these defects. There was a inferior ware, called " Cottage China," decorated with festoons and flowers and sprigs scattered at random over it ; ribbons in bows and knots are also sometimes found on this as well as on the more expensive Bristol porcelain.

The marks on Bristol are various, but perhaps the most characteristic one is the X-like cross, impressed or painted in blue or brown and generally accompanied by a numeral, from 1 to 24, but never above the latter figure. These figures referred to the workmen, each of whom was known by a number. Occasionally there is a dot with a cross and numeral, and when Dresden patterns were used the Dresden crossed swords were used as a mark, often with a dot between the handles. In FIG. 102 is given a group of characteristic Bristol pottery. The two mugs are unmarked ; the pitcher is marked with a cross in brown ; the sugar-bowl with the handles is marked with the cross and numeral " 6," and the other sugar-bowl is Leeds, showing how easily Leeds may be mistaken for Bristol, though the colour of the glaze is different. The sugar-bowl we call Leeds is marked with a " G " in brown. This is one of the regular Leeds marks. This photograph is taken from specimens in the Antiquarian Rooms at Concord, Massachusetts.

It is only the rarity of these pieces which gives them their value, as a comparison with the figurines in Chelsea and Derby shows the greater excellence of the latter two. Within a few months a Bristol porcelain tea-set, painted with flowers in their natural colours, consisting of teapot, creamer, sugar-box and eight cups and saucers, brought $210 in London, while the vases decorated with " exotic birds" bring $1,500 and over.

The city of Bristol to-day one can imagine to be little changed from what it was when the factory for china was in full operation. There is not a scrap of the porcelain to be picked up anywhere and but a few pieces shown in the Museum there, which is famous for its portrait of Oliver Cromwell. There is in use a two-wheeled cart, a sort of chariot affair which seems a survival of Roman days, and the city is quaintness exemplified ; but London, or even our own country, seems better hunting ground for Bristol china than its birthplace.

# Leeds.

In 1760 the Leeds Old Pottery was founded by two brothers named Green. Fifteen years later Humble and Green made cream ware there, and in 1786 the firm was Hartley and Green. At first " Leeds Ware " meant the product from this pottery alone, but later it has come to include the ware made in the County of York, where Leeds is situated, and where there were many potteries in operation late in 1700 and early in 1800. The best of this ware was that made at the Leeds Old Pottery, but as the mass of this ware was quite unmarked it is often difficult to distinguish between the different factories.

Leeds ware, whether cream or white, has peculiarities which, once known, make it easy to identify. In the first place the paste is very light and frail, and, most characteristic of all, the glaze is a most pronounced green in shade, which colour shows plainly around knobs and handles, under the rims of saucers and plates, and in any place where the glaze is not thinly spread. The decorations are in a variety of styles, either under or over glaze painting, printed ware and raised work, ranging from highly finished products to crude and slovenly work on the ordinary pieces. The best cream-coloured Leeds ware, without decoration in colour, is both artistic and beautiful, and is worthy of more attention than is given to it by collectors. There are exceedingly fine candlesticks to be found occasion. ally, and parts of dinner-sets (owing to the frail char. acter of the ware these do not survive entire), the tureens, pitchers and dishes having a certain kind of twisted handle which is very pretty. I have heard recently of two tureens in different parts of the country, one of them coming in way of trade and both being of similar size and decoration. They have the pretty twisted handles and a sort of raised leaf decoration about the body, as well as a graceful shape and a cover with a large and fine knob.

There are basket-work dishes, plates and fruit baskets (though I have seen this same style of pieces with the impressed name, an anchor of Davenport, and also from Herculaneum Pottery). These pieces are cut out and modelled in the paste, not cast in a mould. There is a fine fruit dish of this style in a very creamy tint in the Boston Museum of Fine Arts. The usual Leeds ware found here now, though quantities were sent over, is the more ordinary white earthenware or of a very pale cream tint. The bulk of it is decorated in colours or with gold, and much of the decoration, on the pitchers particularly, is quite crude. Lustre decoration, copper, silver and a purplish pink are much used in bands and little leaf patterns and, more rarely, as a background with the cream ware showing as a pattern. A group of these lustred decorations is shown on the top row of FIG. 103 in the group of Leeds ware, the pitcher on the left side of the lower row being silver lustre with pattern left white—" resist "— and the others copper and purplish pink decoration.

Pepper-pots are not unusual with uneven bands of blue or green, and the swan-knob pieces are not alone confined to Leeds ware, for I have seen them on marked Bristol as well. The fluted teapots with swan-knobs are less common, and I have been offered a fine cup and saucer of fluted ware, decorated prettily in colours, for one dollar, a modest price for a perfect specimen. Very ornamental tea caddies, gaily decorated, come in Leeds ware, and were, no doubt, made for the fashionable tea gardens of the period, when each table was furnished with its little tea caddy, and customers were expected to make their own infusion. The lustre ware of Leeds make, marked or unmistakable, is perhaps the rarest of all.

About 1800 black ware was made here, and up to 1813 between ninety and one hundred different patterns of teapots in black ware were made at Leeds alone. The shapes are very varied in form, size and style of ornamentation. They were round, octagonal, oval or twelve-sided, and I have seen one capable of holding four quarts. The knobs were the familiar seated figure, lions, swan, a flower, etc. Engine-turned mugs and jugs were made at this pottery as early as 1782, and much of this black ware is quite inferior, the handles not being neatly joined, the covers not fitting. While Wedgwood's designs were copied at this pottery in cream ware, they are easily distinguished by the green glaze. This tint was produced by the use of arsenic, which crippled the workmen so that they were not able to follow the trade for more than four or five years. By far the larger quantity of the articles was made for Russia and Germany.

The marks " C " or " G," or both letters together, in brown, are the earliest marks. There will be found, also : " Hartley and Green, Leeds Pottery," or " Leeds Pottery " only. A collection of Leeds pottery is interesting from the variety of shapes and decorations one may find in it, and a cabinet or corner cupboard filled with it is an ornament to any room. As yet it is not difficult to find at moderate prices, and a quart pitcher, with animals and leaves in lustre and colours, may often be had for a couple of dollars.

## *Worcester.*

There is no china that has had so much written about it as Old Worcester. The objects for which certain cities were famous seem to have run in threes. Chelsea was noted for its china, buns and hospital ; Derby for its stockings, cotton mills and china ; and Worcester for its gloves, china and sauce. It is only at the last-named city that the manufacture of its group of three things still keeps on, and to-day you may buy modern china fresh from the factory, gloves made from almost everything from elephant to mouse-skin—to measure at that—and sauce, the odours of whose manufacture float agreeably over the city.

Worcester was only in its infancy, so far as china was concerned, when Derby, Chelsea and Bow had already achieved name and fame. The Worcester Porcelain Company was formed in 1751 for the manufacture of china ware, and, of course, turned its attention first to blue and white, endeavoring to imitate Chinese porcelain in both form and colour. Somewhat later it diverged into the brilliant pigments of the Japanese, and then was led off to more elaborate productions of its own. Who has not seen and handled with delight the beautiful old Worcester, in "Japan Taste"? Many tea-sets of this ware were brought to this country in the fine old ships that took out goods to England and brought back the luxuries with which many a fine mansion was adorned.

The famous Worcester Old Works date from 1751 to 1847, and they passed through many hands. The earliest Worcester china was made of a "frit" body for the finer kinds of china, but an inferior paste was formed for commoner ware. The frit paste may be told by its density and by its green tint when seen with transmitted light. It was formed of sand, gypsum, soda, salt and nitre, melted together in a mass, then broken and pulverized. A light shade of blue was popular for decorations, as well as much more ornate patterns, with landscapes, birds, insects and flowers on them, with much gilding. Worcester was famous for its blues—cobalt, turquoise and enamel blue—and tea and dessert services of every description, compotieres, pierced baskets, cider-mugs, punch-bowls.

jugs, butter-boats, pickle-dishes, etc., were some of the articles made. Figures and groups were not made.

Transfer-printing was early in use, in 1757, and Worcester has always disputed with Liverpool in claiming the invention of this branch of the trade. Richard Holdship and Robert Hancock are two names connected with the early history of Worcester, and much controversy is rife as to which the monogram, " R. H.," so often found on Worcester porcelain, belongs. As has been said, china painters and workmen went from one factory to another, carrying their own styles of work with them, and we have Worcester china " in Chelsea style," as well as in their own. Some of the most famous patterns in Worcester transfer-prints are: George II, with trophy and ship, by Holdship; Queen Charlotte; George III when young, with Fame and Britannia; Marquis of Granby; William Pitt; Shakespeare between Tragedy and Comedy; milkmaids, and other pastoral scenes, from copper-plates engraved by Robert Hancock, these being very rare; tea parties and Chinese landscapes and figures, printed in red, and signed " R. H. fecit "; ruins; fishing and haymaking parties; fortune tellers, and hunting scenes.

Printing from engraved plates was succeeded by what is known as "bat-printing," which is described thus: " The plate was stippled with a fine point by London artists, after choice designs. The copperplate was then carefully cleaned; a thin coating of linseed oil was then laid upon it, and removed by the palm of the hand from the surface, leaving the oil in the engraved lines. Instead of paper, bats of glue were used to take impressions from the plate, and laid on the china so as to deliver the oil marks on to its surface. It was then dusted with the colour required, the superfluous colour being removed with cotton wool, and then placed in the kiln."

Worcester porcelain, undecorated, was sold to be decorated by amateur or professional artists. The marks during Wall's ownership were so many and various it is impossible to enumerate them all. The earliest was a script " W." Then there were crosses and crescents, the Dresden swords, imitation Chinese characters, anchors and lines.

The periods into which Worcester porcelain may be divided are as follows: J. Wall, 1751–1783 ; Flight, 1783–1793; Flight and Barr, 1807–1813 ; Flight, Barr and Barr, 1813. In 1786 two brothers named Chamberlain, employees of the Old Works, started a rival establishment, and, in 1840, under the title of Chamberlain & Co., the Old Works and their factory were united. By 1847 the Old Works practically ceased, and the New Works and the Royal Porcelain works are the present successors.

In 1783 John Flight, who had been agent for the Worcester works in London, bought the concern. Though he and his sons put in energy and capital and did a large business so far as quantity was concerned, the standard of work never rose to that artistic height which made it famous under Wall's management. In the first place the paste they used was inferior and never attained the clearness and transparency of Old Worcester, or, for that matter, of Chamberlain's body either.

The patterns used by Flight were simple painted or printed flowers, and one style, called " royal lily," was a favourite with the nobility. Decorations in " Japan

Taste," a relic of the Old Works, were also a product of this time, as well as full armorial bearings on whole services. From 1783 to 1840 the marks were the name " Flight," or " B," or " B. F. B.," " F. B. B.," with or without a crown. FIG. 104 shows a cup and saucer daintily fluted, and painted in colours, and FIG. 105, an equally charming plate. The pieces are marked with the crescent in blue, which places them as extremely early specimens, for the crescent was used shortly after 1751, when the factory was opened by Dr. Wall.

The Chamberlain concern started in 1786 for decorating only, and the white ware was furnished from the Caughley works. The business increased, and, in 1796, a great impetus was given when the Prince of Orange visited the works and ordered a dessert service. From this time on dinner and dessert sets, elaborate and costly, were produced for royalty and nobility. Lord Nelson and Lady Hamilton ordered, on their visit in 1802, a breakfast-service, a dinner-service and a pair of vases. One of the latter was to have a portrait of Nelson supported by a figure of Fame, and the other a likeness of Lady Hamilton. Nelson's death before anything but the breakfast set was finished and the countermanding of the rest of the order was a blow to the Chamberlains. Specimens of this breakfast service are occasionally met with. They are decorated with a baron's as well as a duke's coronet and the order of San Joseph in a panel, with an Oriental pattern in colours and gold. The services made for the Prince Regent in 1811, in Japan style, and for the Princess Charlotte, in old Sevres style, were their most costly efforts.

Fig. 104. OLD WORCESTER CUP AND SAUCER.

Fig. 105. OLD WORCESTER PLATE.

Fig. 106. PLYMOUTH. HARLEQUIN.
Boston Museum of Fine Arts.

The paste used by Chamberlain is very different from that used by either Wall, or Flight and his successors. It is lighter, more translucent, and made from Wall's original recipe, but improved by the use of better materials discovered since his time. It is pure in colour, and the " Regent's Body " has a closeness of texture that leaves little to be desired. Most of Chamberlain's products are plainly marked with his name, and thus easily identified. The Grainger Works, started in 1801, have been, after a century of operation, absorbed by " The Royal Porcelain Works." It is at these works that " Royal Worcester " is made.

## Plymouth.

The originator of Plymouth porcelain, like the first of European porcelain makers, Bottcher, was a chemist's apprentice. The Plymouth maker was William Cookworthy, who had learned his business in London, and, as early as 1745, wrote to a friend concerning the importation of kaolin and petunse, both necessary ingredients of porcelain, from Virginia. Presumably the difficulty of procuring these ingredients from so great a distance caused Cookworthy to search for them at home, and he was successful, for he discovered at Cornwall both a white plastic clay and a species of granite which gave the vitreous material required. In 1768 Cookworthy took out a patent for the manufacture of " a kind of porcelain, newly invented by me, composed of moorstone, or growan, and growan clay." This was the first English porcelain made from native ingredients. The earliest examples were, as with the other works, blue and white ; but the blue was a dull.

dark shade, which, under much experimenting by Cookworthy gradually became clearer and better.

His knowledge of chemistry was of great assistance to this potter, and he was the first to produce cobalt blue directly from the ore. It is a pity that Cookworthy's experiments took so many years; for when success was at last obtained he was an old man, he had spent a large sum of money pursuing his experiments, and six years after the taking out of his patent, that is in 1774, he sold it out to a relative, Richard Champion of Bristol, already mentioned, and retired from manufacture.

The white porcelain of Plymouth is one of its notable features. The paste is hard with a fine glaze resembling polished ivory, except that the colour is milky white instead of yellow. One of these choice white figures is given in FIG. 106. It is of a harlequin and shows admirable modelling and is full of spirit. The quaint dress comes out well in the snowy paste, and it bears the incised mark of a four. This was really a chemical sign, but it resembles "4" more than anything else.

Cookworthy had a great fancy for marine objects, and shells, limpets and cockles were favourites with him, arranged in tiers and groups. He also used coral forms, exquisitely modelled from Nature; all his pieces are very beautiful and delicate, and, generally, unmarked. The earliest pieces were salt-cellars, pickle-cups and toilet pieces, and are hardly found outside of collections. In white were also made figures, singly and in groups, birds and animals. Among the best known figures were those of Europe and Asia.

The Plymouth tea and coffee pots are very handsome, many of them being tall in shape, with a pattern modelled in the clay, with colour decoration besides. On mugs, jugs, cups and saucers, and vases, birds and flowers are found, exquisitely painted. These were done by a Frenchman, named Soqui, who came from the Sevres factory. A man named Bone, a native of Plymouth, who had been trained by Cookworthy himself, was the one who excelled in blue and white decorations.

The marks on Plymouth are various, a sign, somewhat like the figure 4, and Cookworthy's name being those most in use. Plymouth porcelain is seldom met with in New York State by the china hunter; but it is not so scarce in New England, and, I do not doubt, much is hoarded away in the rich pantries of Salem town, where collections are the rule not the exception.

## *Lowestoft.*

What our great-grandmothers used for their best "chaynie," was this very ornamental porcelain, which may be found to-day all through New England, although like all other wares, except Staffordshire, it is not so common in the interior towns.

While luxury was not characteristic of the early New England homes, yet there were those whose household goods would have seemed rich and elegant to-day, when pretty and tasteful china, glass and silver come within the reach of so many. Mr. Elias H. Derby, who died in 1805, was accounted one of New England's wealthiest men. His estate was estimated at $200,000, and the inventory is long and interesting. Among crowds of other household "stuff" are mentioned two complete sets of china, one valued at $230, and the other at $371. Yet, with all this luxury of china, he owned but eight silver spoons!

It was in the ships belonging to this same Elias H. Derby that crates and rolls of china were brought to Salem. From New Haven went many a staunch vessel, bearing hoards from the friends and neighbours of the captain, and coming home laden with china and stuffs, drugs and rock candy, which were distributed by means of florid advertisements in the papers, or by the milliners or fancy goods merchants, who made little ventures in other lines of business than their own. After the Revolution the merchant marine of Salem increased very fast, and they brought goods from every land. In 1786 the "Grand Turk" was the first New England ship to double the Cape for Canton. In 1805 Salem had forty-eight vessels that sailed around the Cape ; so no wonder the "notable housekeepers" had cupboards full of china.

Lowestoft, while still plentiful in many New England towns, as well as in the South, showing what large quantities of it came to this country, has the most baffling history of any ware made within two centuries. On the question of this porcelain all china collectors may be said to be ranged in two camps : those who believe that Lowestoft was Oriental porcelain, decorated in England at the town of that name, and those who believe that the decoration as well as the porcelain was made in China.

To fully understand the differences of opinion it is well to begin with the geographical position of the

Fig. 107.   CORNER CUPBOARD OF LOWESTOFT.
Antiquarian Society, Concord.

Fig. 108. ROSE-SPRIGGED LOWESTOFT.

Fig. 109. BLUE-BANDED LOWESTOFT.

town of Lowestoft. It is situated in Suffolk on the east coast of England, ten miles south of Yarmouth. Just opposite, across the North Sea, is Rotterdam, in Holland, a great port of entry for Dutch merchantmen trading from the East from as early as 1600. There was a tax, to be sure, on undecorated ware brought into England from China between the years 1775 and 1800, yet it can be seen how easily china could have been shipped in from Rotterdam, there being no embargo between England and that country.

If such large quantities of undecorated china were carried to England it is strange that there is scarcely a piece to be found unpainted. I know of but one such piece in this country, a helmet creamer, which is held in a private collection in Newark, N. J.

It is admitted on all sides that as early as 1756, and until 1762, soft paste pottery was made at Lowestoft in imitation of Delft ware, and decorated in blue and white. Pieces dated and signed are held in and about Lowestoft and in several museums in England. Mr. Jewitt, who has unearthed what facts are known about Lowestoft, says, " the collector will be able to distinguish immediately between those examples painted at Lowestoft on Oriental body, and those which were potted and painted there."

The porcelain which we call Lowestoft is of a fine pearly tint, the usual colour of Chinese porcelain. The decoration has certain characteristics which are all soon learned, and then each collector must make up his own mind as to the position he wishes to take in regard to this much disputed question.

The styles of decoration were various, but the most familiar are those with dark blue bands, or dots, or other figures heavily overlaid with gold, usually with coats of arms ; or decorations in one colour, showing landscapes, figures, flowers and sprigs ; and, most familiar of all, flowers and sprigs in natural colours, with delicate borders in colour and gold.

The richest collection it has been my good fortune to examine gathered under one roof is at the Antiquarian Society, in the historic town of Concord, Massachusetts. Not only is the amount of porcelain very large, but it is of the greatest variety, embracing all the familiar patterns. The pieces are not under glass, but advantageously placed in corner cupboards and on tables and stands, so that the china hunter is at liberty to study at his leisure, and even to handle, if he bears in mind Emerson's injunction, "That the best things in this world are generally a little cracked." See FIG. 107.

The kindly custodian seems to know at a glance the true lovers who may be trusted, and goes about his business, leaving one to touch reverently, compare pastes and patterns and bask in a china lovers' paradise.

To give some idea of how much of this china came to America, it is asserted that all the scores of pieces shown here were collected in the neighbourhood of Concord. It must be remembered, however, that Boston and Salem were ports of entry, and that the early settled and nearby towns had opportunities for purchasing china not granted to more remote places.

In FIG. 108 are shown some of the rose pattern Lowestoft to be found at the Concord Antiquarian Society. One notices the Oriental-looking teapot, with its quaint and prim little English sprigs, the rough nut on top just touched with gold, and the familiar twisted handle. The tall graceful jug is a shape not shown before, and may have been used either for flip or hot water, its use being regulated by the temperance proclivities of its owner. This, too, has the rose for decoration, larger bunches being shown on the sides and little sprigs being scattered about. There are also jugs of this same shape, with covers, but much smaller, from five to six inches high, evidently for hot milk, as they come with the tea-sets. The cup and saucer are also adorned with the rose pattern, and on the inside of the cup is a charming design in several colours. The shapes of all these pieces of pearly tinted Lowestoft are very Oriental in character, the tea caddies, with the rough nut on top, generally coloured or gilded, and the flat twisted handles, have always been characteristic of Chinese porcelain. So were the tiny cups without handles, and the little dog, which is often used for a knob on covers, is Celestial in every line.

But when we approach the decoration it is a different matter. Those pieces with a rose in the decoration are thought to point conclusively to English decoration for two reasons. The first is that one of the chief decorators at Lowestoft was an Englishman named Rose, who used this graceful method of signing his pieces, and the second is that the arms of the borough were the Tudor or full-blown rose. A rose like this is never found on avowedly Chinese porcelain, and these flowers all look as if painted at one place, possibly by one hand.

They tell at Concord an amusing story about this same Lowestoft. The original collector of all the interesting and valuable relics gathered here had a small stock of china lore.  He began to gather what was old long before many of us recognized its beauty. In the early days of these Colonial Rooms—before the founder's death—he used to show his collection himself. A visitor one day, on looking at the china, remarked, " I see you have some Lowestoft here."  The old man thought she called his china " low stuff," and promptly ejected her for running down his collection.  He related the incident, some days later, to a lady who lived in Concord, and she upheld the delinquent and said it was " very fine Lowestoft."  He was convinced, but against his will, and there is still to be seen a slip of paper in his handwriting which says, " Mrs.——says this china is low stuff."  He shuffled the responsibility for its name off his own shoulders at any rate.

In FIG. 109 is shown a group of the blue and gold decoration.  As you see it standing on the quaint fluted tea-table, so it may have stood a hundred years ago, presided over by the mistress of the house in brocade gown and embroidered kerchief.  The straightnosed tea pot and the tea caddy with the little dog a top have been seen before.  The decoration this time is different.  A pair of birds, each with a twig in its mouth, face each other, surrounded by a circle of rich blue starred with gold, and outside that a delicate wreath of gold.  The teapot has a similar bird, but a heavier blue circle and without the wreath, showing a simple variation of a popular pattern which could easily be made, free-hand, in a factory where English decorators were allowed freedom in executing their designs, but highly impossible to an Oriental decorator, who slavishly followed the pattern before him

The beautiful helmet jug, which shows, even in the picture, the irregularity of its surface, and the teacup and saucer belonged to the same set.

To judge of their unsurpassed elegance one should hold them in the hand, note the splendid blue of the border, overlaid with a pattern in gold, and then study the almost classic form of the vase which forms their decoration, its severity mitigated by the delicate sprays of gold surrounding it. The blue border is broken by small medallions, and the contrast of the blue and gold with the pearly tint of the china is very satisfying to the eye.

The other cup is of an unusual shape, has on it a solitary bird surrounded by a wreath, and above it a blue and gold border. The tea caddy stands in a pretty tray, though usually they have parted company years ago. To-day, in shops where they sell Oriental china, you will find caddies of this identical shape, even the little dog on top being cousin to the one on the caddy shown. But, for decoration, blue and white Chinese patterns only.

In the Metropolitan Museum of Art there is a collection of over thirty pieces of Lowestoft, with the blue and gold decoration. It is placed in cases with specimens of other old English china, and is conspicuously labelled Lowestoft many times, showing that the authorities here do not regard it as Oriental. There is the well-known blue border starred with gold, not so rich a pattern as on the cup and saucer and creamer in FIG. 109 but still very handsome. There is a shield with entwined initials in gold, and on some of the pieces the two characteristic birds.

The early history, the entire history of china manufacture at Lowestoft, whether hard or soft paste, is very indefinite. The original proprietor of the works was a Mr. Hewlin Luson. Mr. Robert Browne, who bought the works from him, died in 1771, and was succeeded by his son, also Robert Browne, who made great improvements in the body. In fact the china made was so satisfactory that, in 1770, the year before the elder Browne died, they put their china on sale in London, as the following advertisement duly sets forth :

" Clark Durnford,
Lowestoft China Warehouse.
No. 4 Great St. Thomas the Apostle,
Queen St., Cheapside, London,
Where merchants and shopkeepers may be supplied
with any quantity of said ware at the usual prices.
N. B. Allowance of twenty per cent for ready money."

There is also in existence the original account made by a man sent out by Wedgwood to buy pieces of all well-known wares. This was so that the enterprising Wedgwood might learn of all improvements in paste made by his contemporaries, for the benefit of his own wares. Among other articles of china purchased may be found the following : " May 12, 1775, One Leastoff slop basin." Mention is made in the same account of pieces of Bristol and Chelsea wares, showing that Lowestoft was thought of enough importance to challenge the notice of Wedgwood, the foremost potter of his day.

In FIG. 110 are found three pieces of Lowestoft soft paste porcelain, with a thick glaze and characteristic rose. The tint of the body is creamy, not the pearly tint of the other hard paste porcelains. They were given to the Boston Museum of Fine Arts by a collector of china living in the Isle of Wight. They are labelled " Lowestoft, certified to have been made in England." One of the most unfortunate things about Lowestoft is that it is all entirely unmarked. Only the early blue and white specimens bear any mark whatever.

The pieces shown in FIG. 110 are less delicate than those of the hard paste porcelain. The bands around the saucer are red with yellow dots, and the flowers are in their natural colours. The creamer does not belong to the same set, but the lattice work decoration in deep rose is sometimes seen on the hard porcelain and is not in the least an Eastern pattern, and the shape of the jug is not familiar in the hard paste pieces. I have seen, in the hard porcelain, the tray to a very beautiful fruit basket. It has a rich heraldic device in the centre, enclosed by festoons of flowers, while the rim is in pierced work, each square being decorated by a few dots of enamel. There are the remains of the whole of this set, which was a dinner-service, and even the salt cellars are richly decorated both inside and out.

The end of the manufacture, or, at least, decoration of this china, is quite as mysterious as the rest of its history. It ceased between 1803 and 1804, " owing, it is said, partly to the severe competition of the Staffordshire potters, partly to trade losses, one of which was the seizure by Napoleon, in Holland, of several thousand pounds' worth of their merchandise in that country." There are no traces of a factory left, and no fragments of china have ever been dug up.

## Spode.

In general china ware takes the name of the place where it is made.   In this case it takes the name of the maker, Josiah Spode, who established a factory at Stoke-upon-Trent as early as 1770.   He had all the training necessary to make a good potter, for he was apprenticed to Thomas Whieldon, who made, among many other ceramic products, the beautiful tortoise-shell ware.   Spode was nearly forty years old when he started out on his own account, and he was succeeded by his son who commenced the manufacture of porcelain in addition to pottery about 1800.   William Copeland became a partner of Spode in 1779, and the business is carried to the present day by descendants of the original Copeland.

The first products of the factory were pottery, then porcelain, and finally a superior kind of ironstone china, which was almost porcelain, so superior was it. This was invented by the younger Spode in 1805. The body of the porcelain was soft and white and the glaze fine.   A great improvement was made in the body of the paste when bones were introduced, and many of the shapes of the articles are very beautiful. The dinner and tea services of porcelain, which are not uncommon in this country, are among the finest sets ever sent over here, and even the ironstone has a certain elegance about it.

The first Spode died in 1797, and his son carried on the business until 1827, when he died.   There are

Fig. 110.  CERTIFIED LOWESTOFT.
Boston Museum of Fine Arts.

Fig. 111. SPODE.

Fig. 112. MASON'S STONE.

given the names of some of the patterns which made
the Spodes famous, with the date of manufacture ;

| | |
|---|---|
| Castle, 1806. | Tower, 1814. |
| Roman, 1811. | Peacock and New Temple, 1814. |
| Turk, 1813. | New Nankin, 1815. |
| Milkmaid, 1814. | Italian, 1816. |
| New Japan, 1815. | Woodman, 1816. |
| India, 1815. | Oriental, 1820. |
| Dagger border, 1814. | |

The Blue Imperial was introduced in 1826, one year
before the younger Spode died.

Whiie any of this china and semi-china is good to
own, particularly if it be an heirloom, the Spode which
is really worth a place in a collection is that made by
Spode the elder, which would bring it prior to 1797.

All Spode the elder's work is marked, and his pottery, decorated in gold and colours, commands and is
worth a high price. His black, and jasper wares in
any colour, marked, are rare. From 1784 to 1789 the
mark was simply Spode, in printed letters, impressed.
From 1800 to 1827 the mark consisted of the name
Spode in printed letters, impressed, and usually in
addition, the name of the pattern in blue, purple or
red. On the stoneware the mark was "Spode, Feldspar
Porcelain" or "Spode, Stone China." After this date,
if the name Spode was used, it appeared as "Late
Spode." While there are large quantities of this
china all over the country, it is one of the least familiar
to those who are not collectors. Not long since I had
a letter asking what a "Spode cup" was. The writer
had been reading one of the popular Colonial novels,
and the heroine was depicted as drinking tea from a

Spode cup, and the query arose as to what sort of material it was.

There are three other porcelain manufactories which should be briefly mentioned in any category of English wares. They are "Swansea," Nantgarw and Caughley.

## *Swansea.*

As early as 1750 a pottery was established at Swansea where ordinary wares were manufactured. George Haynes was the original owner, and about 1800 he perfected a paste which he called " opaque china." He made it for a little more than two years only, and then, in 1802, sold the works to Lewis Dilwyn, and the articles sent out during his holding of the works were very beautiful. A painter named Young decorated the china with exquisite birds, butterflies and flowers. All this choice work was put upon the opaque china, for real translucent porcelain was not made till 1814 by Dilwyn. Four years only was this choice product made—the best English porcelain made up to that date. It is very scarce now and very highly prized. The body was soft paste, beautiful in colour and glaze and exquisitely decorated with flowers, birds, etc.

The marks are very plain, " Swansea," impressed or stencilled in red, with occasionally a trident in red. The history of Swansea, like that of so many other pottery works, closed with its absorption by another factory. In 1820 the works were bought by John Rose, of Coalport, and incorporated with his factory at that place.

## *Nantgarw.*

As with Swansea so with Nantgarw. This little town, as one may learn from its name, was in Wales, and from 1813 to 1820 the factory made porcelain objects in a variety of lovely shapes—vases, plaques, and dinner, tea and tête-a-tête services. They made exquisite tinted grounds in many colours, and in addition these were painted with flowers, birds and insects in their natural colours. A very favourite decoration was a sweetbriar rose, and a border of trefoil or clover leaves was very characteristic.

This factory was started by William Billingsley, the flower painter. The career of this man is worthy of note as showing why the decorations of different factories so closely resemble each other. He first appears at Derby as an apprentice, in 1774, and there he stayed and worked for twenty years. In 1794 he went to Pinxton in Derbyshire, where, with John Coke, he established a small porcelain factory, in which Billingsley managed the making of the paste, which was a good soft paste porcelain, with, generally, a decoration in blue and gold, known as the Chantilly sprig.

He is next heard of at Mansfield, where he was painting porcelain on his own account, then a little later at Torksea, also painting. During 1808, on account of some trouble, probably the divulging of trade secrets, he went into hiding, but was soon heard of at Worcester Works, where he remained decorating porcelain till 1813. At this date, with his son-in-law, a man named Walker, he opened the works at Nantgarw, and managed the works at Swansea, until, in

1820, both these works were bought by Mr. Rose and transferred to Coalport, whither Billingsley went also.   Here he seems to have lived and worked until his death in 1828, at the age of seventy.   His handiwork can be seen on porcelain from Derby, Worcester, Swansea, Nantgarw and Coalport, and when he had the opportunity he placed his mark, a " B," on the pieces he decorated.   Most proprietors, however, did not allow this, preferring their wares to go out with the factory mark only.

The pieces of this porcelain which are extant, when not tinted, show a beautiful white ground.   The mark is " Nantgarw," printed, or impressed.

## Caughley.

The original pottery at Caughley, Shropshire, was established as early as 1751, but the works in which most interest is felt were built in 1772, by Thomas Turner, at which were made the Caughley or Salopian wares, many of which were sent to this country.   His pottery and porcelain were of the best quality, for it was Turner's policy to employ the best artisans.   In 1780 he introduced the willow pattern, which was designed by one of his decorators named Minton, from Oriental models.   Turner is said to have made the first complete dinner service of printed ware in England.

The first Caughley ware, like the early output from most of the other works, was blue and white.   Porcelain was made there and sold in an undecorated state to other works.   In 1788, when Robert Chamberlain started his works at Worcester, he bought his china at Caughley, and had it sent by barge down the Severn to Worcester. This was also done at Grainger's works at Worcester.

Printing on porcelain is one of the fields in which Caughley did a large and successful business. Even before this, as early as 1757, both Caughley and Worcester made printed pottery, and Robert Hancock, who has been spoken of in connection with the Worcester works, engraved for Caughley as well, for his name, signed in full, appears on some of their patterns.

Coalport bought up Caughley about 1799, and ran both factories until 1814. Swansea, Nantgarw and Jackfield were bought in 1820, six years after Caughley works had been closed. All the materials and moulds were moved to Coalport, and in 1821 the Caughley works were pulled down, largely on account of the lack of coal in that region. At Coalport many marks were used which had hitherto belonged to separate factories, so there is great confusion.

About 1800 some pieces were marked simply Coalport. Besides the confusion incident to so many factories being purchased and run by one man, good counterfeits of Dresden, Chelsea, Sevres and other wares were made, in which the marks also were counterfeited. The French grounds were used, and the Sevres rose was a favourite pattern they copied. These copies are called counterfeits because they were made with the avowed purpose of deceiving would-be purchasers. A fine object reproduced, with marks showing when and where made, is quite legitimate; but where wares are copied, marks and all, and sold as genuine, then fraud is attempted and that article is a counterfeit. There is one country where this rule does not prevail, and that is Japan. They feel very differently with regard to the matter there, and think a successful reproduction of a master's work, marks and all, but a tribute to that master's excellence. It is therefore not permissible to deface it by the mark of the copyist, who merges his identity in the work of the original artist. This is freely admitted by workers in Japan, and the code holds good in many branches of art.

There is one potter whose claim to recognition rests on the excellence of his work in that comparatively humble branch of ceramic art, stone china.

## Mason's Ironstone China.

At Lane Delph, in Staffordshire, was established, in 1797, a pottery by Miles Mason, whose name may be found on specimens of early wares. It was his son, Charles James Mason, who perfected and patented in 1813 the ironstone china, which became so well known and popular in this country. The paste was made by mixing with the clay pulverized slag or the scoria of ironstones. They also made soft paste porcelain in small quantities, and did a large and flourishing business. In their ironstone they made vases and pitchers with relief ornaments decorated in colours. They were quite celebrated for a rich shade in blue, combined with red and a small amount of other colours, which gave a very rich colouring. See FIG. 112. They mingled printing and painting in a very effective manner, and the designs were Chinese, with landscapes and figures, or conventional patterns touched up with gold. One of their famous patterns was called " Bandana."

An early mark was the name " Miles Mason " in full. Later it was simply " M. Mason," and, from 1813 to 1851, when the business passed out of Mason's hands, it was marked " Mason's Ironstone China." See FIG 113.

### " A COLLECTOR'S DREAM."

" A Dresden shepherdess was, one day,
   Milking a small Delft cow,
   When a Sevres marquis came along—
   I saw him smile and bow ;
   ' O lovely shepherdess, hear my song '
   I think I heard him say,
   ' For thou hast captured my porcelain heart,
   And by my sword I swear thou art,
   A star in the milky way ! "

G. S. HELLMAN.

# CHAPTER VIII.

## BASALTES, LUSTRES, WHITE WARE, ETC.

FOR a collector with an eye to the beautiful, who is looking about for something odd, rather difficult to obtain but always satisfactory, I should recommend the acquisition of a few choice specimens of black ware or basaltes. There is one point in particular which makes this ware valuable for the novice: it has never been reproduced, and when you find a piece you can be quite sure you have an antique. It is a fact, to be sure, that by far the greater number of specimens are unmarked, and that cotemporary potters used one another's models and copied patterns freely. You can learn quite easily to distinguish good work from bad, and the fineness of finish, and delicacy of cutting show for themselves.

Basaltes was one of the earliest products of the English potter's art—indeed its manufacture goes back to Roman days, when it was one of their specialties, and during the Middle Ages there was much black ware used both in utensils and for tiling. The Elers were among the first of the Staffordshire potters who turned their attention to improving this ware. They were said to use red clay and ironstone only. Wedgwood's ware was more complicated and vastly superior, and his Egyptian black, ultimately called basaltes, was made from native clay, ground ironstone, ochre and oxide of manganese. The ochre was obtained

Fig. 113. HERCULANEUM PORCELAIN. Second period.

Fig. 114. BLACK BASALTES.

Fig. 115.  NELSON  TEAPOT.  Black basaltes.

Fig. 116.  QUEEN ANNE TEA-SET.  Silver lustre.

from the deposit of oxide of iron found in coal mines.

Wedgwood calls his basaltes a porcelain, equal in hardness to agate or porphyry and resisting the attacks of an acid. No potter ever quite succeeded in rivalling Wedgwood in the manufacture of this body, but Palmer & Neale and Adams produced beautiful ware.

This basaltes comes in two shades, so to speak: dull and slightly shining. The fine polish was usually obtained by use of the lathe, though some potters used a varnish which was burned in at a red heat. The dead black pieces belong to a later period than the shining ones, and were more admired, Sir William Hamilton, Lord Warwick and other connoisseurs of that time giving their verdict in favour of the dull ware. Busts, medallions, vases and the choicest service pieces were unpolished, as was the body of those vases which were decorated in colours.

From 1770 on this ware gained great favour, and the demand was fairly larger than could be easily supplied. The skilled workmen were given vases, statuettes, busts, medallions and intaglios to model, while the less skillful turned out tea-sets, lamps, tripods and jugs in endless variety. They struggled to take advantage of a rising market, in a manner not very different from that of the tradesmen of a hundred years later. The figure pieces are extremely rare in this country, but sometimes they were from twenty to twenty-five inches high. Smaller groups were modelled by special artists and designed with great care, as were the vases, which were of elegance and beauty.

A vase is not often found out of a museum in this

country, but I have seen a variety of teapots, creamers, sugar-bowls and medallions, all found in the middle and southern states, some of which are illustrated
here. By far the larger part are unmarked, but I
know one small round teapot, marked " Birch," which
has its duplicate in the British Museum. Potters had
a curious fashion for marking the teapot only with
their name; so that when the pieces were scattered, as
followed in due time, the creamers, sugar-boxes and
bowls were nameless. Of the Staffordshire ware it
was generally the sugar-boxes which were marked, a
curious vagary, surely, to mark one kind of ware one
way, and a second ware another way.

This teapot marked " Birch " was found in London
and bought for a very small sum by one of the brother-
hood, who was rummaging through a junk shop for
" finds," after the fashion of his kind.

FIG. 114 shows an interesting group. None of the
pieces is marked, but the middle pitcher was made by
Elijah Mayer, or E. Mayer and Sons, who were potters at Hanley from 1770 to 1830. On the side we
show is a portrait medallion of George, Prince of
Wales, when he was made Prince Regent in 1811.
He succeeded to the throne of England, as George IV,
in 1820. The Prince's feather encircles the medallion, and above it is a very handsome lace pattern,
while the handle is decorated with a beading. An
equally fine portrait of the Duke of York is on the
other side. The Elijah Mayer works made a great
deal of this black ware, which was notable for the
events it celebrated. The marked pieces all have a
high value.

Recently I saw a sugar-bowl of this basaltes, made

by Mayer and having on one side a bust of Wellington being crowned by Britannia, with Fame blowing a trumpet. On the other side is the inscription : " India, Portugal, Spain, Vittoria, 21st June, 1813." This bowl, in perfect condition, with cover and handles, sold for forty dollars.

The teapot and other creamer in FIG. 114 are noticeable for the excellence of their decoration and the beauty of their shape. They both—but the creamer in particular—tend to that ovoid form which Wedgwood declared was the most beautiful for this style of objects and for vases. The groups of figures are elegant, and the photograph does not do justice to the cutting. The side shown has a classic group, vestal virgins at an altar preparing to sacrifice a lamb. On the reverse side are maidens representing History and Fame crowning the bust of Cicero with a laurel wreath. On the base of the teapot is basket work ; on the creamer an incised leaf-like pattern. The knob of the teapot has the seated veiled figure used by so many potters, but always agreeable.

The best class of this black basaltes was made by applying the figures which were cast in moulds after the body of the piece was formed. Then they were fired and the outlines of the figures sharpened, all the rough edges cut off, and every detail carefully attended to. Of such workmanship were all the best pieces, and the pieces shown in FIG. 114 come under this head. The other method was to pour the basaltes in the form of " slip " into a mould, and let it set. These pieces are thinner than those made the other way, less artistic and less regular in shape. Such a piece is shown in FIG. 115, yet it is intrinsically more valuable than the others.    It is one of Mayer's pieces, celebrating Nelson's victories.    The center medallion is a shell, and in the shell are three figures, one placing on a tomb a wreath marked " Nelson."    On the tomb is the word " Trafalgar."    On the other side, in a similar shell-shaped medallion, is the palace of St. James, and in the distance the Pyramids, showing the hero's progress and commemorating his prowess.    Nelson died in 1805, so this piece was made after that date, probably while the glorious victories were still in everybody's mind.    These historic black basaltes are very rare, and always difficult to find.    Only three such pieces have come under my notice.

Tablets of basaltes, with exquisite designs, were set in furniture, or inserted in chimney pieces.    The first produced were found to be too small to be effective for use in this latter manner, but after much experimenting they were made as long as twenty-three by nine and one-half inches.    The early ones were in very high relief, but as skill increased the relief was lowered, still maintaining the artistic elegance and delicacy for which they were so noted.

Many small pieces for toilet articles, pots for ointments, articles for writing tables and cabinet specimens were made, and it is matter of record that some of these were despatched to America.    From the stout nature of the ware they ought still to be in existence, if one only knew where.

Names of some of the potters who made basaltes before 1800 and after are :

E. Mayer & Son, Palmer & Neale, Thomas Wheildon, Lakin & Poole, Eastwood, John Turner, E. J. Birch, Joseph Twyford, Charles Green, H. Palmer.

of Hanley, Josiah Spode, David Dunderdale of Castleford.

## *Lustre Wares.*

The term lustre, as collectors in this country generally apply it, refers to metallic-looking wares of English manufacture. Scarce as genuine pieces of this
pottery are becoming, and fine as much of it undoubtedly is, it holds no more comparison to the old Italian
and Spanish lustre wares than a tallow dip does to the
moon.

To the Saracens were the Italians indebted for the
freedom and luxury of the styles they copied, for the
use of colour without stint and for the beauty of the
lustre which they copied from the Eastern artists.
The most famous lustres emanating from Italy come
from the city of Gubbio. The master artist there was
Georgio Andreoli, and his fame rests on his ruby
lustre, brilliant and gleaming like a polished gem and
shading from ruby to claret; on the silver, with the
effects of moonlight on water; on the gold and golden
shades and on the green, rarest and most jewel-like of
all. Georgio's signed works date from 1519 to 1537,
but he is supposed to have died in 1552.

From 1560 to 1570 the art of making lustre declined,
and disappeared. It has been sought in modern
times, with what success we all know.

The Hispano-Moresque pottery antedates that of
Gubbio, the beginning of this lustre ware being about
1320. Gold or copper with a paler yellow lustre
decorates the earlier specimens, while the deeper copper lustres are assigned to the latter part of the four-

teenth century and from that time on until the beginning of the seventeenth century. These ancient
lustred pieces were ornamented, not covered, with the
lustre as are the specimens of more modern times.

The characteristics of Hispano-Moresque are not
only the metallic lustre with which it is overlaid, but
the beauty of form of the objects, which has acquired
for them the name of " gilded works." This pottery was
sent to every quarter of the globe, and these lustres
had a large share in furnishing models for the dawning
industries of many lands. Barcelona and Valencia, as
early as 1546, were rivals in the manufacture of faïence,
and the modern lustre ware of Barcelona in ruby tints
is very beautiful and decorative. Even now, occasionally, pieces of this old ruby lustre come into the
market, after years of seclusion in collectors' cabinets,
and every bit is of almost priceless value. A dish sold
in London in June, 1902, for seventy-nine pounds sixteen shillings, about four hundred dollars. In addition
to its beauty this dish was further noteworthy for having been mentioned in Macaulay's " History of England " as figuring at the dinner given to Lord Faver-
sham by the Bridges of Weston Zoyland, Bridgewater,
previous to Monmouth's defeat. It has always
remained in the family until the present sale.

Among the modern lustre the silver-tinted comes
first in point of rarity, though the rose-spotted Sunderland lustre, shown in FIG. 96, is a close second and
brings perhaps a larger price. There is a Sunderland
pitcher on sale, like the larger one in the picture, which
is valued at one hundred dollars. It is absolutely perfect and has the original owner's name painted on the
front.

Even in England, silver lustre, once so largely manufactured, is now exceedingly scarce. It has been superseded by a cheaper process giving more durable results. Dealers and collectors hunt for choice specimens in vain, while the prices paid for good pieces are such that the original makers would be astounded. See FIG. 116.

The body of this pottery is earthenware, either brown or white, and is covered with a solution of platinum. This mineral was discovered in 1741 and was used by the Staffordshire potters and still more largely at the pot-works at Preston Pans. Silver lustre originally was but a cheap and glittering imitation of silver, and the very early specimens were lustred inside as well as out, to carry the deception to its extreme limit. I have never seen any specimens so treated except mugs and bowls and the tea-set shown. After the ware became more common and nobody was longer deceived, the potters confined its use to the exterior of vessels and used it in decorations, in patterns and bands, and occasionally in combination with gold lustre.

The largest private collection of old silver lustre of English make, which I know, is held in England, and numbers one-hundred and thirty-eight specimens.

The nearest approach to figures made may be seen in FIG. 133, Neptune modelled as a candlestick by Wedgwood. Plain straight candlesticks, like the shapes in brass, pewter and silver, are run across occasionally and were no doubt cast in old silver moulds, as they followed the sterling patterns exactly.

There are also found tea-pots and coffee-pots, hot-water-jugs, cream-jugs and cider-jugs, sugar-boxes, bowls, egg-cups, mugs, two-handled cups, mustard pots, kettles and salt-cellars as well as vases and candlesticks. Some of the jugs are very handsome in shape and large enough to hold three pints. The fluted or ribbed tea-sets in Queen Anne's style are eagerly sought at large prices.

In 1838 electro plating was invented, and from this time on the manufacture of silver lustre decreased and finally ceased between 1850 and 1860. In FIG. 116 is given one of the fluted Queen Anne sets already mentioned. It is perfect, and the extra teapot belonged to a similar set of slightly different pattern. It stands in one of the trays fashionable at that period and belongs to the collection in the Concord Antiquarian Society.

FIG. 117 shows what must have been the last uses' to which silver lustre was put, for a china merchant who has been long in the business tells me he sold similar pieces about 1860 and worked them off as best he could, for they were "old stock." The cake basket in the centre is very ornamental. It is nine inches high and eleven inches across the top. The body of the ware is grey pottery, and the lines on the base, the leaves and the stem which wreathe the top are of the lustre, and the pendent bunches of grapes are covered with brown enamel. Exactly such a piece is the choicest ornament of the English collection already mentioned, and no doubt there are many tucked away in cupboards here, which the owners would bring out did they know how highly such pieces were esteemed. The vases are of the same grey body, the ornamentation being in the lustre, and on each side is a charming dancing figure modelled in low relief. These three

Fig. 117. SILVER LUSTRE CAKE-BASKET AND VASES.

Fig. 118. GROUP OF LUSTRE JUGS.

Fig. 119. LUSTRE MUG AND GOBLETS.

Fig. 120. GROUP OF LUSTRE JUGS.

pieces are absolutely perfect and were rescued not long since from a hamlet many miles from the railroad, but where enough china lore had penetrated to make the owner know she had a " good thing" and demand a stiff price. The handsomest piece of silver lustre which ever came under my notice is the large jug shown in FIG. 118. It will hold a couple of quarts, is absolutely perfect, and after a more or less eventful career is passing an honoured old age in the possession of a descendant of its original owner. He speaks with great reverence of " Great Aunt Thankful's jug," and relates with unction how he finally became possessed of it, arriving at the vendue where a less reverent relative had put it up at auction, just too late to bid it in, but at last got it away from its purchaser upon the payment of ten dollars. It is beautiful in every way; the shape is nice, somewhat fluted, and the lustre is flawless, rather unusual in so large a piece. When so much lustre was made and despatched to us it seems strange how it has disappeared in a comparatively short time. Most potters made lustre ware, and if one had a list of those who at one time or another put it on the market it would embrace almost every well-known English potter's name.

While the silver lustre was originally made as a sham, the sturdy copper and gold lustre stood on its own feet from the first. It is claimed by the supporters of Wedgwood that he first made the copper and gold lustred wares in 1776, from a receipt given him by Doctor Fothergill. The first idea was to apply it only to frames, but it proved so unexpectedly ornamental that numberless beautiful articles were made. The gold lustre was exceptionally fine, and honey

cups of simple but beautiful form became very popular.   The lustre jugs come in every size, from the tiny
ones holding but a couple of spoonfuls—mere toys—
to the great ones, for tavern use, holding a gallon or
more.   Those shown in the photograph with Great
Aunt Thankful's jug, are all of a deep copper shade
and were gathered from many different places, yet are
presumably of the same period; as the shapes of the
handles of all, save the smallest, are alike.   None are
marked ; little of this ware is.   They all have different
styles of decoration, and the choicest is the one with
the white star-like flower and the line of bead work on
the handle.   They are all on dark pottery body, as is
common, but the oldest one I ever came across was a
child's toy of a deep cream-coloured pottery, with
lovely, rose lustred bands encircling the body.   It belonged to an old lady, over eighty years of age, who
had taken it with her in all her various movings.   It
was one of the few toys she had as a little girl in a
remote Vermont village, and was brought to this
country from England some years before she was
born.   It has suffered somewhat but is carefully
mended and presents an unscarred front to the world.
    The largest of these lustre pitchers were set down
in manufacterers' pattern books and in old inventories as cider-pitchers, and goblets came with them
similar in pattern to the pitchers.   In FIG. 119 is
shown such a pair of goblets and a mug, the exact
counterpart of which, in colour, size and decoration, is
at Mount Vernon and is said to be the one Washington used daily for shaving.   While numbers of these
" cyder jugs " were in use in private families, the
largest ones were used at the taverns, which occupied

a prominence in rural life that is quite done away with to-day. Besides the transient guest, the single men of the town took their meals at them, and certain localities were famous for certain mixtures which were generally compounded in these great jugs. At the taverns where the stage coaches stopped there would be dozens of these pitchers in use, and "calibogus," " mimbo," "spiced ale " and " flip " were some of the savoury condiments served in them.

Flip, especially dear to Yankees' stomachs, was used all over the country and was mixed in many ways, but a favourite recipe ran as follows: " Mix together a pint of cream, four eggs and four pounds of sugar. This is to be kept on hand. To every quart of bitter beer add four great spoonsful of the sugar and cream compound and thrust in the red hot loggerhead." This imparted the burnt taste so highly esteemed. This recipe made a very temperate variety of the drink. The usual receipt called for a gill of rum. " Metheglin " was made from the honey of the wild bee, but this was a summer beverage. Rum, or " Killdevil " as it was known at the time, was the almost universal drink. One old New Englander, however, wrote from Philadelphia : " Whiskey is used here instead of rum but I can not see but it is just as good." Indeed, so potent were the drinks served in some of these innocent looking jugs, that a statute was passed in Massachusetts which forbade the selling of rum to drunkards, and an official was on duty at the tavern to determine when a man was drunk enough. It causes a smile to read, that, in early colonial days, the sale of strong water was forbidden to the Indians, but a later generation decided " that it was not fitting to deprive the Indians of any lawful comfort" and repealed the statute.

Mulled cider was thought a not unhealthful drink for children, and many men commenced the day by drinking a quart of hard cider before breakfast, a sort of eye-opener, as it were. It must have been an unusually temperate man who boasted, "a sup of New England's air is better than a whole draught of old England's ale." Many people are collecting lustre jugs, some fortunate ones with china luck getting hold of thirty or forty pieces. The price is constantly rising. A good jug five or six inches high is easily worth five dollars, while a really fine one, with raised flowers coloured from nature, is worth several dollars more.

A fair enthusiast had a struggle with her conscience and the desire for a lustre jug, which was keen while it lasted. She was stranded for an hour or two by some exigency of travel in a small town in New England and, as the station was desolate and uncomfortable, betook herself to walk. Her travels led her to the graveyard, which seemed to her youthful eyes unusually melancholy, and she was attracted to one grave which had at least a semblance of care, and was adorned by a bunch of flowers. The blossoms were so fresh that our friend pushed aside some of the spreading leaves, to see if they were in water, and then beheld that the vessel containing them was a lustre pitcher, in good condition, and with a band of pale blue on which were bunches of flowers touched in by hand. It seemed, so she confessed afterwards, that she must have that pitcher, and, as fair exchange is sanctioned, she removed the flowers, laid a silver dollar beside them and started station-wards with her prize. She got no farther than the gate of the graveyard ; for a hand clutched her (only a metaphorical hand), and she hurried back and replaced the pitcher, unable "to rob a lonely grave." There was no time to find the owner of the pitcher then, and a lengthy correspondence, conducted through the village postmaster, brought no result. The " owner did not care to part with it ; it was handy for flowers "—a rebuff which often meets the collector who unexpectedly comes on a find. I have in my own mind a copper lustre jug, six inches high, with an ivy wreath on it in a lovely shade of green. The owner is not a collector, does not care for the jug, yet cannot be induced to sell or exchange it, and there it is, at this moment, on a kitchen pantry shelf, holding molasses, with a little saucer over the top, subjected to the cook's unlover-like handling when she is making gingerbread. The owner only sees it when she makes periodical visits to the pantry, and will not let it go because she " always remembers that pitcher held molasses." Such people as these are the despair of collectors. FIG. 120.

There are copper lustre jugs with bands of brilliant yellow and figures or flowers on them in colours, either printed or painted. Very beautiful pieces were made at Longton by Thomas Barlow. Such as these are marked with an impressed "B." Indeed Longton seems to have been a great centre for lustre ware, both the High-street works and Park works turning out silver and copper pieces. Gold lustre was used for decorative purpose at the Gold-street works, which were also at Longton, and sometimes tea-sets of this gold shade, looking very new, may be found in this country. One

of the unpleasant things about all lustre, except silver
and rose spotted, is the fact that the old shapes and
designs have in many cases been reproduced.  But
one who handles china can be almost sure to detect
the new.   In the first place it is perfect, and shows no
marks of wear on the base, where, in old pieces, the
lustre is generally worn off.   The shade is brighter
and has not the depth and richness of the old ware,
and it seems to have a glassy glaze which is not found
on the old.   A search through the china houses of
New York and Boston failed to reveal a single bit of
modern lustre ware in any form whatever.   The dealers said there was no call for it, and they had ceased
importing it.   Finally a piece was secured in Canada,
where it is said much may be obtained, and the differences are quite marked between the old and new,
particularly in weight.

An extremely choice and valuable piece of old copper lustre is shown in FIGS. 121 and 122.   It is called
the Cornwallis jug and comes under the head of historic.   On one side is shown the surrender of Cornwallis, and though we have seen that the English potter was not very sensitive when he came to depicting
our victories, yet in this case he endeavored to smooth
matters over when he put on the inscription.   It
reads, "Cornwallis *resigning* his sword at Yorktown,
Oct. 17, 1781."   Surrendering was an unpalatable word.
On the other side is a portrait of Lafayette with a
laurel crown held above his head by two figures, representing, no doubt, Victory and Fame.

All these Cornwallis jugs are fine and hard to get.
This one, in addition to the historical interest connected
with it, has a personal history which makes it doubly

valuable. It is one of a pair brought from England, soon after the Revolutionary War by a Mr. Dangerfield of Fredericksburg, Virginia, who was an officer in our army. The pair of jugs remained in his family for three generations and have just been sold; the one shown going to grace a collection of one hundred and forty jugs held in Virginia, and the other one being given to the Virginia room at Mt. Vernon as a present from the school children of Virginia.

It is just as well to remember that on the occasion pictured on the jug Lord Cornwallis was not present; he feigned illness and caused General O'Hara to deliver the sword to Washington, who deputed General Lincoln to receive it. In every way these jugs are admirable—shape, proportion, colour and decoration. They are far in advance, in a certain noble simplicity, of many of the present day shapes, out of which it is almost impossible to pour without spilling the liquid. These old-time jugs, no matter what their size, have the same large lip, and it is as noticeable in the lustres as in the Liverpool jugs. FIG. 123.

## Castleford.

Somewhere between the years 1770 and 1790 a pottery was started at the town of Castleford, twelve miles from Leeds, where white ware, known as Castleford ware, black ware, Queen's ware and the choicer kinds of pottery were made. The first potter whose name is connected with these works was David Dunderdale, who came into possession of them about 1800. These works were open, under various managements.

until about 1820, when they were closed. Subsequently they came into the hands of some of the old
workmen, but the plain white paste for which they
were originally known seems to have been discontinued.

The most familiar pieces in America are teapots.
The covers are sometimes attached with metal pins;
occasionally are sliding; but more often have the lift-
ing lid with which we are familiar. The Castleford
pieces are very much like the basaltes in everything
but colour, some of them being dead white, not unlike
parian, which was invented some years later; and some
have a very slight gloss which was obtained, so it is
thought, by smearing the inside of the fire-clay box
where the pottery was fired with the ordinary china
glaze. This vaporized with the heat and deposited a
slight film on the objects being fired. Castleford
ware is translucent if held to the light, and is ornamented with groups of figures—some of the same
classical groups which have been seen in basaltes and
which were original with Flaxman or Lady Templeton or some other of Wedgwood's artists—and the
models were bought or copied from Wedgwood's
pieces. This ware is seldom found with any colour
on it. At most it has only lines or bands of blue,
green or brown. They made a bid at these works for
American custom by making designs of Liberty, the
Arms of the United States, portraits of Washington
and Franklin, etc.; but few of these specimens seem
to have survived, the general run being the classical
subjects referred to before. The same two methods
of procedure followed in the manufacture of basaltes
were followed in Castleford ware :—either the clay was

pressed into moulds—in which case the piece is quite
thick—or, in the form of "slip," poured into moulds,
under which treatment the teapot, or whatever it
might be, was considerably thinner.  An occasional
piece of Castleford comes to hand with the pitted
surface which we ascribe to the method of salt glazing; but this was caused by having the inside of the
mould lined with tiny points which left corresponding
depressions in the surface.

In FIG. 124 is given a very beautiful specimen of
this ware.  The teapot is not uncommon in style, but
the body of it shows the pitted background, and the
floral design is in very high relief and beautifully
finished.  So also is the little border of ferns at the
base and about the cover.  The knob is a daisy, a
flower much used in this ware.  This piece has faint
bands of colour on the edge of the handle, at the base,
above the floral band and on the cover.  The elegance
of such a tea-pot speaks for itself.  It is generally
supposed that some of the pierced, printed or painted
ware which we call Leeds was made also at Castleford.  The so-called Castleford, however, is the white
ware.  Very few pieces are marked, but when they are
it is with the letters " D. D. & Co. : Castleford."  Two
long lines crossing each other in raised slip and the
number " 22," impressed, were also said to be the
marks of this pottery, but by far the larger proportion
of pieces is left unmarked.

Two or three specimens of this white ware amid a
collection of basaltes make a very ornamental shelf in
a corner cupboard.  Indeed a black basaltes tea-set or
a Castleford, if you can bring your mind to think
that your cabinet treasures are not too bright nor yet

too good to hold human nature's daily food, is a very elegant addition to that fast vanishing but delightful meal, supper.  With the addition of some choice old cups and saucers, brilliant in colouring or choice in design, either the black or the white ware looks uncommonly fine, a thousand times more desirable in every way than the gaudy silver which in our day is the end-all and the be-all of every housekeeper.

# CHAPTER IX.

## WEDGWOOD AND HIS WARES.

THE ceramic art of various countries—France, Italy, Germany, China, and Spain—is classed in different epochs or periods. In each epoch there were usually one or two factories or potters whose work was so admirable that it was difficult to award the palm between them. In England it is different; there is one name which expresses the greatest heights which English pottery has ever reached, and that is, Wedgwood. In no branch of art, learning or manufacture is there a royal road. All paths which lead to the heights of success are stony for some part of the way, and it is only by the exercise of patience, energy and perseverance that the goal is reached. It was by the combination of these three qualities that Josiah Wedgwood accomplished the amount and quality of the work he did, and built for himself, day by day, an enduring fame. He came from a family whose members had long been potters at Burslem, and was the youngest of a family of thirteen children. He was born in August, 1730.

His early education was fragmentary, no doubt, as there was but one school in Burslem and that a poor one, and two years after the death of his father, when Josiah was but eleven years old, he was put to work in the pot works, as a thrower. The will of his father provided that when Josiah came of age he should have twenty pounds, not a very large capital with which to start in business, surely. But Josiah was to learn his trade, and that he did, being bound as apprentice to his brother, for whom he worked till he was sixteen years old. Then he contracted the smallpox, "the dregs of which disease settling in his leg," as Mr. Gladstone says, eventually necessitated its amputation. What would have proved to most men a terrible crippling was a weary trial at first, but in the end one factor which tended to make him the great man he was. No longer able to engage in the arduous labour of throwing the clay, his mind was forced to dwell on other branches of the business. From the time he was sixteen till he reached the age of thirty-four he was a constant sufferer from this leg. Only after it was amputated did he recover a measure of health. Wedgwood himself attributes much of his success to the fact that he was frequently laid up with his infirmity, these periods of inaction causing his mind to be all the more active. Mrs. Wedgwood, his mother, who seems to have been an estimable woman, died when Josiah was not yet eighteen. The family of brothers and sisters continued to dwell in the old house, and Josiah worked out his five years' apprenticeship. Possibly he supposed after these five years of faithful work he would be taken into partnership with his brother, but this was not the case. When he came to be twenty years of age he took his small patrimony and started out in life for himself. He went first to Stoke and there made knife handles in mottled agate and tortoise shell ware, which he supplied to the hardware manufacturers of Sheffield and Birmingham.

In the year 1752, three years after his apprenticeship had expired, the young Josiah entered into
partnership with a man named John Harrison and
still continued to make the knife handles. Two years
later came the partnership with Thomas Wheildon,
the best known potter of his day, and this association
lasted for five years. Wheildon's reputation for his
wares was widespread, and most fortunate it was for
Wedgwood to be associated with so desirable a partner. On Wheildon's side the benefit derived from
Wedgwood's taste and skill about balanced accounts.

There are interesting documents extant, covering
the period of this partnership and giving a variety of
curious details with regard to the custom of hiring
potters, and the prices at which some of the wares
were sold in 1754 and a little later. For instance,
potters were always hired from Martinmas to Martinmas, and into the agreements went many strange items.
One man had stockings furnished him, another a
shirt, at sixteen pence a yard, and one employee who
worked for two shillings threepence a week, had, as
further emolument, "an old pr. stockins, or something."

The great Josiah Spode, who came afterwards to be
so well and favourably known, worked for Wedgwood,
in 1749, for two shillings threepence a week, or "two
shillings sixpence if he deserves it." As for the tortoise shell and other wares, plates came as low as
eight shillings a dozen, and one dozen painted dishes
are set down as worth but two shillings. The wares
made by Wheildon and Wedgwood were excellent in
shape, of good quality and carefully made. It is
needless to say how scarce they are now and how

desirable.   There were, besides the tortoise shell, the cauliflower ware, and salts, mustard pots, bread-and-butter plates, coffee pots, teapots, sugar boxes, dishes, mugs, etc.   The famous green glaze which Wedgwood invented the year of the partnership, 1754, and which is described as a " new green earthenware, having the smoothness and brilliant appearance of glass," had much to do with the rising fortunes of the new firm. The partnership expired in 1759, as it was drawn but for five years, and Wedgwood returned immediately to Burslem, intent on perfecting his experiments and bringing them to a successful issue.

He was now twenty-nine years old, and, in the old pot works which had been occupied by his brother, he set to work not only to create new ideals but to rival old ones.   The old pot works did not prove satisfactory, and he moved to those connected with the " Ivy House," as it was called from the profusion of this plant growing upon it, which, no doubt, furnished him with models for the ivy pattern he was so fond of introducing in his work.   This house and works were rented by Josiah from his relatives for the modest sum of ten pounds yearly, and, having a house, his thoughts ran naturally to filling it, so here he brought his bride. Josiah Wedgwood, now somewhat over thirty, was carrying on the old works—Churchyard Works, as they were called—where he made common wares, and the Ivy House Works where the choicer specimens were made.   He was suffering intensely with his leg, the condition of which had become most distressing.   Yet, under all this stress, he personally superintended both works—in fact every article may be said to have passed through his hands—and he increased the product of tortoise shell and marbled wares by making vases with gilt or coloured foliage, jardinieres, white ware medallions, the green glazed earthenware, different dishes to represent different fruits—melons, pears, pineapples, etc.,—and all these had a ready and abundant sale.

With the success coming from his numerous inventions and with the betterment of his health (his leg had been amputated), he naturally sought to increase his output and to do this was obliged to have more extensive works. It was at this time that Wedgwood rented a third pot works, not far from Ivy House, and continued to manage three distinct manufactories in his native town. Besides being constantly on the alert to improve his wares himself and to acquire any new ideas which were being put forth by other potters, he also found time entirely to re-organize the methods of the workmen in his employ, bringing order out of chaos and organizing a system by which he was left comparatively free to experiment and perfect, while still holding the reins of government. With these three establishments under his control he had serious difficulties to contend with. For instance, there were but three modellers in his employ, and of these three only one gave his entire time to Wedgwood. The tools of the trade were still of the most primitive order—a turning lathe, a potter's wheel and a few knives. With ambitions for a higher type of work, this redoubtable man had to set to work and invent his own appliances—new tools, kilns, drying ovens, etc., and teach his workmen how to use them, and oversee their efforts. Day and night he laboured, taking hardly the necessary time for rest. He was early at the bench with his workmen, and generally with his own hands he taught them how to make the object he wished them to form. He often said he did his thinking by night, so that he might be up and doing by day. An infinity of small details crowded on his mind, and it is interesting to see how he met, solved and settled them. It had always been customary to call potters to their work by sounding a horn, though in general they came and went from the works pretty much as they pleased. In the new works which were acquired after the Ivy House Works, Wedgwood sought to overcome this difficulty and had a small cupola built, with a bell hung within it to sound working hours. This gave to the factory the name of Bell House Works. These works were rented by Wedgwood from Mr. Bourne, their owner, till the removal to Etruria.

At the Bell House Works Wedgwood made his finest pieces, and so admirable did they become that he soon gained distinction both in England and on the Continent. In September, 1761, Wedgwood made and presented to Queen Charlotte, upon the birth of her first child, a caudle and breakfast set of his cream-coloured ware, which had by this time reached a high state of perfection. He had it still further embellished by his two best painters, Daniell and Steele, and on the creamy yellow ground were raised sprigs of jessamine and other flowers, all coloured from Nature. The queen was highly delighted and gave orders for a dinner service, and, in token of his gratitude, Wedgwood called this Queen's Ware. He received commands to call himself by the proud title of "Potter to Her Majesty." Of course both potter and his products became immensely fashionable when the queen set the style, and orders flowed in upon him. It is on record that at this

Fig. 125. CREAM WARE. HUSK BORDER.
Boston Museum of Fine Arts.

Fig. 126. BASALTES MEDALLION.

Fig. 127.  BASALTES TEA-SET.
Boston Museum of Fine Arts.

time these cream-ware plates, large size, brought fifteen shillings a dozen and other pieces in propor- tion. It is well to remember that the common type of plate in this ware was of the trencher pattern, or like the old wooden plates, with flat edge and without a rim on the under side. So far only Wedgwood's successes have been mentioned, but his losses were vast and continuous. One disaster followed another, but with that dogged perseverance which was one of his characteristics he kept bravely on. Consider the feel- ings of the potter who labours for months creating and modelling, and, in a few hours, by a deficient kiln, has all this work of brain and hand destroyed !

After arriving at the point of perfection in the Queen's Ware our potter did not reap the whole benefit of his labours and trials. All the potters of the region quickly took to making it and gained the rewards without the losses. The distinctive quality of Wedgwood's cream-coloured ware was the introduction of Cornwall clay, and its superiority was due to im- provements in the processes of its manufacture and its glaze. This cream-coloured ware, so called, varies in shade from an extremely light primrose to the deepest saffron. The variation in the colour comes from the clay, the dark tints being much rarer than the light, and the objects made in them are always of the finest quality and highly desirable. Some splendid speci- mens of basket work—" twigged baskets " Wedgwood called them—are found in this deep tint, as well as centre pieces of various shapes. Vases were made in cream ware of a thin paste, with highly vitrified glaze and of small size. If left uncoloured they were plain, ribbed, fluted or impressed with classical borders.

Then followed serpent, goat's head and dolphin handles and festoons. Inlaying was used and gilding, as well as patterns in blue, red, black or brown. Then the cream ware was sprinkled with colour. Vases marbled with gold and others sprinkled with the same are set down in an invoice of cream ware dated October 15, 1768, and the wholesale price was from eighteen shillings to ten shillings sixpence each. FIG. 125.

Of the cream-ware services there are more specimens to be found. In a catalogue of this ware it is noted that a service of Queen's Ware, consisting of one hundred and forty-six pieces, at wholesale cost three pounds, seventeen shillings, about $19.25. There were round and oval covered dishes, "terrines" for soup, pickle dishes, salt cellars, etc. There were also to be had in addition to the pieces of the regular service. " Root dishes with pans to keep them hot. Covered dishes to stew or keep a dish of meat hot. Dishes for water zootjes (Dutch fish). Ice pails. Egg baskets to keep boiled eggs hot in water. Egg spoons, table candlesticks of different patterns from nine to fourteen inches high. Cheese toasters with water pans, pudding cups, shapes for blanc-mange, asparagus pans, monteths for keeping glasses cool in water, beer mugs with or without covers, croquants or sweetmeat dishes, ice-cream cups and covers, strawberry dishes and stands and dessert spoons."

When it is considered that Wedgwood personally invented most of these dishes, thereby adding to the variety and comfort of daily living, it seems as if what he accomplished in this ware alone would have given him a reputation as a benefactor. Up to this time by far the greater part of household utensils were wood or pewter, most undesirable in comparison with this fresh pretty ware which came within the reach of the middle classes, who had been unable to buy the porcelain or Oriental wares used by the wealthy. The best patterns used on this ware Wedgwood copied directly from the antique. They were the egg-and-tongue, meander, antique, and helix borders. The colours and forms of these varied greatly, and besides being in great demand in England were exported to Italy and Germany. The grape pattern in purple and gold was put on a dessert service for the great Lord Chatham.

That splendid service made for the " Mesdames of France," in 1787, bore this grape border in brown, with trophies and musical instruments in the same colour.

In 1787 there were, in addition to the patterns which had been printed by Sadler and Green, these:

| | |
|---|---|
| Honeysuckle in several colours. | Red and black strawberry leaf. |
| Red Etruscan. | Brown drop. |
| Black and red spike. | Dotted border, bell drops, light |
| Brown edge. | green. |
| Blue morning glory with green | Broad pea-green and mauve. |
| leaves. | Royal pattern, pencilled land- |
| Bell-drops, deep rose colour. | scapes. |

The next year several more patterns were added among them are:

| | |
|---|---|
| Red and black dotted border. | Moss border. |
| Green and black Etruscan. | Green oat with blue lines. |
| Brown strawberry leaf. | Green and purple grape. |

There were also an incredible number of varieties of flowers, fruits, shells, plants, seaweeds, etc. Borders going with arms and crests were often intricate, and, during the period from Wedgwood's death, in

1795, to 1843, the patterns were louder in colour and design, and gold was introduced in spots and dashes.

All the finish in old Wedgwood cream ware was excellent, as might have been expected. The joining of the patterns never shows ; no edging is out of line ; and the colour on the same plane does not vary unless it is designed to.

Wedgwood cut out his models first in paper, and modelled most of the trial pieces himself. So true were these models that his plates and bowls " nest " perfectly, and even the commonest jug for wash-hand basin was moulded to be accurate in its lines, good in form, and perfect in its capacity for pouring. His butter tubs were modelled in the pleasing shapes of melon or pineapple. His honey pots were beehives, and his twigged baskets and dishes are things of beauty. In this same cream ware he made watering pots, large and small milk pans, slabs and tiles for dairies, as the management and care of the dairy was a fashionable fad among his aristocratic customers. He would be pleased could he see the estimation in which even this, the humblest of his wares, is held, for so small objects as a pair of bell-pulls, decorated in green, brought at auction, some years since, twenty-two dollars.

After working on the ware itself and its decoration, Wedgwood then turned his attention to shapes, and from this time on great improvements are noted in the forms of common objects, and convenience and the perfection of each piece was studied.

Wedgwood's taste and artistic sense were so strong that even the silversmiths followed his models, as well as the members of his own craft. In all of the long and prosperous career of this prince of potters only once did he take out a patent, and then only an unimportant one for decorative purposes, in the year 1769.

Previous to this time Sadler and Green had been engaged in printing on Wedgwood's Queen's Ware in biscuit state, and much of it was on the market. It is extremely hard to find any to-day, even in England. The difficulty of getting his wares safely to Liverpool for printing and back again to Burslem, seems to have impressed upon the mind of Wedgwood the importance of good roads or water carriage. So, about 1764, we find him endeavouring to have turnpikes built and canals put through, and it was owing to his efforts that the first turnpike road was run through the potteries district ending at Burslem.

Even with all the expense he was put to, and with his losses by experiments and imperfect appliances, Wedgwood was no longer so much hampered for money. His wife had brought him quite a little fortune, some authorities giving the figures as twenty thousand pounds—an immense sum for those days, and of great assistance to her ambitious husband.

By 1766, owing largely to Wedgwood's own efforts, and to his coming forward with a generous subscription at the proper moment, the canal project was put through. Wedgwood, appropriately, was invited to cut the first sod, and the Grand Trunk Canal, which took over six years to build, became a fact. It was ninety miles long, and opened up the pottery districts, making the receipt and despatch of goods more certain and vastly more speedy, as well as lowering the freight charges.

Finding as time progressed that the cares of overseeing took too much of his attention, which might have been employed to better advantage, Wedgwood took as partner his cousin, Thomas Wedgwood, who for some years had been foreman in his factory. The works at Burslem had become too small, and, in 1766, a year so full of important events to Josiah Wedgwood, he began to build works in the township of Shelton, only about two miles from Burslem, and most advantageously placed, as Wedgwood thought, for it was to be intersected by the proposed canal. Here were built first what were known as the "Black Works," in 1767, by the side of the canal, and here commenced the manufacture of black basaltes, Egyptian, or black ware, as it was variously called. He had perfected this ware the previous year, and describes it, to use his own words, as "Basaltes, or black ware; a black porcelain biscuit of nearly the same properties with the natural stone, striking fire with steel, receiving a high polish, serving as a touchstone for metals, resisting all the acids, and bearing without injury a strong fire; stronger, indeed, than the basaltes itself." So hard was this basaltes that it would strike fire with steel, yet with a surface so soft that it seemed to have the bloom of velvet, and was capable of being moulded and cut into the most exquisite ornament.

In FIG. 126 is given one of the basaltes medallions in the set "English Kings," which were modelled from Astle's portraits. These medallions are two inches long and one and three quarters inches wide, and the particular set from which this one is taken is framed in an old-fashioned silver mount which contrasts admirably with the velvet blackness of the basaltes. No photograph can do justice to the beauty and finish of this ware and to those delicate details to which Wedgwood himself paid so much attention. Fortunately for us, Wedgwood had his works catalogued, showing what and how many sets or pieces were made, and there were six editions of this catalogue beginning with the year 1773, again in 1774, 1777, 1779, 1787, and under the younger Wedgwood in 1817. In no year were there more than thirty-six sets of these "English Kings" made, and in the years from 1779 to 1787, when his art productions reached their highest perfection and greatest number, there were made but sixty-eight sets in all.

There are some details which every collector should know and which should be carefully noted in every piece of this basaltes before purchasing, as there were quantities of counterfeits put upon the market.

The first point to be looked at is the flat surface or body-plane. Those belonging to the Wedgwood and Bently period, from 1769 to 1780, and also to the Wedgwood period 1781 to 1795 are always beautifully perfect, even and smooth. No variation or waviness ever appears on the surface, and there is no "crazing"—that is, minute cracking of the surface glaze— ever to be seen on the elder Wedgwood's ware.

The relief part, or raised work, is, almost without exception, beautifully perfect. The use of a microscope or hand magnifier reveals perfections, not defects, and the minutest pieces, such as were used to set in rings or eardrops, will show up with the finish of antique gems. The draperies and limbs, each tiny finger and toe, the plumage of birds are all perfect and distinct.

No test is more to be relied upon than the accuracy of the under cutting. In modern medallions or cameos, the outlines of limbs, profiles, draperies, etc., lie flat with the surface ; in " Old Wedgwood " the modeller's tool has under-cut these lines, and the relief stands out sharp and distinct from the plane. This gives roundness and the appearance of high relief to the figures, flow to the draperies, and that detachment from the background which gives these reliefs their chief beauty. In those bas-reliefs and portraits modelled by Flaxman this under-cutting is shown in its highest perfection, as is also that polish and finish where not a detail is forgotten nor overlooked. Many fine specimens, however, are not under-cut—that is cut away from beneath the figure—but are, nevertheless, carefully finished on the edges by the modeller's tools. Those specimens lacking under-cutting, or after finish with the tool, are to be regarded with suspicion, and it is extremely doubtful if they were made prior to 1795. These remarks apply to all specimens of black ware and jasper and to all objects made in these wares.

As for the marks, it is well to bear in mind that almost every piece of old Wedgwood bears his mark. Those which are unmarked are trial pieces, when a new body or colour was used or some experiment was being made, or such rare pieces as in the hurry of a great establishment escaped the workman's attention.

To the experienced collector the " feel " of the piece, the finish, and the choice perfection of the details will reveal the master's work, even though the mark be lacking. The name Wedgwood is frequently impressed in small capitals which vary from one thirty second to one quarter of an inch in height. On the small pieces this lettering is extremely minute, so that it needs a magnifier to reveal it. Except letters and figures, generally used singly, the collector will remember that all the more peculiar marks were used after the death of Wedgwood, the elder, in 1795.

The double mark ＼／ dates from between 1805 to 1815, ⫪ is the mark of the period of Oriental patterns, 1810, and the use of three capitals in combination, as " A. T. Q.," " R. S. B.," " T. M. P.," " L. G. Z.," and others of the alphabet taken at random, are not only still used but are never more than fifty or sixty years old. One excellent test of age is the extreme roundness of the two letters " o " in the name Wedgwood, and so is the figure " 3," or the single letter " O " in addition. Besides the printed name Wedgwood, it is found sometimes as if printed by hand, with the old-fashioned letter " d," the upward stroke of which turns backward. This mark is never found on any of the modern ware. In this same hand printing may be found the two names Wedgwood and Bentley, which puts the piece bearing such mark prior to 1780, when Bentley died. This firm name may also be found in a circular raised medallion, with the word " Etruria " added.

There are numberless examples having the impressed stamp of Wedgwood with a single letter added as " Wedgwood A," or " V " or " H," etc. Figures, too, are sometimes combined, as " Wedgwood k," and " 2," or " Wedgwood 43." There are many pieces bearing in addition scratched marks of various kinds, but these are invariably workmen's marks. In addition there are given by Miss Meteyard, who made

Wedgwood and his work a life study, about one hundred other marks which were used *always in connection* with the name Wedgwood.

When the name of the subject is given on the medallions, it is usually on the face of the piece at the base of the portrait. See FIG. 126. If it is not impressed on the front it is scratched on the back by hand. The marks on printed or painted ware are of the impressed name and a mark or two in the same colour as the pattern. Sometimes the name is printed on in red or blue, but *always* in small capitals. In the old ware the impressed stamp is notable for its beautiful clearness. In modern ware it is often blurred and ragged.

Numbers of the finest cameos and portraits have the letters " H " or " G " signifying Hackwood or Greatback, two of Wedgwood's finest workmen. Wedgwood himself did not like his men to do this, and endeavoured to suppress their marks as much as possible, for he wrote to Bentley, on December 22, 1777, as follows: " I cannot resist the temptation of showing my dear friend our new Shakespeare and Garrick, though they are not so well fired as they should be; we put them in our common biscuit oven. You will see by looking over the shoulder of each, that these heads are modelled by William Hackwood, but I shall prevent his exposing himself again now I have found it out. I am not certain that he will not be offended if he is refused the liberty of putting his name to the models which he makes quite new, and I shall be glad to have your opinion upon the subject. Mine is against any name being upon our articles besides " W " and " B," and if you concur with me I will manage the matter with him as well as I can."

Prior to the partnership with Bentley, in 1768, the goods, which were largely cream wares, were simply marked Wedgwood, in large type, and often even this was omitted on many pieces of a set. It is not impossible to buy old Wedgwood in this country to-day. Within the last three years I have bought two of these portrait medallions of the old period, one William, Prince of Orange, size four by three inches, in the set of "Illustrious Moderns" mentioned in catalogues, in perfect condition, and marked, for ten dollars. The other set in silver, two by one and three quarters inches, of William the Conqueror, I bought for fifteen dollars. They were marked simply "Wedgwood" in small, finely executed capitals on the back of the first one, the subject on the front in the second one, and scratched in the back, on the one of William, Prince of Orange.

These medallions were generally sold in sets, arranged in trays or framed, and I find in a sale catalogue of Christies', in London, for the year 1781—which was the year succeeding Bentley's death—that a set of twenty-six of these heads, unframed, brought but one pound, ten shillings, which reduces them to the infinitely small price of a trifle over twenty-one cents each for the medallions, size two by one and three quarters.

Wedgwood did not at first use the black basaltes for vases. In 1766 and 1767 he worked hard in improving the lathe to be used in their manufacture, and it is in 1768 that we first hear of basaltes vases. The earliest of these were bronzed, but did not meet the popular fancy. In the next year, 1769, they were painted or ornamented with festoons in white biscuit, glazed. Small white medallions were also employed, surrounded with a frame, in the same white biscuit. It took some years to bring these vases to their final perfection, and from 1769 to 1776 they were ornamented with flutings, ribbing, strap-work, floral and husk festoons, and with goat's head, mask, satyr and dolphin handles. The surface of these vases was generally highly polished, and the mark on them is the circular raised medallion, with the name Wedgwood and Bentley and often Etruria. This mark always signifies a fine period, with high quality of work, beautiful shape and superior workmanship, and the surface has a velvet touch to the finger. The earliest ones with bas-reliefs, all—vase and decoration—being black, had festoons of flowers and husks or a simple medallion.

In 1776 Wedgwood undertook more artistic flights. He writes to Bentley in June of that year: " I am preparing bas-reliefs for most of our black vases and hope to have a very complete assortment for you to open with the next season ; and such as make a striking and pleasing variety in that part of your show."

Flaxman's exquisite bas-relief of the " Dancing Hours " was first applied to the basaltes vase, and copies of it were sent to London in September, 1776.

A new variety of black belongs to this same year, for Wedgwood, ever alive to meeting popular taste, found that the dead black was more generally liked than the polished, and from this time he used it in busts, medallions and vases. The collector will find that the polish of the earliest vases grows less and less as the potter advanced, and was avoided in the finest period. From 1777 all the bas-reliefs were, as they appeared, adapted to vases as well as to gems and intaglios. In this way the dates of vases, etc., can be closely approximated; as Flaxman's groups and Lady Templeton's small figures could not have appeared till somewhat later, 1782 or 1783, while such well-known groups as "Achilles," or the "Daughters of Lyco-medes," or the "Sacrifice of Iphigenia," came after 1787.

Wedgwood took an honest pride in these exquisite productions and says, in 1779 : "They are from three or four inches high to more than two feet. The prices from seven shillings and sixpence each, to three or four guineas, which does not include the very large ones and those pieces which consist of many parts, and are very highly finished." He speaks of the degree of perfection to which these black vases have been brought, and adds : "On this account, together with the precision of their outlines and simplicity of their antique forms they have had the honour of being highly and frequently recommended by many of the connoisseurs of Europe ; and are being placed amongst the finest productions of the age, in the palaces and cabinets of several princes."

That these pieces were worthy to be so ranked is true, and to my mind the jaspers do not compare with this, the highest, most exquisite and artistic pro-duct of Wedgwood's life.

In FIG. 127 is shown a charming tea-set, with the hot-water kettle which was an invention of Wedg-wood's. The exquisite figures of children and cupids stand out from the background in beautiful relief, and the shapes of the pieces are as graceful as we are led

to expect.  When Wedgwood first began to manufacture, tea and coffee were greater rarities than they
are now, and even well-to-do families often did not use
either drink once a day.  In country districts the use
was more restricted still, so that tea-sets were not
much in demand except for festive occasions.  Then
the higher classes used Oriental porcelain, with tea or
coffee pot and creamer of silver.  Wedgwood, whose
perception was ever alive to creating a demand, saw
that with handsomer and finer ware he could carry
forward public taste and stimulate a desire for these
articles.  This he did and filled modest English
homes with objects of utility and elegance, replacing
and crowding out the coarse and common.

Some of the black ware was painted.  " Encaustic
Painted Ware," it was called, and tea-services and
separate articles were made in it ; even teacups and
saucers are described as having " Etruscan borders in
encaustic paintings," and " Roman cups," and bread-
and-butter plates are also mentioned.  None of this
encaustic ware had the elegance of the plain black.
As an example of the beauty of the basaltes vases,
one is given in FIG. 128.

The price of these vases was necessarily high, the
risk in making large pieces being great, for in putting
on the figures, the models and moulds of which were
costly, there was danger they would crack.  Fluted
vases were more reasonable than those with figures,
and plain handles were less costly than decorated
ones.  Yet what Wedgwood called high seems very
small to us, for in Christies' catalogue for 1781 many
" mantel suites," consisting of three, five, or seven
pieces—candelabra and vases—were sold, and the high.

est price reached was six pounds for " a suit of five, with candelabra." This set was bought by Flaxman. This sale was after the death of Bentley and was held apparently to reduce stock. In addition to the tea-sets, hot-water kettles, vases and candelabra, there were also made in basaltes, statuettes, even cups and saucers, salt-cellars, tea-trays, flower-pots, flower-holders and " tazze," as they were called. They were flat cups or dishes, each with a foot and handles, copied from Etruscan and Greek examples. The largest sizes of these tazze were used for fonts in churches. Frames were also made in this material, generally for the medallions.

Rarest objects of all, in basaltes however, are figures of elephants, lions and horses. The latter were made from models by Mrs. Landre, but, while on record in the catalogue, no specimens are known. A wonderfully fine pair of lions is in a private collection in England.

The fourth great invention made by Wedgwood was what he eventually called jasper ware ; but before speaking of this a few words must be given to a most important event in his life, his partnership with Bentley.

Wedgwood was one of those wonderful men, who by system, by never quitting an object until they had effected their purpose, and by a careful management of time, seemed always to have leisure at command. Yet he found that all the vast details of such a great establishment were more than he could manage, and, roughly dividing his products into two classes, the useful and the ornamental, he invited his friend Mr. Bentley to become his partner in the ornamental

branch. Just why Wedgwood should have chosen
Mr. Bentley, who was a literary man rather than one
of business, cannot be told ; yet the partnership, lasting
twelve years, till Bentley's death, was one of the
wisest acts of Wedgwood's life. It began in 1768. The
"Black Works" were finished and work on the other
manufactory and the dwelling house was soon commenced at Etruria. In 1770 these were finished, and
Wedgwood named the whole estate, with its works
and mansion house, Etruria.

The extraordinary care and resources of Wedgwood
had been brought to bear on the new manufactory,
and it was not only the largest but the most complete
which had yet been built. No sooner were the works
set in order and filled with competent workmen than
they were fully occupied in both branches of the
business, ornamental as well as useful. When the
factory was well started, Wedgwood turned his attention to the comfort of his workmen, and built for them
a village where they could be comfortably and happily
housed.

With Mr. Bentley situated in London, looking after
and introducing the products of Wedgwood's fertile
hands and brain, the latter gave himself up to improving and beautifying his work. Sir William Hamilton
assisted him in his studies of antique forms and models,
and urged him to take out a patent for painting in
encaustic colours ; this he did, and it was the only one
he ever had. So free was he from professional jeal-
ousy that he regretted having taken even this precau-
tion to protect himself, saying to his friends, he
" would be better pleased to see thousands made happy
and following him in the same career, than he could

be at any exclusive enjoyment." This single patent was granted on November 16, 1769. The first problem Wedgwood had to struggle with after perfecting his methods of encaustic painting was to reduce the price of the objects so treated. The vases were large, some as tall as twenty inches, and the price varied from one to ten or twelve guineas each. For the exceedingly choice ones even more was charged, and one painted for Lord Carlisle was fifteen guineas.

"The Grecian vases we have are sadly too dear," wrote Wedgwood to Bentley in 1772. "When I tell our noble customers ten guineas for a small pair of vases with a single figure upon each, I am sure of a full stare in the face from them." So Wedgwood went to work to reduce cost and make their manufacture rapid and economical. At first each vase was painted separately, the outlines being drawn upon it in chalk. But this was soon given up and the outlines printed and the colours filled in afterwards. Even in the body of the vases new mechanical aids were employed which facilitated production. The body oftenest used was basaltes with some slight chemical differences to give it a bluish or brownish tone. There were also vases of a red biscuit body, painted like the black ones, but these were never so popular and were not made in large numbers.

The best period of the painted vases was 1780 till 1795, and quantities were made, the purchasers including many of the highest rank in England, St. Petersburg, Amsterdam, Genoa, and Leghorn. The subjects which were used to decorate them were not only taken from antique Etruscan vases but from gems, antique paintings and bas-reliefs, as well as Hamilton's " Antiquities."

On the thirteenth of June, 1769, in one of the rooms of the " Black Works," the first product of the new factory was thrown. It was a great day for Wedgwood, his family and friends. At the potter's bench sat Josiah Wedgwood, arms bared and encircling the plastic ball of clay, while beside him stood his partner, Thomas Bentley, and his wife. The clay was moulded with his accustomed care, and on the board in front of him grew a row of classical urns, fashioned by his skillful hands. These pieces all were fired, painted with purest Etruscan design, and each was marked :

" June XIII, MDCCLXIX.
One of the first day's production
at
Etruria in Staffordshire
by
Wedgwood & Bentley.
Artes Etruriae Renascunter."

The body of these vases was basaltes, and the figures and inscriptions are in red. The vases are of two sizes, ten, and ten and one half inches high, and they bear groups of Hercules and his companions in the garden of the Hesperides. Each group is varied slightly on every vase. So popular did this style of vase become that they were thrown in Etruria and painted at Chelsea in order to supply the demand. In this latter place were many excellent artists to be had, who worked under the superintendence of Mr. Bentley. These Etruscan vases, etc., were sold largely on the Continent as well as in England, and the material of

Fig. 128. BASALTES VASE.
Boston Museum of Fine Arts.

Fig. 129. JASPER FLOWER-HOLDER. GREEN AND WHITE

which they were made is so durable that many of them still exist.

In the year 1770, Wedgwood had the satisfaction of receiving large orders, not only from the King and Queen of England, but from Catherine of Russia as well. The set ordered by Catherine must have grieved Wedgwood's artistic soul, for his patroness did not leave the decoration to him, but gave positive orders concerning it. On each piece was to be painted in black enamel different views of the palaces, castles of the nobility, and different places of interest in the kingdom. Also upon every piece was to be painted a green frog or toad, as the service was to be used at a palace that bore this name.

Wedgwood rose to the occasion and the set was finished in 1774. Twelve hundred original sketches had been made of palaces, etc., to decorate it, and the chatty Mrs. Delaney writes of the " sensation " the service caused when exhibited in London: " I am just returned from viewing the Wedgwood ware that is to be sent to the Empress of Russia. It consists, I believe, of as many pieces as there are days in the year, if not hours. They are displayed at a house in Greek street, Soho, called Portland House. There are three rooms below and two above, filled with it laid out on tables ; everything that can be wanted to serve a dinner. The ground, the common ware, pale brimstone, the drawings in purple, the borders a wreath of leaves, the middle of each piece a particular view of all the remarkable places in the King's domin-ions neatly executed. I am sure it will come to a princely price ; it is well for the manufacturer, which I am glad of, as his ingenuity and industry deserve encouragement." She does not mention the green frog as being a part of the decoration, yet the Empress showed this service to Lord Malmesbury when, in 1795, he visited the palace of La Grenouilliere.

In 1773 Messrs Wedgwood & Bentley issued their first catalogue of goods. It is a curious document, and seems to have been designed for customers who did not have the opportunity of visiting the ware-house in Great Newport Street.

It does not include the cream ware, in which Bentley had no share, but specifies :

" *First*. A composition of terra-cotta resembling porphyry, lapis lazuli, jasper and other beautiful stones, of the vitrescent or crystalline class.

" *Second*. A fine black porcelain, having nearly the same properties as the basaltes.

" *Third*. A fine white biscuit ware or terra-cotta, polished or unpolished."

The last of the three was used for vases, medallions, stands, etc., and sometimes for portraits on a field of black basaltes.

In the second edition of the catalogue there was a fourth ware enumerated.

"*Fourth*. A fine white terra-cotta of great beauty and delicacy, proper for cameos, portraits and bas-reliefs."

This was the first appearance of what became the most popular, and, to many people, the most beautiful of Wedgwood's productions, jasper ware. A flower holder is given in FIG. 129.

In the last catalogue published, 1787, this ware had arrived at its greatest perfection and was now widely known as jasper. This is how the catalogue sets its merits down :

" *Fourth.*  Jasper a white porcelain bisque of exquisite beauty and delicacy, possessing the general qualities of the basaltes together with that of receiving
colours through its whole substance, in a manner
which no other body, ancient or modern has been
known to do.  This renders it peculiarly fit for cameos,
portraits and all subjects in bas-relief, as the ground
may be made of any colour throughout without paint
or enamel, and the raised figures are the pure white."

The magnificent productions of the Wedgwood
Works and the fame acquired by the Catherine of
Russia and other royal services had given an impetus
to the sales of the wares outside of England.  There
was such a call for them on the Continent that as
early as 1774 what was called a third edition of the
catalogue was issued, translated into French.

The broad spirit of this noble potter is shown in
his turning his attention from these objects of beauty
which were his delight to such simple matters as
inkstands and eye-cups, these latter being sold at one
shilling each.

The catalogue was next translated into Dutch, and
was issued at Amsterdam in 1778.

Somewhere about this time Wedgwood and Bentley
took into their service a young and unknown man,
named John Flaxman, and it was due to the steady employment and encouragement given by these potters
that the sculptor was gradually able to work his way
upward.

No adequate list of the patterns and groups designed
and modelled by Flaxman for Wedgwood is extant.
With the characteristic generosity of Wedgwood the
prices paid to Flaxman from the very first were liberal.

In 1783, the year after the marriage of Flaxman to Ann Denman—his guiding star—he got as much as two pounds ten, for modelling a portrait for a ring and one pound five, for one of the chessmen which later became so famous. Some of the original models of these seventeen figures in wax are still preserved at Etruria, in a sadly dilapidated condition, it is true, but showing how they were first made in white wax, the "cores," or "strengtheners," being of twisted wire. It was not known just where or when the game of chess originated, some authorities making it an Eastern amusement, some dating it from the fifth century in England. So Flaxman felt himself at liberty to choose as he would, and his figures are of the Middle Ages. He selected effigies, figures on tombs, and pictures in glass as his models for kings and queens, knights and ladies.

The figures were often in white jasper, but were also made in blue, black, or green, the bases remaining white. The shape of the base varied also, and was either oval, round, or square, the oval shape being the earliest. In an invoice of December 6, 1787, the various figures are charged at three shillings, one penny, each. Flaxman drew these designs at various times between October, 1783, and March, 1785. It was his method to draw a rough sketch, submit it to Wedgwood, and, if approved, to make a careful drawing. The drawings from which these chessmen were finally modelled were sent to Etruria in March, 1785, and the price charged was six pounds, sixpence. The modelling seems to have been paid for in addition. It is not known whether chess boards were made to go with these exquisite figures. Cribbage boards in pale blue jasper, with decorations in white relief, were made a few years later, and are occasionally seen, but chess boards would have been larger objects than could have been easily made in this composition. In 1867, at Christies, were sold five pieces of one of these sets of chessmen, a king, queen and three pawns. They brought twenty-one dollars.

All the original models were made larger than they were intended to be, so as to allow for the shrinkage by fire. When the model had been made a mould was made from it, and into this mould, when dried, the prepared clay was pressed. If the original model was, say, eight inches high, its copy in clay would be eight inches also. After passing through the kiln, however, and being fired, it would shrink as much as one-eighth, in every way. Thus it would come out but seven inches high, and proportionally smaller in every other measurement.

It caused much wonder how pieces could be produced precisely alike, yet varying in size, say from ten inches to such tiny things as were fit for an ear-drop or a jewel in a ring. It was easily managed. A mould was taken, say from the piece just mentioned, which had shrunk from eight to seven inches, and from each successive size, the reduction being a loss of one-eight of its then size, till it was reduced to the wished-for dimensions.

In the year 1770, on the twenty-sixth of November, Thomas Bentley died, and later on Wedgwood took as partners his own sons and Thomas Byerley. In 1783 there occurred at Etruria a "bread riot," which was quelled, and peace restored, chiefly by Wedgwood's own efforts. By 1785, Wedgwood, never

pausing in his efforts at improvement, introduced a
" jasper dip " in which clay vessels were immersed and
so received a coating of jasper instead of being formed
of it throughout.  It made the goods more costly,
however, and Wedgwood writes to Bentley:  " The
new jasper, white within, will be the only sort made
in the future ; but as the workmanship is nearly
double the price must be raised.  I think it must be
about twenty per cent."

In the next year, 1786, came the sale of the marvel-
ous collection of antiquities and bric-a-brac belonging
to the late Duchess of Portland.  In this sale was included that unique work so highly extolled, the
" Barberini Vase," so called from having belonged to
the famous Barberini family at Rome.  It came from
them by purchase to Sir William Hamilton, who, in
his turn, sold it to the Duchess of Portland, when it
became known as the Portland Vase.

Every one knows how Wedgwood admired this
vase, attended the sale, bid against the son of the
Duchess, who desired to retain the treasure, and rose
in his bids till the Duke crossed the room and asked
his reasons for wishing to own the piece.  Wedgwood
told of his desire to copy it, and the Duke of Portland
promised to allow this if Wedgwood would stop bid-
ding and allow the Duke to keep it.  This arrangement was accepted by Wedgwood ; the Duke paid
1,029 pounds ($5,145 dollars) ; and Wedgwood took
home with him this gem.  He says: " I can not suffi-
ciently express my obligation to his Grace, the Duke
of Portland, for entrusting this inestimable jewel to
my care, and continuing it so long—more than twelve
months—in my hands, without which it would have

been impossible to do any tolerable justice to this rare work of art. I have now some reason to flatter myself with the hope of producing in a short time a copy which will not be unworthy the public notice."

The copy was made in due time, and as an example of modern ceramic art could not be excelled. Fifty copies were made, all of which were subscribed for. The vase was made by Wedgwood with both black and dark blue grounds. The original moulds are still in existence, and copies are even now produced by the Wedgwoods at their own works.

At this time, in his own manufactory at Etruria, Wedgwood was making such perfect works of art as that shown in FIG. 130. The earliest one of these was made in 1781, and shown to the public in the show rooms in Greek Street, Soho.

In some way the notion had become prevalent that Mr. Bentley was the originator of the most beautiful works put forth since his connection with the ornamental branch, and it was largely to counteract this idea that the exhibition was held the year after his death. All the Wedgwood and Bentley stock was shown, and in separate cases the newest and most artistic productions of Wedgwood himself, for by 1761 the difficult operation of firing large masses of jasper had been mastered, and he had been able to colour his composition sea-green, light and medium blue, and also black. The finest vases of this period were decorated with Flaxman's designs, " The Dancing Hours," " Apollo and the Nine Muses," " An Offering to Flora," " Tragedy, Comedy and Apollo," and others.

These subjects were, of course, continued during the whole period of vase making, with infinite variety of detail as to ornament.   Wedgwood speaks of these vases in a letter to Sir William Hamilton, dated June 24, 1786: "One thing I persuade myself you will observe, that they have been objects of very great care, every ornament and leaf being first made in a separate mould, and then laid upon the vase with great care and accuracy, and afterwards wrought over again upon the vase itself by an artist equal to the work ; for from the beginning I determined to spare neither time nor expense in modelling and finishing my ornaments, and I have the satisfaction to find that my plan has hitherto met with the approbation of my friends, for the purchasers of every nation declare them to be the highest finished and cheapest ornaments now made in Europe."

The vase shown in FIG. 130 is absolutely faultless. It is in a medium shade of blue, with the figures in white.   Observe the grace of the festoons of flowers, the perfection of the signs of the Zodiac.   No detail but can bear the closest scrutiny, and it will but reveal fresh excellences under the magnifying glass.

Lady Templeton's small groups of children, etc., first appeared about 1786.   Lady Diana Beauclerk's came later, as did Miss Crewes's.

The pedestals and tripods often used as supports to the jasper vases must be noted too.   Suitable size seems to have been the chief factor sought in their choice, for there never seems to have been any matching of patterns.   If size and colour were adaptable, this was sufficient.   The height of these vases ranges from seven and one-quarter inches to nineteen and one-half, the average being from ten and one-half to thirteen and one-half inches.   Many of the choicest vases

Fig. 130.  JASPER VASE, BLUE AND WHITE.
Boston Museum of Fine Arts.

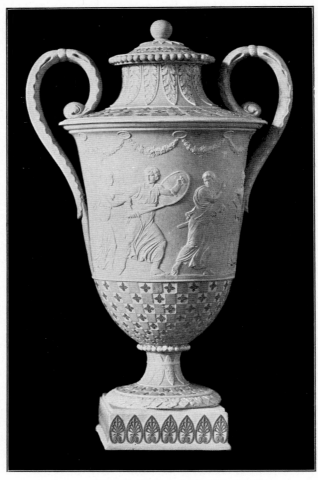

Fig. 131.  JASPER VASE, LILAC AND WHITE.
Modelled by Hackwood.  Boston Museum of Fine Arts.

are from eleven to sixteen and one-half inches in height.

In 1787 the scale of prices was as follows, nothing being said as to decoration: Seven and one-half inches, one pound, one shilling. Nine inches, one pound, eleven shillings and sixpence. The prices rose in proportion to size and ornament until the maximum of thirty guineas was reached, a price cheerfully paid to-day for one of the smallest ones.

The vase shown in FIG. 131 has more variety in colour than is usual in these pieces. The body of the vase is lilac. The diaper pattern on base of vase and cover is alternate squares of blue and white, the white square being decorated with quatrefoil ornaments in green. The beautiful pattern on pedestal is also green.

These old vases are fastened to the pedestals by nuts and screws, and these bits of metal have become one of the methods by which the old Wedgwood— prior to 1795—may be told from the more modern. If the objects were made before 1780 the nuts and screws are of iron, not cast but beaten, and the metal is rough and scaly and always very black. In some cases the screw works in a sunk box, but this is unusual. Later there were used brass nuts and screws, and these will be found much tarnished with age and very small. In July, 1775, Wedgwood mentions twenty dozen screws being sent from London to Etruria for vases, but the greater part of the work was done in London by a man named Palenthorpe. Spurious pieces of Wedgwood often have the nuts covered with cement or plaster of Paris so as to conceal their newness, and of all such appliances one should beware.

Writing as late as 1789, in regard to this jasper ware, Wedgwood says : " For when the workman has finished with them they have a long and hazardous fire to pass, which with the polishing and finishing afterwards, takes near a week, and in this burning they are liable to various and unavoidable accidents in which case we are obliged to make them over again and this doubles the time."

No one can help admiring the fine spirit of this great man, whose ambition was to excel in whatever he laid his hand to.   England, a land of blossom, had hitherto had small attention paid to articles in which to grow her plants in houses and conservatories.  The varieties of shapes and forms invented by Wedgwood are admirable, and lend themselves to picturesque arrangement never before approached.

Beginning with the common red flower-pot, and passing a little later to those of stone ware, both grey and white, great improvements were introduced.  The red ones became more shapely, harmonious colouring was applied, the stoneware had simple decorations in festoons or medallions, or moulded patterns.  The famous green glaze, one of Wedgwood's earliest achievements, was applied to what he called "flower, bough and root pots," as was the well-known cream ware, and flower pots of this became as popular as table sets.  The very largest myrtle-pots were hooped, and on many of the smaller sized ones were repeated the popular patterns.  Goat's heads, masks and dolphins were used for handles.  Then basaltes and terra-cotta bodies were employed and more classical forms adopted.  Bas-reliefs were applied, and stands, pedestals, and plinths were used as supports.

In FIG. 132, modelled by Hackwood, is shown the highest perfection these elegant flower stands achieved. It is in a brownish lilac with figures and ornaments in white, with perforated cover in which the stems of the plants were held in place. There are collections containing myrtle pans, bouquetiers and root pots only, and the number of these articles is exceedingly large. There are some of these pieces to be met with even yet, and the plainest is to be eagerly seized upon. Within the last eighteen months I have seen a fruit stand, cabbage leaf pattern, with base of tortoise shell ware, which was sold at auction in a small house in the interior of New York State. A woman bought it for ten cents, and a china fancier who happened in asked to see it. It was marked with the name "Wedgwood," impressed, and as well as could be told in the hasty glance given it, belonged to the old period. An offer was made to the purchaser, of a brand new pretty white dish in its stead, which was eagerly accepted, the purchaser declaring she only "bought it because it was going so cheap." It proved to be an old piece, for after Wedgwood had made his green glaze satisfactory he no longer combined it with mottled ware.

In 1787 the sixth and last edition of the catalogue in English issued during Wedgwood's life was published. There have been two English reprints since, one in 1817 and one in 1873. The title reads:

"Catalogue of Cameos, Intaglios, Medals, Bas-reliefs, Busts and small Statues; with a general account of Tablets, Vases, Escritoires, and other ornamental and useful articles. The whole formed in different kinds of porcelain and terra-cotta, chiefly after the

antique and the finest models of modern artists. By
Josiah Wedgwood, F.R.S. and A.S.; Potter to Her
Majesty, and to his Royal Highness, the Duke of
York and Albany. Sold at his rooms in Greek Street,
Soho, London, and at his manufactory in Stafford-
shire. The sixth edition with additions. Etruria,
1787."

This catalogue, a pamphlet of seventy-four closely
printed pages, gives lists of the products in double
columns. It speaks of the four bodies already
mentioned and gives two others which he had perfected
since the previous edition in 1779. They are:

"*Fifth.* Bamboo, or cane-coloured porcelain.

*Sixth.* A porcelain bisque of extreme hardness,
little inferior to that of agate. This property, together with its resistance to the strongest acids and
corrosives, and its impenatrability by every known
species of liquids, adapts it happily for mortars and
different kinds of chemical vessels."

Of the bamboo or cane-coloured ware specimens
exist in most collections, and Wedgwood mortars have
a world-wide reputation.

In 1788, on October 20, the partner in the "useful
wares," Thomas Wedgwood, died, and Josiah was left
with both branches of his large business on his hands.
On January 18, 1790, Josiah Wedgwood took into
partnership his three sons, John, Josiah, and Thomas,
and also his nephew, the style of the firm being Josiah
Wedgwood, Sons, and Byerley. The latter held a one-
eighth interest in the firm until his death in 1810.

In 1795 on January 3, Josiah Wedgwood died, and
on the sixth his remains were buried in the Church of
St. Peter, Stoke-upon-Trent. Unfortunately his last

Fig. 132.  JASPER FLOWER-POT OR "BOUGH-POT."  LILAC AND WHITE.
Modelled by Hackwood.  Boston Museum of Fine Arts.

Fig. 133.   SILVER LUSTRE CANDLE-STICKS.
Boston Museum of Fine Arts.

illness was painful, probably cancer of the mouth, called in those days "mortification," and he lingered in suffering for three weeks.

A tablet has been put up in the Church of St. Peter, rehearsing his virtues and his works, but a more enduring monument was built by the man himself in sending out into the world works of so fine a character that each one was as perfect as its nature permitted. To-day as yesterday his name sets a standard by which other potters are measured, and in more than one hundred years since his death no work can equal his.

Although many examples of his handiwork have been illustrated, there were many others equally fine which have not been touched upon. Wedgwood himself divided his ornamental productions into twenty classes which, briefly, are as follows :

*Class One.* This comprised intaglios and medallions cut from antique gems and from the finest models which can be procured from modern artists. By 1787 no less than 1032 separate designs had been issued. There were two sections into which this first class was subdivided, first the cameos and second the intaglios. Roughly speaking a cameo stands out in relief from the background, while the intaglios are cut into the background. The cameos were made in jasper with coloured grounds, or in plain white bisque. As early as 1775 Wedgwood wrote he was absolutely sure of blue " of almost any shade, and likewise a beautiful sea-green and several other colours for grounds." In the cameos were subjects taken from Egyptian, Grecian and Roman mythology, War of Troy, Roman history, Illustrious Moderns, etc. The intaglios took

a fine polish and were often made in imitation of various coloured agates or other stones.  Most of these
intaglios were made for rings, seals, bracelets or
brooches, and were generally to be mounted in gold.
Portraits of people were also cleverly produced in seals,
the original model being made in wax by Flaxman,
Hackwood, or some other of Wedgwood's best artists.
Wedgwood's quaint way of setting forth his wares
shows how well he appreciated their excellence :—

  " If gentlemen or ladies choose to have models of
themselves, families or friends made in wax, or cut in
stones of proper size for seals, rings, lockets or bracelets, they may have as many durable copies of these
models as they please either in cameo or intaglio, for
any of the above purposes at a moderate expense.  If
the nobility and gentry should please to encourage
this design, they will not only procure for themselves
everlasting portraits, but have the pleasure of giving
life and vigour to the arts of modelling and engraving,
etc."

  The cost of these wax models, to be produced of a
proper size for ring or bracelet, was three guineas each.
After the first model was made copies were much
cheaper—at five shillings each—and not fewer than ten
could be ordered.

  These intaglios, when of antique subjects, were
" pirated " boldly.  One of the worst offenders was
Voyez, who even forged Wedgwood's name.  Many
of these spurious intaglios are scattered abroad, but a
moment's comparison with an original will reveal the
copies' lack of polish, colour, and finish.

  *Class Two*, in Wedgwood's division, included bas-
reliefs, medallions and tablets.   Three hundred and

more distinct groups were made by him and his staff of artists. The bas-reliefs were generally made in jasper of two colours, and were used to set in furniture, cabinets, fireplaces, etc. Some of the fine old English country seats are still decorated with these tablets, which date from Wedgwood's own day. Owing to difficulty in firing, these early bas-reliefs were small, six inches long by nine high ; but, at last, twenty-seven and one half inches long, and eight and one half inches high were obtained for such subjects as " Diana visiting Endymion, etc."

These tablets were, from the first, very costly, even at wholesale. In 1787 one invoice gives the prices of a lot of tablets :—" One long square tablet, blue ground, Apotheosis of Virgil, 7½ by 14¾ £16-16s. One ditto, green ground, Apotheosis of Homer, £18-18s."

Wedgwood says, in 1777, long before they arrived at their perfection, " The jasper tablets want nothing but age and scarcity to make them worth any price you would ask for them."

*Class Three* consisted of medallions and portraits, etc., of kings, queens and illustrious persons of Asia, Egypt and Greece. There were more than one hundred of these.

*Class Four* dealt with ancient Roman history, from the foundation of the city to the end of the Consular government, including the age of Augustus. Sixty medals, from Dassier, were in this class, at one guinea a set, or sixpence each.

*Class Five.* Forty heads of illustrious Romans.

*Class Six* embraced the twelve Caesars, in four sizes, and their Empresses in one size only.

*Class Seven.*  Sequel of Emperors from Nerva to Constantine, fifty-two in all.

*Class Eight.*  The popes, two hundred and fifty-six medallions.  To those who took the whole set, they cost threepence each.  Singly, sixpence each.

*Class Nine.*  Kings and queens of France and England, one hundred heads, sold only in sets.

*Class Ten* included heads of " Illustrious Moderns." In 1787 there were two hundred and thirty heads named in the catalogue, which were made not only in basaltes, and in blue and white jasper, but also in jasper of one colour only.  These latter sold at a shilling each.

Under such favourable conditions medallion portraiture became very popular.  Numerous private individuals, as well as whole families, sat to a modeller.  Many such portraits are still to be picked up, but only a portion of these can be identified.  Among the many people not classified in the catalogue are Erasmus Darwin, Richard L. Edgworth, Bentley and his wife, Dr. Small, Flaxman, William Penn, etc.  Many of the nobility sat for their portraits, and in the cases where individual beauty was marked there was a good sale of the portraits on this account.  Some of the most successful portraits were those of Lady Finch and her beautiful daughters.  Flaxman modelled many of these portraits, though it is impossible to say definitely just how many.  It is known positively, however, that Mrs. Siddons sat to him for her portrait.  So did Herschel, Dr. Johnson, the King of Sweden, the Queen of Portugal, Sir Joshua Reynolds, the Duchess of Devonshire, Queen Charlotte, and a long list of other notables.

The most numerous portraits in this class, modelled by any one man, were those made by William Hackwood. All the Wedgwoods and Bentleys and their families and friends sat to him, and almost all visitors of note who came to England visited Etruria and left models of their faces.

*Class Eleven.* This was ' headed, " Busts, small statues, boys and animals." It included many of his notable works, chiefly the large busts of distinguished persons which have now become so rare. Black basaltes was the material used, and some busts were twenty-five inches high, while eighty others of well-known persons ranged from twenty-two to four inches in height. There were also ornamental figures of sphinxes and of various animals.

Busts were made occasionally in red, in white and in cane-coloured terra-cotta. Rousseau and Voltaire were made in this latter material. In Russia these busts had a great vogue, and in Holland after the issue of those of the De Witts, Prince of Orange, Grotius and others the demand became extraordinary. Amsterdam was the center of trade and agents were needed in nearly every town.

Hackwood's skill in modelling was truly wonderful when it is considered that he made these busts, life-size from small statues, prints or antique gems. I refer to such busts as Homer, Cicero, Venus de Medici, Sappho, etc. They were most spirited and life-like, and they brought very large prices, even at wholesale costing three pounds, three shillings, and the smallest bringing one pound, eleven shillings and six-pence. The bust of Voltaire, in black, had a large sale among the clergy. No doubt the colour seemed indicative of the philosopher's connection with the devil.

Copies of these old busts are still made at Etruria, but the beauty and finish of the old ones seem lacking. The modern busts are almost always marked with three letters in combination. As for the animals mentioned in this class few survive. Pug dogs are specified and elephants. The production of these latter ceased probably because they did not sell well. "I will send you no more such ponderous animals till you have sold what you have. For, as the lad said, 'I fear we made a bull when we first made an elephant.'" So writes Wedgwood. These figures were sixteen and one half inches long by fourteen and one half inches high. Lions and bulls were made in high relief in ivory composition.

Under this class come the little groups of children, the tritons, griffins, tripods and candelabra. Some of these were modelled by Wedgwood himself, but the larger number by William Bacon. A pair of tritons in " brown earth " were made for Thomas Lombe, Esq., in 1774, and cost four guineas. Sometimes the tritons were bronzed and sometimes gilt. In FIG. 133 is shown a most unique pair, of dark earthenware, silver lustred. This lustre was first applied in 1791, and was seldom used to cover the objects entirely, but usually was laid on in a pattern upon a body of black. The modelling of these figures is exceptionally fine and full of strength.

It must be remembered that up to the time of leaving Burslem, in 1769, Wedgwood, like the other Staffordshire potters, made many small figures and ornaments in earthenware. As he carried all his moulds and patterns with him it is probable that these were made for many years longer, for they were exceedingly profitable, and there was a brisk demand for them to ornament dressers, buffets, mantel shelves, etc., and besides being on sale at warehouses, they were sold at fairs and carried all over the country by hawkers and dealers. The figures varied from seven and a half to eight and a half inches, and were brightly coloured and highly glazed, after similar productions from Dresden, Bow, and Chelsea. The preference was for shepherds and shepherdesses, à la Watteau, singly or in groups, and there were some larger figures, of Daphne, Apollo, cupids, etc. These are found marked "Wedgwood" in large letters, and exact copies are also found unmarked, leading one to suppose that when Wedgwood made finer bodies and more elegant objects, he grew ashamed of these inartistic pieces. Marked groups and pieces of this early period are always desirable, and show in the strongest manner the wonderful advance which was made in figure work under Wedgwood's impetus.

*Class Twelve* included lamps and candelabra. These were made in variegated pebble and black basaltes, and sometimes in jasper of two colours. There were never many of these made and they have now become scarce and rare.

*Class Thirteen* is one of the most important in the whole catalogue. It embraces all the tea and coffee services of every variety, as well as chocolate sets, sugar dishes, cream ewers, with cabinet cups and saucers, and all the articles of the tea-table and dejeunér made in bamboo and basaltes, plain or enriched with Grecian and Etruscan ornaments. For

the very choicest cabinet pieces jasper was used, and
it was of the finest and most transparent character,
and of intense hardness, yet presenting to the touch
the velvety bloom which is always found on fine pieces
of this ware.

*Class Fourteen* consisted of flower- and root-pots.

*Class Fifteen* comprised the ornamental vases of antique form, of agate, jasper, porphyry and other stones
of the crystalline kind.

*Class Sixteen* included the vases of black porcelain
or artificial basaltes.  These graceful and choice vases
were put to more than ornamental uses, for one was
used as a part of the monument to Viscount Chetwynd,
in Ashley Church, in 1770.

*Class Seventeen* was composed of all the styles of
objects, vases, tablets, etc., which were decorated with
encaustic paintings of Etruscan and Grecian subjects.

*Class Eighteen* included all the magnificent works
of art formed in jasper with coloured grounds and white
relief figures.

*Class Nineteen* seems hardly to come under the head
of " ornamental," for in it is included inkstands, paint-
chests, eye-cups and chemical vessels.  Among the
many useful inventions made by Wedgwood, one of
the most useful was an inkstand which its inventor
claimed prevented the ink " from evaporating, growing thick and spoiling, as it does in all the common
inkstands."  These stands were sold in connection
with sand and wafer boxes, and were in jasper of two
colours as well as basaltes.  Some of the shapes of the
pieces were extremely elegant, the inkstands and boxes
being in the forms of Grecian urns, standing in a long
graceful tray, ornamented with heads and small pat-

terns on the edge. While one can but admire the artistic spirit and ambitious desire to have his work as excellent as it could be made, which always animated Wedgwood, it is also admirable to see how he worked to make his productions a success financially, and to spread their fame world-wide. He sent these ink-stands broadcast over the Continent, England, Ireland and America, and there is scarcely a collection which does not include one or two.

The paint-chests were for water-colour painters, and the eye cups, made of compositions imitating different pebbles, were used for bathing the eyes. There were toilet-boxes, also, in terra-cotta, basaltes and jasper bodies, which were exquisite. They were used to hold pins, patches, pomatum, rouge, gloves and bows, tassels, gold and silver ornaments, lace, buckles, rings and knick-knacks. They could be bought for from three shillings up to twelve. These little articles have survived time and change in small numbers, as have the paint-boxes, for people no longer grind and mix their own colours as they did in Wedgwood's day.

*Class Twenty*, the last, was "Thermometers for measuring strong fire, or the degrees of heat above ignition."

Besides these twenty classes of goods, which were chiefly ornamental, at the end of the catalogue is the an-nouncement: "The Queen's Ware of Mr. Wedgwood's manufacture, with various improvements in the table and dessert services, tea equipages, etc., continues to be sold as usual at his warehouse in Greek Street, Soho, and at no other place in London."

Included in these classes already enumerated, but particularly specified, are many objects of the greatest beauty. Such tiny objects as strings of beads for the neck and arms were made of all shades of jasper, daintily decorated in white, and formed ornaments of exquisite workmanship and colour.

Drinking cups, copied from antique specimens in the British Museum, were made as early as 1774. They were basaltes, usually, the rims edged in silver. There were some in the form of a fox's head mounted in silver, "Druid Mugs," "Sportsmen's Drinking Mugs," with the well-known design of hare and hounds and huntsmen, with which we are familiar on jugs. The earliest of these have a brown-glazed ground. Pipe heads, also came under his notice, and he formed beautiful ones in basaltes, and jasper, these latter having, usually, a blue body with white figures. These heads were used with reeds for drawing the smoke through, and snuff and tobacco-boxes are also mentioned. Wedgwood made hookah vases for export to the East. Jasper was the body employed and the decoration was very elegant, the metal appliances being silver or silver gilt.

Trays of every size and shape were made to hold various objects. They were oval, octagonal, square, elongated, or round, fluted or engine-turned, and decorated with reliefs. Always charming, the jasper trays were of great beauty, as were the encaustic ones. The cream-ware trays were simply fluted, and of varying shades of cream. In jasper you might choose to grace a boudoir in pale sea-green, olive, lilac, slate, light, medium or dark blue. Many of these trays with their services are still extant. Mr. Gladstone, who was a china collector himself, had one of slate-coloured jasper, with ornament in white, and quatrefoil decorations.  These trays are generally found with the name "Wedgwood" incised upon them, and in connection with the letter "o" or figure "3" or both together.

Wine-coolers, made upon the principle of absorption and evaporation were introduced before 1787. They were in an unglazed red ware were elegant in form, and appropriately decorated with garlands of grapes and vine leaves.

Brown glazed tart and pie-dishes were made in quantities, and from 1793 to 1802 they were largely in demand.  During Josiah Wedgwood's life Champion's patent for the sole use of certain Cornish clays prevented his making porcelain, and it was with difficulty that he kept his choicer wares from assuming this texture, so it was never made at Etruria until about 1805-1806, when soft paste porcelain was manufactured, and continued until 1815 when it was discontinued.

Frames in earthenware were made at an early date, but were found too perishable to become popular. Friezes were made of many of the choicest designs, and the dining-room and drawing-room at Etruria Hall, as well as these same rooms in Mr. Bentley's house at Turnham Green were thus decorated, as well as several houses for the nobility.  There were pastile burners in many shapes and sizes in which pastiles or perfumed paste could be burned.  Like the pot-pourri vases they have perforated lids for the odour to escape.  They were made of a variety of bodies, but most often in red and black.  The pot-pourri jars were made in Josiah Wedgwood's time, but the pastile burners were introduced about 1805, and were made in the old moulds. They were used not only in cases of sickness but were set on stairways in halls and rooms for perfuming the whole house.

There are specimens of a shiny black ware which are not at all uncommon in tea-sets and coffee-pots, decorated with gaudy flowers, either peonies or chrysanthemums, which are sometimes declared to be old Wedgwood. This is not true. They were not made till about 1805, and continued in vogue till 1815.

Supper sets are very rarely met with now. They consisted of four separate covered dishes either flat or raised, which nest together and form four divisions of a circle, the central space being occupied by a pile of twelve plates, and surmounted by a sauce-dish. The trays were of the same material as the service, or of some rich inlaid wood.

I am occasionally asked if it is possible to obtain specimens of Wedgwood in this country. Certainly it is, though the choice pieces, of course, command large prices. In another part of this chapter I have spoken of the cabbage-leaf compote which was picked up for a few cents, and since then I have seen an exquisite dish of the old " green glaze," twelve inches long, and oval in shape, with raised decoration in strawberry leaves and fruit. It was bought for one dollar at a second-hand store, both buyer and seller thinking it a piece of " Majolica," and the purchaser taking it for its fine colour. On the back is the mark " J. W." impressed in script under the glaze, and every detail of the pattern is carried out with great care. The printed cream-ware with pretty patterns can sometimes be had for one dollar a plate, and there are many jugs with his well-known patterns on them, some quite unmistakable for their fineness and finish.

Fig. 134. WEDGWOOD'S PATTERNS.

Fig. 135.  TOBY AND OTHER JUGS.

Fig. 136.  LAVENDER PORCELAIN JUG.

In FIG. 134 is shown a group, not all Wedgwood's, but bearing designs he originated. They have been slowly gathered in the South and one of particular interest is the smallest in the front row, which belonged to Thomas Jefferson, and from which, for many years, he drank his milk and water tea.

The two large ones on the upper row are in cane-coloured ware with bunches of grapes, and different grains on the panels of the sides.

Most of the museums, all over the country, have specimens of the basaltes and jasper wares, and no doubt there is much of the less choice wares still tucked away awaiting recognition.

The product of no other factory so well repays study as that of Wedgwood, and the eulogy on his monument seems not too fulsome.

SACRED TO THE MEMORY OF

### JOSIAH WEDGWOOD, F.R.S. AND S.A.

Of Etruria, in this country.

Born August, 1730, died January 3, 1795.

Who converted a rude and inconsiderable manufacture into an elegant art and an important part of a national commerce.
By these services to his country he acquired ample fortune.
Which he blamelessly and reasonably enjoyed,
And generously dispensed for the reward of merit and the relief of misfortune.
His mind was inventive and original, yet perfectly sober, and well regulated.
His character was decisive and commanding, without rashness or arrogance,
His probity was inflexible, and his kindness unwearied ;
His manners simple and dignified and the cheerfulness of his temper was the reward of the activity of his pure and useful life.

He was most loved by those who knew him best
And he has left indelible impressions of affection and veneration on the minds of his family who have erected this monument to his memory.

# CHAPTER X.

## JUGS, TEAPOTS, AND ANIMALS.

### FIG. 135.

THE passion for collecting old china extends to all sorts and conditions of men, and, in certain localities, seems to run to one class of objects. In a certain city of New York State with which I am familiar there are more than six collections of jugs of which I have personal knowledge, and in certain other places teapots are the objects sought. A great many jugs—what true collector would call them pitchers?—have been shown already, and mentioned, but there are legions more, some of them presenting puzzles which the collector would gladly solve.

In FIG. 136 is shown a jug which is still open to study. It is of porcelain body, of a splendid shade of lavender, and decorated with a graceful pattern in white. It can easily be seen that the piece was made by pouring slip into a mould, for there are many irregularities, particularly in the base, but its colour is so lovely and the decoration is so fine that the smaller details are overlooked. The maker was probably Ridgway, though the piece is unmarked, for there are jugs of similar material but less graceful shape, lavender in colour, and decorated in white, marked with his name. The patterns on these specimens, which are marked Ridgway, are very ornate, winged lions, with fauns pouring wine from a cup, and a head of

Bacchus forming the lip. There is a beautiful border of grapes and leaves, and, except in the matter of shape, this is a handsomer jug than that in FIG. 136. The wholesale copying of wares which were in the least popular makes one cautious about naming unmarked pieces. I have seen only these two patterns in this lavender porcelain, which is very brittle in its composition, and has an extreme high glaze.

FIG. 137 is a nice example of Davenport. It is an earthenware jug in the Nautilus pattern, which was so popular, and is painted over glaze, not printed. The works at Longport were opened in 1793 by John Davenport, who made stone china as well as earthenware. The body of this jug is the fine cream colour to which we have been accustomed in the Staffordshire wares, and the decoration is black, pink and green. John Davenport believed in employing the best artists obtainable to decorate his wares, and he made very choice and handsome dinner and tea services, as well as many minor pieces. He got some of the artists from Derby to work for him, and his porcelain sets, which were made later, were very fine. The name is generally printed on the pieces in red, small capitals being used. An impressed anchor is also used with the name "Davenport–Longport," surrounding it in a circle. This piece is comparatively modern, it is marked with the anchor, dated 1838, and has, besides, the initials of the person it was made for. The factory is still working, and sends many goods to this country ; the name of the firm at present is John Davenport & Sons.

A pretty jug is also given in FIG. 138. It is Staffordshire, not the old choice blue, but brown. It is by

Clews, and belongs to his " Picturesque Views " series.
The view is Newburg, Hudson River, though it is
sometimes labelled " Hudson City," an error by some
careless workman, no doubt.  This jug is twelve inches
high, and was intended for milk or cider.  No collection is complete without as many of these Staffordshire pieces as one can get hold of, old blue preferably,
and if not that, whatever one can.  There is infinite
variety in the shapes and scenes, and in the colours
and combinations.  Insensibly these jugs, Staffordshire particularly, lead one on to a pastime as beguil-
ing as collecting old china.  When you have some
piece with a view unmarked, the next point of interest
is to settle what it is.  You turn immediately to
second-hand book shops and look over all the old histories of this country you can find—everything marked
" pictorial " that comes to hand—in hopes of verifying
your china.  There are many of these old books, and
somehow they gravitate to the ten or fifteen cent
counter.  Even if you don't find what you were in
search of, you find something that claims your attention, the price asked is so small, and lo, before you
know where you are, you are on the road to becoming
a bookworm !

FIG. 139 is called the Minster jug, and was made
by Charles Meigh.  Job Meigh, the grandfather of
Charles, started the " Old Hall Works " at Hanley
about 1770.  The works descended from father to
son, and then to grandson, by whom they were continued till 1861.

Besides the blue pottery already mentioned, Charles
Meigh made many other wares, and this jug of stoneware is marked and dated 1846.  While these jugs are

Fig. 137. DAVENPORT JUG.

Fig. 138. NEWBURG JUG.

Fig. 139. MINSTER JUG.

Fig. 140. ARIADNE JUG. *Alcock.*

Fig. 141. ALCOCK JUGS

not rare, they are by no means common, and the beauty of the modelling and finish makes them an ornament to any collection. Age has given them a creamy tone which is very beautiful, but sometimes they develop spots, which may be cleaned off with bread, or, if these are deep-seated, warm water, soap, and a soft brush will generally remove them.

The factory started by the elder Job was sold in 1861, as has been mentioned, and it is now largely devoted to the manufacture of white ware. Its proprietors claim that they are the originators of an entirely new branch of ceramic art, and I should be afraid to say how many thousand pieces of porcelain they turn out yearly. Their circular claims that they make about one thousand different shapes and sizes of porcelain teeth, varying in tint from the pearly one of the poet's fancy to the dark brown one of him who uses tobacco. These articles are moulded, dipped and fired like any other porcelain goods, and a motto from some of Wedgwood's writing about the necessity of doing well whatever you attempt, hangs in a conspicuous place in the office. One wonders if they classify their products as Wedgwood did, into the ornamental and the useful!

In FIG. 140 is shown a pair of singularly beautiful jugs, from the works of Samuel Alcock & Co., who owned the "Hill Top Pottery," or "Hill Pottery," at Burslem, which had formerly belonged to Ralph Wood. If one may judge from the jugs they made, their work must have been very fine, and it is a pity that more of it is not to be found. These works were rebuilt in 1839, and the Alcocks had worked them for many years previously. In 1860 the works were sold.

but the date of the jugs is said to be about 1830, and M. Protat is given as the modeller. He was a Frenchman, who came to England and worked for several potters:—at Etruria for the Wedgwoods, for the Mintons, and for the Alcocks. The pair of jugs shown are of an ivory tinted parian, with the figure of Ariadne in an exquisite shade of lavender, as is the vine decoration about the top. The edge and inside of the lip are richly gilt. In the Boston Museum of Fine Arts is a single pitcher on loan exhibition, exactly like this pair save that the colours are reversed, and that the body is lavender of a most exquisite shade, and the figures and decorations white.

The shade of lavender used by this firm is very beautiful; it is hard to compare it to any known tint, for violets are too blue and lilacs are too cold to give any idea of its warm rosiness. The next illustration, FIG. 141, shows four more Alcock jugs belonging to the same collection as the one previously shown, and the owner of which has the most phenomenal luck, getting her jugs in pairs, though often each one comes from a different source. Such a pair is seen in the first and third pitchers, which bear on the bottom these words, "The Distin Family, the Saxe Horn Performers." On the jugs are five panels, each being a portrait of a member of the family with his instrument in his hand. These pitchers have the interesting variation of being white figures on a lavender ground in one case, and lavender on a white ground in the other. The handle has a horn for decoration, and there is a wealth of delicate ornament about the top and on the base. The tall graceful jug between them has an Eastern scene, white figures on a pale blue ground, and the fourth and last, a gypsy tent in white and lavender. All six jugs bear the Alcock mark which is variously, "Alcock & Co., Hill Pottery, Burslem," or "S. Alcock & Co.," either printed or impressed, which I fancy was the earliest mark of the firm, though very little is to be learned about them.

These jugs of Alcock's are all moulded ware, as were most of Wedgwood's and all the early English potters. This process has been nearly superseded during the past forty or fifty years by what is called by the French term, "pâte-sur-pâte." This process gives an effect similar to that of the jasper wares, except it has a high glaze. The colours used for the background are grey, green in two shades, and a dark and medium brown. On these backgrounds the design is applied in white paste, which is laid on in successive layers with a brush, till it has a given thickness, and forms a rough shape. This mound of paste is trimmed and rounded with sharp and cutting tools, or by means of a small scraper until it has the required form and thickness. After the bas-relief is made, it has the first firing, which welds the parts together and gives it sufficient consistency to be dipped into the glaze. Then comes the final firing, and if the piece is successful—a large proportion is not—the result is charming. The final firing fuses the white paste to such a degree that only the thicker portions remain white, the thinner parts, as draperies, etc., permit the background to show faintly through, which gives an ethereal character to the work. It is used in all sorts of fanciful designs, on vases, tablets, placques, and the colours, particularly the browns, are very charming. To Wedgwood's fine and sharp reliefs it bears about the same relation as a water-colour to one of Rembrandt's oils. Each style has its admirers.

The sharply cut relief is admirably shown in FIG. 142 where the jugs shown come under the head of " Makers Unknown." The pair of tall jugs are quite remarkable examples of bold relief and the undercutting brings them out wonderfully. You may almost hear the twang of the bowstring on the left-hand jug, the tenseness of the figure being admirable. The whole design is very spirited, birds as well as boy, and the pure white gives it the look of marble. It is the central jug, however, to which one turns again and again. Silenus, quite overcome with his potations, is supported on either side by a satyr, their goat's legs and pointed ears being most delicately modelled. All about hang bunches of grapes, and on the other side the infant Bacchus, deserted by his drunken nurse, is stealing a ride on his mule, and full of pleasure with his prank. Who would ever dream of calling this bacchanalian vessel a pitcher? This latter word is so suggestive of such temperate fluids as milk or water, while the good old-fashioned word "jug" is fairly redolent of those spiced and steaming mixtures which formed so potent an element in the daily rations of several generations ago. It seems as if almost any drink would taste better from such a beaker, and I do not doubt it was often supped from the jug itself. Certainly that scallop in the rim seems admirably formed for the mouth. Even the handle, twisted stems, is appropriate to the rest of the design. Nothing now-a-days is choice enough for such a jug but the golden wine of Andalusia, made from such grapes as Bacchus himself loved.

More distinctly formed for convivial pleasure is a sort of jug called Toby, named, so it is said, from a thirsty old soul, Toby Philpot, whose habit, as you might say, was not that of temperance. In our head-piece the central ornament is such a Toby, and an uncommonly genial one. He is rather unusual from the fact that both hands are occupied, as he holds both mug and jug, and from the benign expression of his face, which is really delightful in its genial benevo-lence. The faces on many of such jugs are disagree-able and leering visages, quite enough, one would think, to dispel all wish for any liquor they contained. Our own Toby is so amiable that you smile with him; no doubt it was such a jug that Gabriel Varden had, and which he constantly requested Dolly to keep re-plenished, and near his hand on the table. This Toby is unmarked, probably of Staffordshire, and very gay in his colours, as most of them were. His red coat and green trousers make a fine showing on the high shelf from which he smiles down, and this smile is re-flected in his owner's countenance whenever a sugges-tion is made of buying him.

In FIG. 143 three other Tobys are shown. The cen-tral one is the most unique, as it is of silver lustre on pottery. It is most unusual in every way, and has, like the Toby in FIG. 135, a cheerful, happy smile. It bears signs of age and use, and, like its companions in the picture, came from the City of New Orleans, a treas-ure house indeed for the hunter of antiques. The large Toby is a famous pattern, Benjamin Franklin taking snuff. It is a very fine example, in good condi-tion, and its record is known for eighty years back. Jugs very similar to this are made in England to-day.

but they are not of this creamy old bone paste, which surprises you by its extreme lightness every time you lift an article made of it. The decoration is different also, and the old and the new are as clearly marked as if the Tobys were dated. The last member of the trio is a caricature of Charles II, made in reference, no doubt, to the time he spent wandering about England after the defeat at Worcester, in 1651, before he was able to effect his escape to France.

The number of jugs which one may gather is only to be limited by one's patience, length of purse, and place to put them. The chief objection to them is the space they occupy, which is equally to be thought of in regard to teapots. The earliest one recorded of these latter articles, of European make and hard porcelain, was that formed by Bottcher in Saxony, sometime in the year 1708. He had been experimenting for some years to make hard porcelain, and succeeded, in 1708, in drawing out of a furnace a saggar containing a teapot, which was plunged into cold water in the presence of the King of Saxony, Augustus II, and sustained no injury.

Between 1690 and 1710 the Elers Brothers made teapots of red clay in imitation of Japanese wares, but how much earlier they had been made in China or Japan it is impossible to say. I have seen some very early specimens, Chinese, with a spout on each side, and a division through the center, so that one vessel could hold both black and green tea. I do not believe these pots were used by the Chinese in their own households. Certainly not for the "Cha-no-yu," or ceremonial tea-drinking, which is not to be confused with the ordinary absorption of the liquid.

The " Cha-no-yu " is a form of entertainment which the uneducated foreigner cannot appreciate. Every movement is regulated by laws known to the initiated only. The subject of conversation does not touch on every-day affairs, but the host produces some work of art. or reads a poem, and that is what must be considered. The kettle containing the boiling water, the bowl and other utensils must all have some historic or artistic interest, and the cup from which the infusion is drunk is the gem of all the service, often an example of archaic pottery.

How can the Occidental, a creature of to-day, regard with sufficient reverence a performance where the rules governing it have not been changed for centuries? True there are various schools which differ as to minor details,—whether the little straw broom with which the drink is stirred should be laid afterward on the seventh or thirteenth seam of the matting, and things of that character, which seem of infinitely small importance to the ignorant, but make a vast difference to the connoisseur. The spoon seems to us a necessary factor to a cup of tea; the Chinese would not know what to do with such a barbaric tool. Neither would they condescend to drink the boiled fluid which poses for a large portion of the Western World as tea.

In Stockbridge among the Berkshires, in Providence, Rhode Island, and in Utica, New York, are the largest collections of these fascinating objects yet heard from. The smallest of these gatherings numbers over five hundred and the largest is creeping towards two thousand.

In FIG. 144 is shown a group of teapots, in printed wares—black, mulberry, red and green—and one

Castleford. They vary in size from the one holding scarcely more than one cup to the family comforter; —and each one of them is agreeable in shape and decoration. The two in the background are similar in shape and in the pattern of the handle, the one on the left being sparingly decorated with lustre. The teapots with the cover setting down in a box-like recess antedate those in which the cover sets over the top. Many of the "Old Blue" pots are of this same shape, with the front of the rim rising up sharply. It was in teapots like these that the infusion was served, at those functions which have since been superseded by the afternoon tea. In Colly Cibber's "Lady's Last Stake" come these lines: "Tea, thou soft, thou sober, sage and venerable liquid; thou female-tongue-running, smile-smoothing, heart-opening, wink-tipping cordial, to whose glorious insipidity I owe the happiest moment of my life, let me fall prostrate."

From just such vessels as these did our patriotic grandmothers drink those odious herb decoctions which their fervid hearts preferred to tea taxed by England, even though their palates rebelled. It was the custom to have the tea served on what were called tea-poys, little stands of Chinese make, with mandarins or pagodas on them, and brilliantly lacquered. These often came in sets, "nesting" into each other, so that when not in use they would occupy small space in the best room.

From China, tea had been introduced into Japan in the beginning of the ninth century, and presumably the same customs prevailed with regard to making it. no true Oriental ever adding milk or sugar, or even the lime juice preferred by the Russian.

About 1770 Sir Charles Williams wrote a poem called " Isabella," which is intended to show the morning occupations of Lady Isabella Montague. One of her admirers has the following speech put into his mouth.

> " To please the noble dame the courtly squire
> Produced a teapot made in Staffordshire !
> So Venus looked, and with such longing eyes,
> When Paris first produced the golden prize.
> ' Such work as this,' she cried ' can England do ?
> It equals Dresden and outdoes St. Cloud.
> All modern china now shall hide its head,
> And e'en Chantilly must give o'er the trade.
> For lace let Flanders bear away the bell,
> In finest linens let the Dutch excel,
> For prettiest stuffs let Ireland be first named,
> And for best fancied silks let France be famed ;
> Do thou, thrice happy England still prepare
> This clay, and build thy fame on earthenware ! "

Ten years later this prophetic jest had been made actual truth by the notable productions of Wedgwood and others, who, even at this date, 1770, were on the way to perfecting these sources of comfort.

In FIG. 145 is presented a bevy of beauties that, may have been in this country at the time of Boston's largest and most notable tea-party, or shortly after. All china collectors know how Franklin's name and face are continually occurring on china and pottery, and how, as well, it is connected with this stirring event in Boston Harbour. The affronts to Franklin had inflamed the Colonists, and England was incensed by the speech of Wedderburn with reference to the letters of Hutchinson and Oliver, which Franklin had brought to America. Both sides were ready for a fray, and England determined to bring the Colonists to a realizing sense of their dependence. The tax on tea still existed, and it was to be enforced. The reception meted out to the three ships which sailed into Boston Harbour that December day, 1773, is known to every school boy in America, and, no doubt, some New England dames regretted the three hundred and forty-two chests which were flung into the briny waters of the harbour, particularly when they were sipping some of the bitter infusions made from the leaves of such shrubs as could be conveniently gathered and dried.

At many an afternoon gathering the comparative merits of "New Jersey tea," as the drink made from the dried leaves of the red-root was called, was discussed, and one cannot blame the good women if they silently acknowledged the superiority of the leaves of the China plant.

The teapots shown in FIG. 146 are all worth particular study. The shapes are fine, the wares various, and the decorations, painted in colours, very beautiful. No wonder such teapots as these called forth expressions of admiration, and were copied to a great extent.

That delightful traveller, Arthur Young, writes in August, 1788, of a fair held at Guilbray, France, where much merchandise was sold. He finds here examples of porcelain and Queen's Ware, English goods, and French imitations of a very poor quality. He asked the Frenchman who was selling them, if the treaty of commerce would not be very injurious, since the French goods were so very manifestly inferior to the English. " Precisely the contrary," answered the merchant

Fig. 142. EAGLE AND SILENUS JUGS.

Fig. 143. TOBY JUGS.

Fig. 144.  GROUP OF TEAPOTS, PRINTED WARES.

Fig. 145.  GROUP OF TEAPOTS, LUSTRE DECORATIONS.

"these goods are the best yet made in France. Next year you will see still further improvement, and ten years from now, we will excel you at every point."

The round teapot at the left is a favourite shape with early makers. I have seen its counterpart, decorated with printed designs and marked " Sadler & Green, 1756." The one next to it is a familiar Bristol pattern and has beautiful decoration in flowers, similar to the pot at the extreme left, which is ribbed all the way down, while the right hand one is ribbed only half way down.

Even the person who is not a china lover, pure and simple, must admire each of these specimens. The quaint shapes, the creamy ware, the gay posies shown thereon make each one an ornament for a dining-room not to be despised, and very different from those specimens made by the Elers Brothers, even though they cast the very first refining influence upon the trade of potting. Their work seems crude enough in comparison with what was produced one hundred years later.

In the Metropolitan Museum of Fine Arts is a most interesting collection of tea-bowls, some of them dating back as far as 1500. They are all rather small, made of a rough, brownish, mottled ware, and each one is accompanied by a little tea-jar, with a cover of pottery, or an ivory button. They are small and dainty in shape and can hold but a spoonful or two of the dried leaves.

There are also, among the many specimens shown, examples of kettles for water or wine which are exactly in shape and size what we call teapots. Several of them are centuries old, but the first one which is called a teapot is from Japan and dated 1720. One remarkable quality of the Oriental was the way he adapted himself to the wants of the Occidental market, and strove in every way to meet its demands.

Gombron, opposite to Ormus in the Persian Gulf, was the first port opened to the English East India Company, and from this place the commodities of India and China were exchanged for those of Europe, and China was called "Gombron Ware," before it became known by the general name of china. The Dutch and the Portuguese had been importing before England was able to secure a footing, and i.l 1690 the Dutch were allowed to export annually one hundred bales of china from Japan. We are wont to regard the Chinese as barbarians, yet can trace back many of our comforts and elegancies to their shores, from which source they filtered to us, often by way of Japan.

When the "China drink" became fashionable in the last quarter of the seventeenth century, even though the tax upon it was five shillings a pound, the modish people would have it. With it came fine porcelain, dainty cups without saucers,—the Oriental himself did not use them,—and the pretty kettles for hot water, small enough to be heated upon the little brasier which is, even to this day, the Chinese apology for a cooking arrangement. Our English cousins wanted the drink; they did not care a fig for the ceremonies which surrounded the brewing of it ; and the hot water kettle seemed a good thing to prepare it in. So they popped the leaves into the kettle and, no doubt, boiled them, a much quicker process than boiling water. pouring it into a cup, then dropping in a few leaves, allowing them to uncurl and fall to the bottom before stirring with a few straws.

Saucers were made to gratify the Western market, so were the handles on cups. Be sure no tea-cup with a handle is much more than one hundred years old, for such an addition was not thought of till the end of the eighteenth century. Coffee cups had handles earlier than this. The oldest piece of porcelain known in England is a celadon cup brought from China between the years 1504-1532, and given to New College, Oxford.

On every style of ware the world over, flowers, birds and butterflies are used as decoration. We use these things because the colour is pretty and the shape pleasing, but that ancient people from whom we copied never made a stroke which did not have sentiment or meaning. When Darby went forth to purchase a tea-pot for his Joan, why did he select one with butterflies and bees? Just because it was gay. Yet the workman sitting cross-legged in his bamboo studio put butterflies on a tea-pot, which was copied in England, because they were to him a sign of conjugal felicity. They may almost be called the Chinese cupid; and what the bee signifies even our less symbolic ideas appreciate. What prettier combination could be brought together for a marriage gift than the emblems of conjugal happiness and industry?

There is very little that is poetical in the Staffordshire figures which are by no means difficult to find scattered in many humble homes, chimney-piece ornaments even yet. Some of them are small, four or five inches high, in single figures, groups or pairs. One quite out of the common run is given in FIG. 147. It is one of a pair, twelve inches high, and they are marked on the base " The Lion Slayers." It is hard to say just why the costume of a Highland laddie should be chosen in which to hunt the "King of Beasts," combined moreover with such an Oriental looking headdress. These figures are creamy white, sparingly touched with colour, the stockings, sword and lion's mane being the most brilliant. The smaller groups are often every highly coloured, but the use of gold is apt to be meagre.

The little country lad shown in FIG. 148 is for use. He is four inches high and a pepper-box. There is a hole in the base into which the pepper is poured, and closed with a cork. It shakes out through the little openings in his cap. He is a very lively little person— red trousers, blue coat, and yellow vest and hat. It is quite impossible to give any idea of the hundreds of patterns made for this use. The largest collection known contains between three and four thousand, and of every variety of ware. Napoleon in a cocked hat is a not uncommon device; so is John Bull, and even Franklin's stocky figure has been pressed into service. A shelf of such figures, intermingled with the plain banded pots of Bristol and Leeds and some of the rich copper lustre, makes a very ornamental showing in a corner cupboard, or they mix in well in a collection of larger and more gravely coloured pieces. Another merit of these smaller pieces is their comparatively small price. I saw two or three very good ones this past summer in a little shop at the top of a long flight of stairs in one of the interior towns of New York State, at one dollar, and one dollar and a half each. Very pretty little figures in groups were to be found here also, at two dollars each, also a large white dog, with the rough mane made by dropping

shavings of paste on the glaze before firing. Some
dogs and other animals were made in the United
States at Bennington, Vermont; but they are lighter
in colour than to the English ones, and inferior to
them in make.

All this ware, which is seldom marked, is ascribed to
Nottingham, but it was also made at Chesterfield and
at Brampton. One of the famous patterns made in this
brown Nottingham ware is a bear, rampant (FIG. 149).
His head is separate from the body and forms a drinking cup, the body answering for a jug. This bear is
supposed to be copied from the celebrated " Bear of
Bradwardine," mentioned by Sir Walter Scott in his
novel of " Waverley." The House of Bradwardine is
described as having bears of all sizes and descriptions
carved over the windows and doors, terminating the
gables, answering for water spouts, and supporting
the turrets. Under every one of these creatures was
cut the family motto, " Bewar the Bar." The last and
choicest bear was a drinking cup, kept in an oaken
casket mounted in brass, and carefully locked. It
was only used on special occasions, and when at the
banquet to Waverley the Baron of Bradwardine un-
locked the casket and drew forth the cup, which was
of pure gold, he said, " It represents the chosen crest
of our family, a bear, as ye observe, and rampant."
The cup was wrought to commemorate the doughty
deeds of one of the Baron's ancestors, and was called
the " Blessed Bear of Bradwardine." The story goes
on to say that the bear held nearly a pint, and each
guest was expected to drain it at a draught. Whether
or not the Nottingham bear was fashioned from the
Bradwardine cup one cannot say, yet, no doubt, it was

copied from some famous jug which was known to that mine of information, Sir Walter Scott. The pottery bear is rough all over, forming a good surface to grasp by hands whose steadiness was somewhat lost by frequent potations.

Our last illustration (FIG. 150) shows an animal more useful, and, perhaps, more honoured, yet which would never be dignified by being used for a family crest! She performs the simple office of a candlestick, or, as the opening in the tree-trunk behind her is not quite round, a flower-holder, and looks mildly out at you, this humble friend, the old red cow. She is in Staffordshire, is red and white, stands on a plot of green grass, with a blue brook running beneath her feet, and around the base runs the single touch of elegance, a line of gold.

She stands as an emblem of sorrow, and there is such in every collection, for mingled with the satisfaction of owning her comes the mental picture of her owner's grief. This is the story of her purchase. A china hunter, who scented a "find" in every breeze that blew, got the knowledge that this cow was a treasured possession in a humble little home. He went and made an offer for it, handled it, noted that it was perfect, Staffordshire, and unusual in pattern. His offer was almost laughed at. The middle-aged woman whose property it was said, "Why, that cow was mother's. I never remember when she did not have it. I would not think of selling it."

To any one but a china collector this would have proved sufficient, but our collector could not give up the chase. His daily walks led him, against his will, past that small house, and as often as he could muster courage he stopped and increased his bid. At last he had reached the limit of his patience and his purse, and saying to himself, "This is the last time," he betook himself to the home of his ambition. He held his breath and made his offer. It is proverbial that she who hesitates is lost, and so it was in this case. Who can tell if visions of what could be got for the round sum offered flashed through the owner's mind? The collector saw his advantage, the money was in her hand, the cow in his, and he fled through the open door lest she should change her mind. When he got to the gate, like Lot's wife, he looked back, and it nearly proved his undoing, for the former owner stood in the doorway wiping away with the corner of her apron the fast dropping tears.

# LIST OF VIEWS,
## AMERICAN, ENGLISH & MISCELLANEOUS.
### BY
# ENGLISH POTTERS.

ENOCH WOOD & CO.        ENOCH WOOD & SONS.

*Colour, dark blue.*

*Border*. Opening in centre round, with border of shells, cockle shell being conspicuous.

1. Albany, New York State.
2. Baltimore & Ohio Railroad.
3. Baltimore & Ohio Railroad, uphill.
4. Belleville, New Jersey.
5. Capitol at Washington.
6. Castle Garden and Battery, New York.
7. Catskills.
8. Catskills, Hope Mill.
9. Catskill Mountain House.
10. Catskill Mountains. View of Hudson River.
11. Catskills, Pine Orchard House.
12. Franklin's Tomb.
13. Gilpin's Mills.
14. Greensburg.
15. Highlands, Hudson River.
16. Highlands at West Point.
17. Highlands near Newburg.
18. Lake George, New York.
19. Mount Vernon, seat of late Gen'l George Washington.
20. New York Bay.
21. Niagara Falls.
22. Niagara Falls, Table Rock.
23. Passaic Falls.

Fig. 146.   GROUP OF TEAPOTS. PAINTED WARES.

Fig. 147.   LION SLAYER.

Fig. 148.   PEPPER POT.

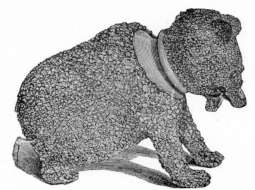

Fig. 149. NOTTINGHAM BEAR.

Fig. 150. COW AND CALF.

24. Transylvania University, Lexington, Ky.
25. Trenton Falls.
26. Trenton Falls, with solitary figure.
27. West Point Military Academy.
28. White House, Washington.
*Border.* Irregular opening for central view, border of various shells, without cockle shell.   Name of view on front.
29. Cadmus.
30. Cadmus at anchor.
31. Cadmus under sail.
32. " Chief Justice Marshall," steamboat.
33. " Constitution " and " Guerriere."
34. MacDonough's victory.
35. Marine Hospital, Louisville, Ky.
36. Union Line steamboat.
37. Wadsworth Tower, Conn.
             *Border.*   Flowers and scrolls.
38. " Chancellor Livingston," steamboat.
             *Border.*   Medallions and scrolls.
39. Landing of Pilgrims.
             *Border.*   Flowers, poppies, etc.
40. Entrance of canal into Hudson River at Albany.
41. Little Falls, New York, Aqueduct Bridge.
42. Rochester, New York, Aqueduct Bridge.

*Celtic china.   Other colours than dark blue.*
             *Borders.*   Various.
43. Buffalo.
44. Fairmount Waterworks, Pennsylvania.
45. Harvard College.
46. Hudson River, near Fishkill.
47. Natural Bridge, Virginia.
48. New York from Staten Island.
49. Niagara Falls.
50. Pass in Catskill Mountains.
51. Port on the Ohio, Kentucky.
52. Transylvania University, Lexington, Ky.
53. Trenton Falls.

54. Washington, Capitol.
55. Washington Vase.
56. Washington Memorial.

### VIEWS IN CANADA.

*Border.* Opening for central view circular, shell border.
57. Falls of Montmorency, near Quebec.
58. Quebec.

### ENGLISH VIEWS.

ENOCH WOOD & SONS.
*Colour, dark blue.*

*Border.* Shells and flowers, irregular opening for central view. Name of scene on front.
59. Beach at Brighton.
60. Cowes Harbour.
61. Dartmouth.
62. Dublin, View of.
63. East Cowes, Isle of Wight.
64. Eddystone lighthouse.
65. Firth on the Thames.
66. Liverpool, View of.
67. Ship of the Line in the Downs.
68. Southhampton, Hampshire.
69. Whitby.
70. Yarmouth, Isle of Wight.
*Border.* Grapevines with fruit, central view in medallion.
Marked, " London Views."
71. Bank of England.
72. Coliseum, Regent's Park.
73. Cumberland Terrace, Regent's Park.
74. Dover, Cliffs of.
75. Doric Villa in the Regent's Park.
76. East Gate, Regent's Park.
77. Hanover Lodge, Regent's Park.
78. Macclesfield Bridge, Regent's Park.
79. St. Phillip's Chapel, Regent's Park.
80. The Holme, Regent's Park.
81. The Lake, Regent's Park.

# LIST OF VIEWS. 257

82. The Limestone Dock, Regent's Park.
*Border.* Grapevines with fruit and flowers. View filling
    entire centre. Name on back.
83. Armitage Park, Staffordshire.
84. Barlborough Hall, Derbyshire.
85. Bedfords, Essex.
86. Belvoir Castle.
87. Bickley, Kent.
88. Brancepeth Castle, Durham.
89. Cashiobury, Hertfordshire.
90. Cave Castle, York.
91. City of Canterbury.
92. Cokethorpe Park, Oxfordshire.
93. Compton Verney, Warwickshire.
94. Dalguise, Perthshire.
95. Dorney Court, Buckinghamshire.
96. Dunraven, Glamorgan.
97. Durham Cathedral.
98. Esholt House, Yorkshire.
99. Fonthill Abbey, Wiltshire. Large view.
100. Fonthill Abbey, Wiltshire. Small view.
101. Goodridge Castle, Kent.
102. Gunton Hall, Norfolk.
103. Guy's Cliff, Warwickshire.
104. Harewood House, Yorkshire.
105. Hollywell Cottage, Cavan.
106. Huntley Castle, Perthshire.
107. Kenilworth Castle, Warwickshire.
108. Kenmount, Dumfrieshire.
109. Lambton Hall, Durham.
110. Maxstoke Castle, Warwickshire.
111. Orielton, Pembrokeshire.
112. Richmond, View of.
113. Rochester Castle.
114. Ross Castle.
115. Shirley House, Surrey.
116. Taymouth Castle, Perthshire.
117. The Rookery, Surrey.

118. Thryberg, Yorkshire.
119. Wardour Castle, Wiltshire, with tree.
120. Wardour Castle, Wiltshire, without tree.
121. Warwick Castle.
122. Wellcombe, Warwickshire.
123. Windsor Castle.
124. York Cathedral.

*Border.* Scrolls and medallions. " English Cities " marked on back.

125. Chichester.
126. Coventry.
127. Coke Denton.
128. Ely.
129. Leeds.
130. Lincoln.
131. Litchfield.
132. Liverpool.   View of city from river.
133. Liverpool.   View of buildings.
134. London.
135. Norwich.
136. Peterborough.
137. Rochester.
138. Wells.
139. Worcester.

## VIEWS IN FRANCE.

### WOOD.

*Border.* Hollyhocks, grapes, etc.   Name of scene on back.

140. La Grange, château of Lafayette.
141. La Grange, east view.
142. La Grange, northwest view.
143. La Grange, southwest view.
144. Cascade de Gresy Pres Chambery.
145. Château Coucy.
146. Château Ermenonville.
147. Hermitage en Dauphine.
148. Moulin sur la Marne.
149. Moulin sur la Marne with figures.
150. Vue Peise en Savoie.

## AMERICAN VIEWS.

Andrew Stevenson.

### *Colour, dark blue.*

*Borders.* Different floral arrangements, **scrolls, large** flowers and small wreaths.

151. Columbia College. W. G. Wall.
152. Dutch Church at Albany.
153. Fort Gansevoort, New York.
154. Junction of Hudson and Sacadaga.
155. Lafayette portrait.
156. New York City Almshouse. W. G. Wall. (Two views, one is marked on back with eagle perched, and the other with eagle flying.)
157. New York City Hall. W. G. Wall.
158. New York Catholic Cathedral. W. G. Wall.
159. New York from Brooklyn Heights. W. G. Wall. (Two views, one on platters, one on plates.)
160. New York from Weehawken. W. G. Wall.
161. New York, Murray St. W. G. Wall.
162. On road to Lake George. W. G. Wall.
163. The Temple of Fame, Perry. W. G. Wall.
164. Troy from Mt. Ida. W. G. Wall.
165. View of Governor's Island. W. G. Wall.
166. Niagara with portraits.

## ENGLISH VIEWS.

Andrew Stevenson.

### *Colour, dark blue.*

*Border.* Roses and other **flowers.**

167. Barrington Hall.
168. Boreham House, Essex.
169. The Chantry, Suffolk.
170. Culford Hall, Suffolk.
171. Enville Hall, Staffordshire.
172. Foulkbourn Hall, also with four medallion portraits, and view of Rochester Aqueduct Bridge at bottom.
173. Foulkbourn Hall. Four medallion portraits, and view

of " Entrance of Erie Canal into the Hudson River at Albany," at bottom.

174. Foulkbourn Hall.  Two medallion portraits, Washington and Clinton.  Aqueduct Bridge at Little Falls, at bottom.
175. Foulkbourn Hall.  Two medallion portraits, Washington and Clinton.  Aqueduct Bridge at Rochester, at bottom.
176. Haughton Hall, Norfolk.
177. Mereworth House.
178. Oatlands, Surrey.
179. Summer Hall, Kent.
180. Tunbridge Castle, Surrey.
181. Walsingham Priory.  Norfolk.
182. Wansted House, Essex.
183. Writtle Lodge.  With four medallion portraits.
184. Writtle Lodge.  Without portraits.

## AMERICAN VIEWS.

### J. AND R. CLEWS.

*Colour, dark blue.*

*Border.*  Scallops bearing names of fifteen States with stars between.  Central views various.
185. White House.  View with sheep on lawn.
186. White House.  View with figures in row boat.
187. White House.  View with curved drive leading to house.
188. Unknown buildings with women on lawn.
189. Unknown buildings with fisherman.
190. Unknown buildings with deer.
191. Unknown buildings with six wings.  Sheep on lawn.
192. Unknown buildings three stories high.
193. Mt. Vernon.
194. Custom House.
195. Castle, with sail boat in foreground.
*Border.*  Scrolls and flowers.
196. Almshouse, New York.

197. Brooklyn Heights, New York from, (same view as Stevenson's.)
198. Columbia College, New York.
199. Erie Canal at Albany.
200. Lafayette, portrait. Made for J. Greenfield's china store, No. 77 Pearl St., New York.
201. New York Bay.
202. New York City Hall.
203. New York Insane Asylum.
204. Peace and Plenty.
205. Pittsfield elm, Winter view.
206. The Temple of Fame. In memory of Commodore Perry. By W. G. Wall.

---

## PICTURESQUE VIEWS.

### J. AND R. CLEWS.

#### *In different colours.*

*Border.*   Birds, flowers and scrolls.
207. Baker's Falls.
208. Fairmount Waterworks.
209. From Fishkill.   On the Hudson River.
210. Fishkill. Near.   On the Hudson River.
211. Fort Edward.   On the Hudson River.
212. Fort Miller.   On the Hudson River.
213. Fort Montgomery.   On the Hudson River.
214. Hadley's Falls.   On the Hudson River.
215. Hudson City.   On the Hudson River.
216. Hudson City, Near.   On the Hudson River.
217. Hudson River View.
218. Hudson River near Sandy Hill.
219. Jessup's Landing.
220. Junction of Hudson and Sacandaga.
221. Little Falls at Luzerne.
222. Newburg.   On the Hudson River.
223. New York.   View of Governor's Island.
224. New York.   View from the bay.
225. Penitentiary at Allegheny, Pa.

226. Pittsburgh. Pennsylvania steamboat.
227. Pittsburgh. View with three steamboats.
228. Troy from Mount Ida.
229. West Point. On the Hudson River.

---

### SYNTAX DESIGNS.

#### J. AND R. CLEWS.

*Colour, dark blue.*

*Border.* Large flowers with small scrolls.

230. Doctor Syntax disputing his Bill with the Landlady.
231. Doctor Syntax copying the Wit of the Window.
232. Doctor Syntax bound to a Tree by Highwaymen.
233. Doctor Syntax Sketching from Nature.
234. Doctor Syntax Entertained at College.
235. Doctor Syntax Sketching the Lake.
236. Doctor Syntax sells Grizzle.
237. Doctor Syntax Reading his Tour.
238. Doctor Syntax Returned from his Tour.
239. Doctor Syntax Taking possession of his Living.
240. Doctor Syntax Mistakes a Gentleman's House for an Inn.
241. Doctor Syntax and the Dairymaid.
242. Doctor Syntax Setting out on his Second Tour.
243. Doctor Syntax and the Gypsies.
244. Doctor Syntax and the Bees.
245. Doctor Syntax Painting a Portrait of his Landlady.
246. Doctor Syntax Setting out in Search of a Wife.
247. Doctor Syntax and the Blue-Stocking Beauty.
248. Doctor Syntax turned Nurse.
249. Doctor Syntax Presenting a Floral Offering.
250. Doctor Syntax Star-Gazing.
251. The Harvest Home.
252. The Garden Trio.
253. The Advertisement for a Wife.
254. Pat in the Pond.
255. Death of Punch.
256. A Noble Hunting Party.

## THE WILKIE DESIGNS.

### J. AND R. CLEWS.

*Colour, dark blue.*

*Borders.* Flowers and small scrolls.

257. The Valentine.
258. The Escape of the Mouse.
259. Christmas Eve.
260. Playing at Draughts.
261. Letter of Introduction.
262. Rabbit on the Wall.
263. The Errand Boy.

## DON QUIXOTE DESIGNS.

### J. AND R. CLEWS.

*Colour, dark blue.*

*Borders.* Flowers and scrolls, with a scallop of beading.

264. Don Quixote.
265. Don Quixote and Princess.
266. Don Quixote and Shepherdess.
267. Don Quixote and Sancho Panza.
268. Knighthood conferred on Don Quixote.
269. Library of Don Quixote.
270. Mambrino's Helmet.
271. Knight of the Wood.
272. Sancho and Dapple.
273. Sancho Panza and the Messenger.
274. Sancho Panza at Boar hunt.
275. Sancho Panza's debate with Teresa.
276. Sancho Panza and the Duchess.
277. Sancho Panza hoisted in a blanket.
278. Sancho Panza, the Priest and the Barber.
279. Peasant Girl mistaken for Lady Dulcinea.
280. The Shepherd Boy.
281. The Repose in the Wood.
282. The Enchanted Barque.
283. Attack upon the Mills.
284. Zanguesian Conflict.

## ENGLISH VIEWS.

### J. AND R. CLEWS.

*Colour, dark blue.*

*Border.* Blue-bells and other flowers.

285. Dulwich Castle.
286. Fonthill Abbey, Wiltshire.
287. Lumley Castle, Durham.
288. Rothesay Castle, Buteshire.
289. St. Mary's Abbey, York.
290. Stratford-on-Avon, Warwickshire.
291. Warkworth Castle, Northumberland.
292. Wells Cathedral.
        *Border.* Scrolls and foliage.
293. Canterbury Cathedral.
294. Greenwich.
295. Rochester Castle.
296. St. Catherine Hill near Guilford.
297. Windsor Castle.

### "SELECT VIEWS."

### J. AND R. CLEWS.

*Colour, dark blue.*

*Border.* Large flowers.

298. Cheddar, Somersetshire.
299. Fountain's Abbey.
300. Kilcoman Castle.
301. Repon.
302. St. Catherine's Hill near Guilford.

### ZOÖLOGICAL GARDEN VIEWS.

### J. AND R. CLEWS.

*In various colours.*

*Border.* Twisted scrolls.

303. Bear Cages.
304. Bird Cages.

# LIST OF VIEWS. 265

## AMERICAN VIEWS.

### JOSEPH STUBBS.

#### *Colour, dark blue.*

*Border.* Scrolls, eagles and flowers.

305. Boston State House.
306. Church in New York.  Doctor Mason's.
307. Highlands, North River.
308. Hoboken, New Jersey.
309. Mendenhall Ferry, above Philadelphia.
310. Nahant Hotel, near Boston.
311. New York Bay.
312. New York City Hall.
313. Philadelphia, Bank of U. S.
314. Philadelphia, near Fairmount.
315. Philadelphia near Fairmount, large view on platters.
316. Philadelphia, Woodlands near.
317. Steven's House, Hoboken, N. J.
318. Upper Ferry Bridge, Philadelphia.
319. View at Hurlgate, East River.

## ENGLISH VIEWS.

### JOSEPH STUBBS.

#### *Colour, dark blue.*

*Border.* Foliage and pointed scrolls.

320. Jedburg Abbey.

## AMERICAN VIEWS.

### J. & W. RIDGWAY.

#### *Colour, dark blue.*

*"Beauties of America,"* Series, name of view on back.

*Border.* Conventional medallions of roses.

321. Almshouse, Boston.
322. Almshouse, New York.
323. Athenæum, Boston.
324. Bank, Savannah.
325. Capitol, Washington.

326. Charleston Exchange.
327. City Hall, New York.
328. Court House, Boston.
329. Deaf and Dumb Asylum, Hartford, Conn.
330. Harvard College.
331. Hospital, Boston.
332. Insane Hospital, Boston.
333. Library, Philadelphia.
334. Mount Vernon, near Washington.
335. Octagon Church, Boston.
336. Pennsylvania Hospital, Philadelphia.
337. State House, Boston.
338. Staughton's Church, Philadelphia.
339. St. Paul's Church, Boston.

### AMERICAN VIEWS.

#### WILLIAM RIDGWAY.

*Colour, light blue or black.*

*Border.* Small sprays of moss.

340. Caldwell, Lake George.
341. Columbia Bridge, on Susquehanna.
342. Delaware Water Gap.
343. Harper's Ferry, Potomac side.
344. Peekskill Landing, Hudson River.
345. Pennsylvania Hospital, Pennsylvania.
346. Port Putnam, Hudson River. View from.
347. Newburg. View from Ruggle's House.
348. The Narrows from Fort Hamilton.
349. Undercliff, near Cold Spring, N. Y.
350. Valley of the Shenandoah, from Jefferson Rock.
351. Vale of Wyoming, Wilkesbarre.
352. View of Capitol, Washington.

### "C. C." CHINA.

#### WILLIAM RIDGWAY.

*Colour, light blue.*

*Border.* Catskill moss, bits of moss over small scale pattern.

353. Albany and Schenectady Railroad.
354. Boston from Chelsea Heights.
355. Capitol, Washington.
356. Kosciusko's Tomb.
357. Washington's Tomb, Mount Vernon.

## AMERICAN VIEWS.
### JOHN RIDGWAY.
***Colours, light blue, black, brown, etc.***

*Border.* Large and small five pointed stars.

358. Log Cabin, side view with plow.
359. Log Cabin, side view without plow.
360. Log Cabin, end view.
361. "Delaware."

## ENGLISH VIEWS.
### J. AND W. RIDGWAY.
***Colour, dark blue.***

*Border.* Flowers, with medallions of children, etc.

362. All Soul's College and St. Mary's Church, Oxford.
363. Cambridge, Caius College.
364. Cambridge, Downing College.
365. Cambridge, King's College.
366. Cambridge, Library of Trinity College.
367. Cambridge, Pembroke Hall.
368. Cambridge, Senate House.
369. Cambridge, Sidney Sussex College.
370. Cambridge, St. Peter's College.
371. Cambridge, Trinity College.
372. Oxford, Christ Church.
373. Oxford, Christ Church, another view.
374. Oxford, Radcliffe Library.
375. Theatre and Printing House, Oxford.

## AMERICAN VIEWS.
### RALPH STEVENSON.
***Colour, dark blue.***
*Border.* Vine leaves.

376. Almshouse, Boston.
377. Almshouse, New York.

378. Battery, New York.
379. Battle of Bunker Hill.
380. Boston Hospital.
381. Boston Hospital with canal in foreground.
382. Brooklyn Ferry.
383. Charleston Exchange.
384. Columbia College, New York.
385. City Hall, New York.
386. Esplanade and Castle Garden, New York.
387. Fort Ganzevoort, New York.
388. Fulton Market, New York.
389. Hospital, New York.
390. Lawrence Mansion, Boston.
391. Massachusetts Hospital, Boston.
392. Savannah Bank.
393. Washington, Capitol.

## AMERICAN VIEWS.

### R. STEVENSON & WILLIAMS.

*Generally marked,* " *R. S. W.* "

**Colour, dark blue.**

*Border.* Oak leaves and acorns.

394. American Museum (Scudder's), New York.
395. Baltimore Exchange.
396. Boston Court House.
397. Boston State House.
398. Columbia College.
399. City Hotel, New York.
400. Harvard College (showing one building).
401. Harvard College (showing group of buildings).
402. Harvard College (showing buildings, figures, etc)
403. Nahant Hotel, near Boston.
404. Nahant Hotel, near Boston, with large tree.
405. Park Theatre, New York.
406. Philadelphia Water Works.

407. Washington, Capitol. This view is found with acorn and leaf border, or with white embossed border, or with four medallion portraits, of Washington, Lafayette, Jefferson and Clinton.

## PORTRAIT AND MEDALLION PLATES.

### R. STEVENSON AND WILLIAMS.

#### *Colour, dark blue.*

*Border.* Flowers and scrolls.

408. Portraits of Lafayette and Washington.
409. Washington, Jefferson, Lafayette and Clinton (portraits). Aqueduct Bridge at Rochester. Erie Canal as it enters the Hudson at Albany.

## AMERICAN VIEWS.

### "R. S."

#### *Colours various.*

*Border.* Lace pattern with roses.

410. Erie Canal at Buffalo.
411. View of City of New Orleans.

## ENGLISH VIEWS.

### R. STEVENSON.

#### *Colour, dark blue.*

*Border.* Acorns and oak leaves

412. Endsleigh Cottage.
413. Harewood House.
414. Kenmount House.
415. Oxburgh Hall.
416. Windsor Castle.
417. Windsor Castle, with four portraits, Washington, Lafayette, Jefferson and Clinton, and having view of Rochester Aqueduct Bridge at base.

## "PANORAMIC SCENERY."

R. S.

*Colour, dark blue.*

*Border.* Foliage.

418. Fonthill Abbey.

## ENGLISH VIEWS.

R. S.

*Colours, various.*

*Border.* Lace pattern with flowers.

419. Eton Hall.

## "BRITISH LAKES."

R. S.

*Colours, various.*

*Border.* Flowers, scrolls, etc.

420. Lake Windermere.

## AMERICAN VIEWS.

E. G. PHILLIPS & CO.

*Colour, dark blue.*

*Border.* Foliage.

421. Franklin's Tomb.

## ENGLISH VIEWS.

E. G. PHILLIPS & CO.

*Colour, dark blue.*

*Border.* Flowers and scrolls.

422. Eton College.

## AMERICAN VIEWS.

T. MAYER.

*Colour, dark blue.*

*Border.* Trumpet flowers and wheels.

423. Arms of Connecticut.
424. Arms of Delaware.

425. Arms of Georgia.
426. Arms of Maryland.
427. Arms of Massachusetts.
428. Arms of New Jersey.
429. Arms of New York.
430. Arms of North Carolina.
431. Arms of Pennsylvania.
432. Arms of Rhode Island.
433. Arms of South Carolina.
434. Arms of Virginia.

*Border*, Foliage.

435. Tomb of Washington.

## AMERICAN VIEWS.

### W. ADAMS & SON.

### (W. A. & S.)

*Colour, dark blue.*

*Border.* Foliage.

436. Mitchell and Freeman's china and glass warehouse, Chatham St., Boston.

## COLUMBUS VIEWS.

*Colours, various.*

*Border.* Medallions, animals and flowers.

437. Columbus Landing. Two Indians seated in foreground, white men walking up from beach.
438. Columbus with fleet in distance. Two figures in foreground.
439. Columbus with fleet in distance. Three figures in foreground.
440. Columbus. Tent view. Columbus and horse, four tents, and two Indians.
441. Columbus and mounted soldiers. Five Indians, etc.
442. Columbus. Squaw seated and Indian standing. Fleet at anchor.
443. Columbus with dogs and Indian. Tents and boats in distance.
444. Columbus, Indians shooting at bird, seated figures also.

AMERICAN VIEWS.

(W. A. & S.)

*Colours, various.*

*Border.* Roses, medallions, and scrolls.

445. Catskill Mt. House, United States.
446. Falls of Niagara, United States.
447. Fort Niagara, United States.
448. Harper's Ferry, United States.
449. Headquarters of the Juniata, United States.
450. Humphreys, United States.
451. Lake George, United States.
452. Military School, West Point, New York, United States.
453. Monte Video, Connecticut, United States.
454. New York, United States.
455. Schenectady on the Mohawk River.
456. Shannondale Springs, Virginia, United States.
457. View near Conway, New Hampshire, United States.
    *Border.* Medallion of sailor and ship.
458. New York (Man and woman in foreground).

ENGLISH VIEWS.

W. ADAMS.

*Colour, dark blue.*

*Border.* Foliage. Name of scene on back.

459. Bank of England.
460. Regent's Park, London, Clarence Terrace.
461. Regent's Park, London, Cornwall Terrace.
462. Regent's Park, London, Hanover Terrace.
463. Regent's Park, London, The Holme.
464. Regent's Park, London, York Gate.
465. Regent's Street, London.
466. Regent's Street, St. George's Chapel.
467. St. Paul's School, London.
468. The London Institution.
469. Villa in Regent's Park. Two persons in foreground.
470. Villa in Regent's Park. Horse and carriage in scene.
471. Villa in Regent's Park. People and dogs in background.

*Border.* Bluebells and various flowers.
*Marked on back with view and name.*

472. Beckenham Place, Kent.
473. Bothwell Castle, Clydesdale.
474. Branxholm Castle, Roxburghshire.
475. Brecon Castle, Brecknockshire.
476. Bywell Castle, Northumberland.
477. Dilston Tower, Northumberland.
478. Hawthornden, Edinburghshire.
479. Jedburgh Abbey, Roxburghshire.
480. Melrose Abbey, Roxburghshire.
481. Morpeth Castle, Northumberland.
482. Scaleby Castle, Cumberland.
483. St. Mary's Abbey, York.
484. Windsor Castle, Berkshire.

*Border.* Large flowers, leaves and scrolls.

485. Armidale, Invernesshire.
486. Blenheim, Oxfordshire.
487. Braham Park, Yorkshire.
488. Carstairs, Lanarkshire.
489. Denton Park, Yorkshire.
490. Fleurs, Roxburghshire.
491. Gracefield, Queen's County, Ireland.
492. Glanbran, Carmarthenshire.
493. Murthly, Perthshire.
494. Pishobury, Hertfordshire.
495. Rode Hall, Cheshire.

*Border.* Foliage and flowers.

496. Denton Park, Yorkshire.

*Border.* Scroll edge and foliage.

497. Northumberland Castle.
498. St. Catherine's Hill, near Guilford.

### AMERICAN VIEWS.

J. AND J. JACKSON.

*Colours, various.*

*Border.* Flowers, bunches of roses.

499. Albany, New York.
500. At Richmond, Virginia.

501.   Battery, New York.
502.   Battle Monument, Baltimore.
503.   Catskill Mountain House, New York.
504.   Castle Garden, N. Y.
505.   City Hall, N. Y.
506.   Deaf and Dumb Asylum, Philadelphia.
507.   Fort Conanicut, Rhode Island.
508.   Fort Ticonderoga, New York.
509.   Girard's Bank, Philadelphia.
510.   Hancock House, Boston.
511.   Hartford, Conn.
512.   Harvard Hall.
513.   Iron Works at Saugerties.
514.   Lake George.
515.   Little Falls, Mohawk River.
516.   Monte Video, Hartford.
517.   Newburg, New York.
518.   New Haven, Conn.
519.   Richmond Court House.
520.   Shannondale Springs, Virginia.
521.   Skenectady, Mohawk River.
522.   State House, Boston.
523.   The President's House, Washington.
524.   The Race Bridge, Philadelphia.
525.   The Water Works, Philadelphia.
526.   White Sulphur Springs, Town of Delaware, Ohio.
527.   Yale College and State House, New Haven.


## AMERICAN VIEWS.

### J. ROGERS & SON.

#### *Colour, dark blue.*

*Border.*   Roses and forget-me-nots.
528.   Boston State House, without cows or chaise.
529.   Boston State House, with cows.
530.   Boston State House, with chaise.

# LIST OF VIEWS.

## AMERICAN VIEWS.

### Thomas Godwin.

*Colours, various.*

*Border.* Morning-glory and Nasturtium.
531. Boston and Bunker Hill.
532. Brooklyn Ferry.
533. City of Baltimore.
534. Columbia Bridge, Pennsylvania.
535. Schuylkill Water Works.
536. The Capitol, Washington.
537. The Narrows from Fort Hamilton.
538. Utica, N. Y.

## AMERICAN VIEWS

### S. Tams & Co.

*Colour, dark blue.*

*Border.* Foliage.
539. United States Hotel, Philadelphia.
540. State Capitol, Harrisburg, Pa.

## PORTRAIT PLATES.

*Colour, medium blue.*

541. General W. H. Harrison.
542. Henry Clay.

## ENGLISH VIEWS.

### S. Tams & Co. Tams, Anderon & Co. etc.

*Colour, dark blue.*

*Border.* Foliage.
543. Drury Lane Theatre.
544. Dublin Post Office.
545. Opera House, London.
546. Royal Exchange, London.
547. Somerset House, London.

## AMERICAN VIEWS.

### JOSEPH HEATH & CO.

#### (J. H. & CO.)

*Colours, various.*

548. Ontario Lake Scenery.
549. Monterey.
550. The residence of Richard Jordan.


## AMERICAN VIEWS.

### CHARLES MEIGH.

#### (C. M.)

*Colours, various.*

*Border.* " American cities and scenery " series, small flowers, etc.

551. Baltimore.
552. Boston Mill Dam.
553. Boston from Dorchester Heights.
554. City Hall, New York.
555. Hudson City, New York.
556. Little Falls, New York.
557. Schuylkill Water Works, Philadelphia.
558. Utica, N. Y.
559. Yale College, New Haven.


## AMERICAN VIEWS.

### THOMAS GREEN.

*Colours, various.*

*Border.* Geometric patterns in pointed design.

560. Penn standing with two other figures, squaw kneeling.
561. Penn standing. Other figures and man kneeling.
562. Penn seated. Two figures standing, squaw kneeling.
563. Penn and Indian standing, man seated, squaw lying down.

564. Penn and man standing. Indian and squaw also standing.
565. Penn and man standing. Three Indians seated and
lying down.

## AMERICAN VIEWS.

### J. & T. Edwards.

#### *Colours, various.*

*Border.* " Boston Mails " series, medallions of steamships,
566. Ladies' Cabin.
567. Gentlemen's Cabin, with three figures.
568. Gentlemen's Cabin with four figures.

## AMERICAN VIEWS.

### Mellor, Venables & Co.

#### *Colours, various.*

*Border.* Medallions of State Arms and small flowers.
569. Rear View of White House.
570. Capitol Buildings of different States.
571. Caldwell, Lake George.
572. Fort Hamilton, New York.
573. Little Falls, New York.
574. View of Mount Vernon.
575. Washington's Tomb.

## AMERICAN VIEWS.

### Makers Unknown.

#### *Colour, dark blue.*

*Border.* Large flowers and scrolls.
576. Albany, N. Y.
577. A View near Philadelphia.
578. Baltimore, Maryland.
579. Chillicothe, Ohio.
580. Columbus, Ohio.
581. Detroit, Michigan.
582. Hobart Town.

583. Indianapolis, Indiana.
584. Louisville, Ky.
585. Near Fishkill, N. Y.
586. Penn's Tree, Philadelphia.
587. Quebec.
588. Richmond, Virginia.
589. Sandusky, Ohio.
590. South America, Buenos Ayres.
591. Washington, District of Columbia.
592. Wright's Ferry on the Susquehanna.
            *Border.*  Flowers, narcissus, etc.
593. Cadmus.
594. B. & O. Railroad.
595. Fulton's Steamboat.
            *Border.*  Fruit and flowers.
596. Court House, Baltimore.
597. Exchange, Baltimore.
598. Dam and Water Works, Philadelphia (side-wheel boat).
599. Dam and water works, Philadelphia (stern-wheel boat).
            *Borders.*  Various.
600. Almshouse, Baltimore.
601. Arms of Connecticut.   Marked " Oliver Stoke."
602. Boston Harbour.
603. Castle Garden, New York.
604. Harvard University.
605. Mount Vernon, " The seat of the late Gen'l Washington."
606. Mason's Temple, Philadelphia.
607. St. Patrick's Cathedral, Mott Street, N. Y.
608. University of Maryland.


## INSCRIPTION PLATES OR OTHER PIECES.

### Makers Unknown.

### *Colour, dark blue.*

*Borders.*  Various.

609. Eulogy plate.   De Witt Clinton inscription.
610. Utica plate.

611. Lovejoy design.
612. Millennium plate.

## AMERICAN VIEWS.

### Makers Unknown.

#### *Colours, various.*

*Border.* Phoenix and engine.
613. Merchant's Exchange, burning.
614. Merchant's Exchange, ruins.
615. New York, Coenties Slip, burning.
*Borders.* Various.
616. Albany.
617. Albany Theatre.
618. American Flag.
619. America Triumphant.
620. Arms of the United States, blue or coloured.
621. Aqueduct Bridge at Little Falls.
622. Battery, New York.
623. Boston Court House.
624. Boston State House.
625. Bunker Hill Monument, Boston.
626. Capitol, Washington.
627. City Hall, Albany.
628. " Constitution." (Ship.)
629. Dumb Asylum, Philadelphia.
630. Executive Mansion, Washington.
631. Fight between " Constitution " and " Guerrière."
632. Fort Hudson, New York.
633. Fort Niagara.
634. Franklin.
635. Harrison Log Cabin.
636. Harvard College.
637. The Narrows, Fort Hamilton.
638. Mount Vernon. Man and horse.
639. Mount Vernon. Seat of the late Gen'l Washington.
540. Mormon Tabernacle.
641. New York from Weehawken.

642.  Old Cathedral, New Orleans. (Municipality No. 1 on face of design.)
643.  Niagara.
644.  Niagara Falls.
645.  Pennsylvania.
646.  Primitive Methodist Preachers.
647.  Thorps and Sprague, Albany, N. Y.
648.  Utica, N.Y.
649.  Virginia.
650.  White House, Washington.

## MEDALLION AND OTHER PORTRAIT PLATES.

### MAKERS GIVEN WHEN IDENTIFIED.

#### *Colour, dark blue.*

##### FOUR PORTRAITS.

651.  Washington, Lafayette, Jefferson and Clinton.
Windsor Castle (17 inch platter.)
Rochester Aqueduct Bridge.  R. S. W
652.  Washington, Lafayette, Jefferson and Clinton.
Park Theatre, New York.  (ten inch plates.)
(This may have at the base either Aqueduct Bridge at Rochester, or at Little Falls, or Entrance of Erie Canal into the Hudson at Albany.)     R. S. W.
653.  Washington, Lafayette, Jefferson and Clinton.
Niagara.  (ten inch plates.)
(This may have at base either Erie Canal at Albany, or Rochester Aqueduct Bridge.)  A. STEVENSON.
654.  Washington, Jefferson, Lafayette and Clinton.
Faulkbourn Hall.  (Nine and ten inch plates.)
(This may have at base either Entrance of Erie Canal into the Hudson at Albany, or Rochester Aqueduct Bridge.)  A. STEVENSON.
655.  Washington, Lafayette, Jefferson and Clinton.
Aqueduct Bridge, Little Falls.  (Fruit dish.)  R. S. W.
656.  Washington, Jefferson, Lafayette and Clinton.
Albany Theatre (vegetable dish).  R. S. W.
657.  Washington, Jefferson, Lafayette and Clinton.
Dutch church at Albany (vegetable dish).     R. S. W.

**658.** Washington, Jefferson, Lafayette and Clinton.
Writtle Lodge. (Ten inch soup plates.)
(Rose border at base.) A. STEVENSON.

**659.** Washington, Jefferson, Lafayette and Clinton.
Rochester Aqueduct Bridge on one side.
Erie Canal at Albany on the other side. (Pitcher.)
R. STEVENSON and WILLIAMS.

**660.** Washington, Clinton, Chancellor Kent and Peter Stuyvesant.
Capitol at Albany. (Wash bowl and pitcher.)
R. S. W.

## TWO PORTRAITS.

**661.** Washington and Lafayette.
City Hotel. N. Y. (Nine inch plates.)
(This may have at base either Little Falls Aqueduct
Bridge ; or Rochester Aqueduct Bridge ; or Erie Canal
at Albany.) R. S. W.

**662.** Washington and Lafayette.
Capitol at Washington. (Ten inch plate.)
Little Falls Aqueduct Bridge.

**663.** Washington and Lafayette.
(Two portraits in centre, surrounded by heavy scrolls.)
R. S. W.

**664.** Washington and Clinton.
Boston Hospital. (Nine inch plates.)
(Erie Canal at Albany, or Aqueduct Bridge at Little
Falls.) R. S. W.

**665.** Washington and Clinton.
Faulkbourn Hall. (Nine inch plates.)
(This may have at base either Rochester, or Little Falls
Aqueduct Bridge.)

**666.** Washington and Clinton.
Park Theatre. N. Y. (Nine inch plates.)
(This may have at base either Rochester, or Little Falls
Aqueduct Bridge.)

**667.** Washington and Clinton.
Capitol at Washington. (Nine inch plates.)
Erie Canal at Albany.

668. Washington and Clinton.
     Niagara.   (Nine inch plates.)
     Erie Canal at Albany.
669. Jefferson and Clinton.
     Boston Hospital.   (Nine inch plates.)
     Rochester Aqueduct Bridge.
670. Jefferson and Clinton.
     Park Theatre, N. Y.   (Nine inch plates.)
     Little Falls, Aqueduct Bridge.
671. Jefferson and Clinton.
     Albany, Capitol.
     Little Falls Aqueduct Bridge.
672. Jefferson and Lafayette.
     Boston Hospital.
     Rochester Aqueduct Bridge.
673. Jefferson and Lafayette.
     Capitol at Washington.
     Rochester Aqueduct Bridge.
674. Clinton.
     St. Paul's Chapel, N. Y.   (Six-inch plates.)
     Rochester Aqueduct Bridge.   R. S. W.
675. Jefferson.
     Columbia College, N. Y.   (Seven and one-half inch
     plates.)
     Little Falls Aqueduct Bridge.   R. S. W.
676. Bainbridge, with motto—" Avast,"—etc.
677. Brown, with view of Niagara and emblems.
678. Captain Jones, of the "Macedonian."
679. Decatur.   Free trade and Sailors' rights.
680. General Jackson.
681. Hull.   Captain of the Constitution.
682. Jackson, " Hero of New Orleans."
683. Paine, Tom (on mug).
684. Perry, (small head).
685. Perry, full figure, also with motto, " We have met the
     enemy, and they are ours."
686. Pike, (small head with motto, " Be ready," etc.)
686a. Lafayette (small head with inscription), " He was born
      at Auvergne," etc.)

# LIST OF VIEWS. 283

## ENGLISH VIEWS.

### R. HALL.

*Colour, dark blue.*

*Border.* Fruit, flowers, lace edge. Scroll on back, with " Select
Views."

687. Biddulph Castle.
688. Boughton Castle, Northamptonshire.
689. Bramber Church, Sussex.
690. Castle Prison, St. Albans.
691. Conway Castle, Carnarvonshire.
692. Eashing Park, Surrey.
693. Gyrn, Flintshire.
694. Luscombe, Devonshire.
695. Pain's Hill, Surrey.
696. St. Charles' Church.
697. Valle Crucis Abbey, Wales.
698. Warleigh House, Somersetshire.
699. Wilderness, Kent.

## PICTURESQUE SCENERY.

*Border.* Large flowers.

700. Broadlands, Hampshire.
701. Cashiobury, Hertfordshire.
702. Dunsany Castle, Ireland.
703. Fulham Church, Middlesex.
704. Llanarth Court, Monmouthshire.

## ENGLISH VIEWS.

### J. W. RILEY.

*Colour, dark blue.*

*Border.* Large scrolls.

705. Bickley, Kent.
706. Cannon Hall, Yorkshire.
707. Goggerddan, Cardiganshire.
708. Hollywell Cottage, Cavan.
709. King's Cottage, Windsor Park.
710. Kingsweston, Gloucestershire.
711. Taymouth Castle, Perthshire.

# WORKS ON POTTERY AND PORCELAIN CONSULTED.

Jewitt's " Ceramic Art of Great Britain."
Chaffer's " Marks and Monograms."
Mrs. Bury Palliser's " The China Collector's Pocket Companion.'
Miss Metayard's " Life of Wedgwood."
Miss Metayard's " The Wedgwood Handbook."
Downing's " English Pottery and Porcelain."
" History of Staffordshire."
" Aikin on Pottery."
Binn's " A Century of Potting in the City of Worcester."
Dossie's " Handmaid to the Arts."
Faulkner's " History of Chelsea."
Nash's " History of Worcester."
Owen's " Two Centuries of Ceramic Art in Bristol."
Litchfield's " Pottery and Porcelain."
Young's " Ceramic Art."
Marryat's " Pottery and Porcelain."
Jacquemart's " History of Ceramic Art."
Audsley Bowes' " Keramic Art of Japan."
Shaw's " History of Staffordshire Potteries."
Haslem's " Old Derby China Factory."
Church's " English Porcelain."
Prime's " Pottery and Porcelain."
Barber's " Anglo-American Pottery."
Earle's " China Collecting in America."
" Old China Magazine."

# INDEX.

| | |
|---|---|
| Abbey, Fountains | 34.   Fonthill 54 |
| Abbey, Richard | 104, 106 |
| Abbey and Graham | 106 |
| Aqueduct at Rochester | 18, 21, 89, 91, 92 |
| Acorn border, china | 89, 91 |
| Adams, W. & Sons | 64, 66, 83, 167 |
| Adams' borders | 34 |
| Advertisement for a Wife | 32 |
| Africa, views of | 26 |
| Albany, N. Y. | 76 |
| Albany, Entrance of Canal at | 22 |
| Albany & Schenectady R. R. | 44 |
| Alcock, Samuel & Co. | 237, 239 |
| Almshouse, N. Y. | 27, 42 |
| America, view | 74 |
| America Independent | 21 |
| American Cities and Scenery Series | 73 |
| American Marine | 74 |
| American Views   22, 23, 24, 27, 28, 34, 35, 37, 44, 47, 54, 83, 88 | |
| Andreoli, Georgio | 171 |
| Antiquarian Society at Concord | 6, 110, 138, 152, 174 |
| Apostle pitcher | 44, 45 |
| Apotheosis jug | 90 |
| Arms jugs | 104, 106 |
| Arms of Delaware | 62 |
| Arms of Liverpool | 107 |
| | |
| Baker's Arms jug | 105 |
| Baltimore, view of | 70, 77 |
| Baltimore & Ohio R. R. | 77 |
| Baltimore Exchange | 45 |
| Bainbridge, Commodore | 97 |

Barlow, Thomas . . . . . . 179
Barber, E. A. . . . . . . 29, 75
Basaltes . . . . 96, 141, 166, 185, 196
Bat printing . . . . . . . 144
Battery, The . . . . , 18, 19. 20, 77
Battle of Bunker Hill view . . . . . 48
Battle of Stonington view . . . . . 113
" Beauties of America " Series . . . 41-45
Bell House Works . . . . . . 190
Bellarmines . . . . . . . 2, 9
Bentley, Thomas . . 201, 202, 205, 206, 207, 213, 215
Billingsley, Wm. . . . . 135, 161, 162
Birch, E. J. . . . . . . 168, 170
Biscuit . . . . . . . . 7
Blacksmith's Arms jug . . . . . 105
Black ware . . . . . . . 15
Black Works . . . . . . 206, 208
Bloor—Derby . . . . . 135, 136
Borders on china . . . . 73, 75, 77, 81, 103
Boston,    20, 21, 30.   Common, 36.   Octagon church 42, 47, 49,
        50.   Tea Party, 245, 246
Boston Hospital . . . . . 42, 92
Boston Mail Series . . . . . 74
Boston Museum of Fine Arts . . 15, 140, 157
Boston State House . . . . 36, 69
Bottcher . . . . . . 147, 242
Bow . . . . . 7, 125, 127-129, 143
Bow—Chelsea—Derby . . . . 136
Branxholm Castle view . . . . . 66
Bristol . . . . . 7, 125, 136-139
British Flowers Series . . . . . 57
British Lake Series . . . . . 54
British Museum . . . . . 133, 168
Brittannia . . . . . . . 132
Buck's Arms jugs . . . . . 105
Buckhorn Tavern . . . . . 52
Bucknall & Stevenson . . . . 27
Burke, Edmund . . . . . . 137

Burleigh, Lord . . . . . . 4
Burslem . . . 12, 35, 61, 67, 74, wharf, 70
Burton-upon-Trent . . . . . . 136
Butcher's Arms jug . . . . . . 105
Byerley, Thomas . . . . . . 213

" C. C." . . . . . . . 44
" Cadmus " . . . . . . 15, 76, 77
Calcutta . . . . . . . 26
Caldwell, James . . . . . 16, 17
Canal, Erie . . . . . . 21, 89
Canadian views . . . . . . 23
Cape Coast Castle . . . . . 26
Capitol at Washington . . . 42, 44, 50
Castles, English . . . 24, 25, 30, 33, 34
Castle Garden, N. Y. . . . 18, 19, 29, 45
Castleford ware . . . . . 181-184
Cathedrals, English . . . . 33, 34
Catherine of Russia . . . . . 209
Catskill . . . . . . . 18
Catskill Mountain House . . . . 20, 46
Catskill Moss Series . . . . . 44
Caughley pottery . . 59, 125, 146, 162, 163, 164
Cauldon Place pottery . . . . . 43
Celtic china . . . . . . 22
Chaffers, Richard . . . . 37, 104
Chamberlain Bros. . . . . . 145
Chamberlain Works . . . . 146, 147, 162
Champion, Richard . . . . 136, 137. 148
" Chancellor Livingston " . . . . 30
" Cha-no-yu " . . . . . . 242
Chelsea . . . 7, 125, 127-133, 138, 142, 143
Chelsea Derby . . . . . 134, 136
Cheyne Walk . . . . . . 130
" Chickweed " border . . . . . 73
Chinese ware . . . . . . 137
Christ and the Woman of Samaria . . . 23
Churchyard Works . . . . . 188

City Hall, N. Y. . . . . 47, 69
City Hotel, N. Y. . . . . . 51, 52, 84
City of New Orleans . . . . . . 53
Clay, Henry . . . . . . . 71
Clementson, J . . . . . . . 58
Clews, Ralph and James   26, 27, 29, 30–32, 34, 35, 38, 45, 46, 66, 92
Clinton, De Witt . . . . 89, 91, 92
Clive, Kitty . . . . . . 127
Coalport . . . . . . 163
Cobridge . . . . 12, 27–29, 35, 48, 92
Coenties Slip, N. Y. . . . . . 82
Collection, Walpole's . . . . 10, 133
Colles, Christopher . . . . . 9
" Colour blue " . . . . . 124
Columbia College . . . . 27, 52, 53
Columbus Series . . . . . 65
Comb, William . . . . . . 32
Conway, N. H. . . . . . . 65
Continental Views Series . . . . 119
Cookworthy, William . . . 137, 147–149
Cornwallis jug . . . . . 180
Cottage china ware . . . . . 138
Country Seats and Castles . . . . 25
Cowes . . . . . . . 25
Cremorne Gardens, Eng. . . . . 130
Cromwell, Oliver . . . . . 139
Crouch ware . . . . . . 3
Crown-Derby . . . . 134, 135, 136
Crown Works, London . . . . 71
Cup plates . . . . 45, 46, 53, 55
Custom House . . . . . 30
Cyrene design . . . . . 83

Dale Hall Works . . . . . 35, 61
Davenport . . . . . 140, 235
Delaware, Arms of . . . . . 62
Delft . . . 2, 10, English 124, 125, Old, 125, 137
Derby . . . 7, 125, 129, 133–136, 138, 142, 143

Diana . . . . . . . . 133
Dillon . . . . . . . . 83
Don Quixote designs . . . . . 31, 33, 46
Downing's " English Pottery and Porcelain," . . 66
Dr. Syntax designs . . . . . 32–34
Dragon pattern . . . . . . 60
Dresden models . . . . 132, 137, 138
Dublln, Ireland . . . 25, 27, view of, 71
Duesbury, Mr. . . . . . 133, 134, 136
Duesbury and Kean . . . . . . 136
Duke of York . . . . . . . 20
Dulwich Castle. . . . . . . 34
Dunderdale, David . . . . . . 181
Dutch . . . . . . 3, 20, 130

East India Trading Co. . . . . . 3, 4
East Indies . . . . . . 3, 5
Eaton Hall . . . . . . . 54
Edwards, J. and T. . . . . . . 74
Egyptian Black ware . . . . . . 166
Elers Bros. . . . . . 5, 166, 242
Encaustic painted ware . . . . . 204
England, Potter's Art . . . . . 2, 3
English Cities Series . . . . . . 25
English Delft . . . . . 124, 125
English Views 23, 24, 28, 33, 34, 37, 44, 46, 47, 53, 57, 91, wares 27, 59
Entrance of Canal at Albany . . . . 22–89
Erie Canal . . . . . . 21, 89
Erie Canal at Buffalo . . . . . . 53
Eton College . . . . . . . 57
Etruria . . . . 12, 83, 103, 190, 206
Eulogy plate . . . . . . . 78
Exchange, N. Y. . . . . . . 81

" F. M." . . . . . . . 74
Faïence . . . . . . . 2, 8
Falls of Montmorency . . . . . 23
Falstaff . . . . . . 133, 134

" Fame " . . . . . . . 133
Farmer's Arms . . . . . . 105
Faulkbourn Hall . . . . . . 91
" Faulkstone Hall " . . . . . . 91
Fenton . . . . . . . 12
Figure work . . . . . . . 14
Fishkill on Hudson . . . . . 76
Flat ware . . . . 8, 14, 18, 21, 133, 136
Flaxman, John . . . . 202, 211, 212
Flight, John . . . . . . 145
Flight and Barr . . . . . . 145
Flip . . . . . . . . 177
" Flow blue " . . . . . . . 13
Ford, Thomas . . . . . . . 74
Forgeries . . . . . . . 84
" Four Elements," figures . . . . 137
" Four Seasons," figures . . . . 137
Franklin, Benjamin . . . 54–56, 86, 95–97, 108
Franklin's Tomb . . . . 54, Toby, 241
French Views . . . . . 26, 42
" Frit " body . . . . . . 143
Fulton Steamboat . . . . . . 30

George II. . . . 130, 132; III 123; IV 118, 168
Gilbert Sale . . . . . . . 19
Glaze . . . . . . 3, 7, 12, 14
Godwin, Thomas . . . . . . 70
Gombron Ware . . . . . . 248
Grainger Works . . . . . 147, 163
Greatback . . . . . . . 200
" Greased " . . . . . . . 9
Green Bros. . . . . . . . 139
Green, Chas. . . . . . . . 170
Green, Guy . . . . . 101, 102, 103
Green, Thomas . . . . . . . 73
Greenfield Works . . . . . . 64
Gubbio, City of . . . . . . 171
Guilds . . . . . . . . 106
Guy's Cliff . . . . . . 25

Hackwood, William . . . . . . 200
Hall, I. & Sons . . . . . . . 58
Haigh Sale of China, Boston . . . . . 21
Hancock, John . . . . . . 36, 67, 68
Hancock House, view . . . . . 67, 68
Hancock, Robert . . . . . 144, 163
Hanly . . . . . . . 12, 41, 72
Hard Glaze . . . . . . . . 7
Hard Paste . . . . . . 7, 136
Harewood House, view . . . . 54, 91
Harpers Ferry, view . . . . . 65, 71
Harrison Campaign Series . . . . . 43
Hartley & Green . . . . . . 139
Harvard College plate . . . . . . 52
Harvard Hall, view . . . . . . 52
Hatters Arms jug . . . . . . 105
Heath, Joseph & Co. . . . . . . 72
Henry VIII. . . . . . . . 129
Herculaneum Pottery . . . . 106, 113, 140
Hertford, Marquis of, collection . . . . 11
Hispano-Moresque Pottery . . . . 171, 172
Holdship, Richard . . . . . . 144
Hollis Hall, view . . . . . . 52
Holworthy Hall, view . . . . . . 52
Hudson City, view . . . . . . 77
Hudson River, views . . . . . 20, 28
Hudson River near Fishkill, view . . . 28
" Hudson River Portfolio " by Wall . . . 31
Humble & Green . . . . . . 139
Hylton, North . . . . . . . 114

Impressed stamp . . . . 15, 17, 22
India, views of . . . . . . 26
Indian Scenery Series . . . . . 58
Independence inscription . . . . 30
Inscription pieces . . . . . . 78
Intaglios . . . . . . . 222
Inventories and Wills . . . . 121, 122
Iron-stone ware . . . . . . 58

Ironworkers' Arms jug     .       .       .       .       . 105
Isle of Wight .       .       .       .       .       .       . 25
Italian Faience     .       .       .       .       .       . 2, 8
Italian Scenery Series .       .       .       .       .       . 58
Italy, Views of.       .       .       .       .       .       . 26
" Ivy ' ware     .       .       .       .       .       .       . 58
Ivy House Works, Wedgwood's     .       .       188, 189, 190

" J. B." .       .       .       .       .       .       .       . 74
Jackson, Andrew     .       .       .       .       .       . 98
Jackson, J. & J.     .       .       .       .       .       67, 68, 83
Jameson, Mrs. .       .       .       .       .       .       . 93
" Japan taste "       .       .       .       .       .       . 143
Jasper ware     .       .       .       .       .       .       15, 96
" Jassamine " ware     .       .       .       .       .       . 58
Jefferson, President     .       .       .       . 57, 89, 91, 92, 95
Jewitt .       .       .       .       .       .       .       . 105
Johnson, Dr. .       .       .       .       .       .       . 135
Jordan, Richard, Residence, view     .       .       .       72, 83
Jugs     .       . 2, 9, 16, 44, 45, 104, 107 108, 109, 110, 234
Justice, figure of     .       .       .       .       .       . 133

Kenilworth Castle     .       .       .       .       .       . 25
Kent     .       .       .       .       .       .       .       . 37
King's College .       .       .       .       .       .       . 53

Lafayette     . 15, 26, 29, 53, 56, 57, 68, 84, 86, 89, 91, 93, 94, 97
Lafayette at Franklin's Tomb, view     .       .       .       . 56
Lake George, view     .       .       .       .       .       18, 77
Lake Windermere, view     .       .       .       .       . 54
Lakin & Poole .       .       .       .       .       .       . 170
Lambeth     .       .       .       .       .       .       . 125
Landing of Lafayette, view     .       .       .       29, 45, 84
Landing of the Pilgrims, dinner service     .       .       . 21
Lane End     .       .       .       .       .       .       . 12
Lawrence Mansion, Boston, plate     .       .       .       . 50
Lead glaze     .       .       .       .       .       .       . 3
Leeds Old Pottery     .       .       .       .       .       . 139
Leeds ware     .       .       .       . 115, 138, 139–142, 183

Limehouse Dock, view . . . . . 25
Little Falls . . . . . . 21, 22
Little Falls, aqueduct at . . . . . 21
Liverpool . 7, 103, 125,144 ; ware 88, 100–123 ; delft 100
London View Series . . . . . . 25
Log Cabin design . . . . . . 43
Longport . . . . . . 12, 37, 54
Longton Place . . . . . . . 179
Lovejoy Cup-plate . . . . 46 ; plate 79, 84
Lowestoft . . . 150, 151 ; china 37, 125, 149–157
Lumley Castle view . . . . . . 34
Lustre decoration . . . 141, 166–181 ; goblets 176

Majolica . . . . . . . 8
" Makers Unknown " . . . . . 28, 75–81
Marks on China :
    Alcocks . . . . . . . 239
    Bristol . . . . . . . 138
    Castleford . . . . . . 183
    Caughley or Salopian ware . . . . 60
    Clews . . . . . . . 35
    Davenport . . . . . . 235
    Derby . . . . . . 134, 135
    Heath . . . . . . . 72
    Herculaneum . . . . . . 107
    Leeds . . . . . . . 142
    Mayer . . . . . . 61, 63
    Mason . . . . . . . 165
    Phillips . . . . . . 54, 58
    Plymouth . . . . . . 149
    Ridgway . . . . . . 41, 44
    Riley . . . . . . . 59
    Sadler & Green . . . . . . 103
    Spode . . . . . . . 159
    Stevenson . . . 28, 53, 54, 88, 89, 91, 94
    Stubs . . . . . . . 37
    Swansea . . . . . . . 160
    Tams . . . . . . . 70

Marks on China, *Continued.*
   Wedgwood . . . . . 199, 200
   Wood . . . . . 14, 16, 17, 22, 25
   Worcester . . . . . . 146
Mason . . . . . . . 5, 83
Mason's Ironstone China . . . . 164, 165
Masonic jugs . . . . . 111, 112, 113
Mayer, Elijah . . . . . . 168, 170
Mayer, T. . . . . . . . 5, 61
Meakin . . . . . . . 83
Medallions on flat ware
     21, 25, 28, 30, 89, 91, 92, 95, 96 ; basaltes 196, 201
Meigh, Charles . . . . . 5, 72, 236
Mellor, Venables & Co. . . . . . 74
Mendenhall Ferry cup-plate . . . . 46
Metropolitan Museum of Art, N. Y. . . 88, 96, 155, 247
Mill at Charenton plate . . . . . 26
Millennium plate . . . . . . 80
Milton, John . . . . . . 132
Milk-maid designs . . . . . . 37
Minton figure . . . . . , 83
Minerva figure . . . . . . 133
Mirror-knobs . . . . . . 96, 97
Mitchell & Freeman Warehouse . . . . 64
" Monument " pitcher . . . . . 110
Montgomery, General . . . . . 113
Morris, Robert . . . . . . 55
Mount Vernon views . . . . . 30, 45
Mt. Vernon . . . . . . 181
" Myrtle " Ware . . . . . . 58
Music Lesson, group . . . . . 132
Museum of Practical Geology . . . . 105

Nadin, Dr. . . . . . . 136
Nahant plate . . . . . . 37
Nantgarw . . . . . 125, 1611–62
Narrows, The . . . . . . 20
Neale . . . . . . . 167

Neptune, figure of . . . . . . 133
Newburg on the Hudson . . . . 20, 77
Newcastle . . . . . . . 115
New Hall Works . . . . . 119, 137
New Orleans, City of, view . . . . . 53
New South Church, Boston . . . . . 42
New York Arms . . . . . . 62
New York City . . . 19, 46, 51 ; view of, 65
New York from Brooklyn Heights, views of . . . 27
Niagara . . . 28, 95 ; urn 94 ; Table Rock 22
North Hylton . . . . . . . 113
Nottingham Bear . . . . . . 251

Octagon Church, Boston . . . . . 42
Old Delft . . . . . . . 125
Old Worcester Works . . . . . . 145
Ontario Lake Scenery . . . . . . 72
Oriental China . . . . 2, 7, 10 ; patterns 131
Oriental Scenery Series . . . . . 58

Palestine designs . . . . . . 83
Palliser, Mrs. Bury . . . . . . 129
Palmer & Neale . . . . . 167, 179
Painted Ware . . . . . . . 6
Paste . . . . . . . 5, 7
Pâte-sur-pâte . . . . . . . 239
Penn's Treaty view . . . . . . 73
Pennsylvania Arms . . . . . . 61
Pepys . . . . . . . . 4
Perry, Commodore O. H. . . . . 97, 98, 113
Philadelphia, views of . . . . . 55, 77
Phillips, E. J. & Co. . . . . . 54-58
Phillips, J. . . . . . . . 113
" Phœnix & Engine " border . . . . . 8
Picturesque Views Series . . . . 35, 46
Pilgrims, Landing of, design . . . . . 21
Pinxton . . . . . . . 125
Pitchers . 12, 17, 18, 21, 44, 88, 107, 109, 110, 111, 113
Pittsfield Elm plate . . . . 31 ; cup-plate 46

Planche . . . . . . . 134
Plymouth . . . . . 7, 125, 147–149
Porcelain . . . . . . 3-8, 59, 136
Portland vase . . . . . . . 214
Portraits . . . . . 28, 53, 86-99
Possett-pots . . . . . . . 3, 9
Potter, Jonas . . . . . . . 6
" Pottery and Porcelain," by W. C. Prime . . 47
Preble, Commodore . . . . . . 112
Preston Pans . . . . . . . 173
Prime, W. C. . . . . . . 37, 47, 129
Printing on pottery . . . . . . 13, 14
Printed ware . . . . . . 6, 100–112
" Proof " condition . . . . . . 9

Quebec, Falls of Montmorency near, view of . . 23
Queen Anne . . . . . . 6 ; sets 174
Queen Caroline . . . . . . 118
Queen Charlotte . . . . . 136 ; ware 190
Queen Elizabeth . . . . . . 2, 3
Queen Mary . . . . . . . 10
Queen's Ware . . . . . . 62, 192

Ranelagh . . . . . . . 130
Regent's Body . . . . . . 147
Regent's Canal. . . . . . . 25
Regent's Park . . . . . . 25, 66
Revolution . . . . . . 12, 55
Rhode Island Arms . . . . . . 62
Ridgway, Job . . . . . . . 41
Ridgway & Sons . . . . . . 41
Ridgway, J. & W. . . . . .41, 47, 83, 84
Ridgway, Son & Wear . . . . . 53
Riley, J. & R. . . . . . . . 5
Ripon, view of . . . . . . . 34
Rochester, City of, N. Y. . 18, 21, 94 ; aqueduct 89, 91, 92
Rockingham . . . . . . .7, 125
Rogers, potter . . . . . . . 69

Rose, William . . . . . . . 153
Rowlandson . . . . . . . 32
Royal Worcester . . . . . . 147
Ruins of Exchange, N. Y., view of . . . . 81

Sadler, John . . . . . . 100, 102, 104
Sadler & Green . . . 100, 101, 193, 195, 247
Sadler, Richard . . . . . . . 13
Sailor pitchers . . . . . . 113, 116, 117
Salopian Works. . . . . . . 59, 162
Salt glaze . . . . . . . 3, 12, 14
Sancho Panza at the Boar Hunt design . . . 33
Sandusky, view of . . . . . . 75
Saucers . . . . . . . . 249
Savannah Bank cup-plate . . . . . 46
Scudder's American Museum . . . . . 52
Scriptural design . . . . . . 81, 83
Second Tour of Dr. Syntax . . . . . 32
Select Views Series . . . . . . 34
Semi-china . . . . . . 5, 7, 8, 15, 57
Sèvres . . . . . . . . 131
Shakespeare Piece . . . . . . 132
Shaw, Ralph . . . . . . . 12
Shelton . . . . . . . . 12
Ship of the Line in the Downs design . . . 26
"Smith set" of China . . . . . 137
Smollett . . . . . . . 130
Soft Glaze . . . . . . . 7
Soft Paste . . . . . . . 7
Spode, Josiah . . 187 ; ware 158—160, 171 ; patterns 159
Southampton, Hampshire, plate . . . . 46
South Carolina, Arms of . . . . . 62
"Spurs" on China . . . . . . 84
St. George's Chapel, London, view of . . . 66
St. Paul's Chapel, New York City, view of . . 89
Staffordshire . . 7, 12—59 ; ware 98, 108, 136, 249, 250, 252
Stamp Impressed . . . . . 15, 17, 22
State House at Boston, plate . . . . . 47

"States" pattern . . . . . . 29, 3c
Steele . . . . . . . . 130
Stevenson, Andrew . . . . 26, 29, 53, 92, 94
  Ralph . . . . . 28, 47—54, 83, 92
  Ralph & Sons . . . . . 92
  R. & Williams. . . . 33, 48, 51, 53, 88
"Stilts" on China . . . . . 8, 33, 131
Stoke-on-Trent . . . . . . 12
Stoke, Works at . . . . . . 64
Stonington, Battle of, view . . . . . 113
Stoughton Church Cup-plate. . . . . 46, 53
Stoughton Hall, Harvard College . . . . 52
"Stourbridge Lion" Locomotive . . . . 44
Stratford-le-Bow . . . . . 126, 129
Strawberry Hill . . . . . . 10, 133
Stubbs, Joseph . . . . . 35—37, 61, 69
Stubbs & Kent . . . . . . 37
Sunderland Inscription . . 80 ; pitchers 114, 115, 172
Sun of Righteousness Series. . . . . 23
Swansea . . . . . . 125, 160
Swift . . . . . . . . 130
Sydenham . . . . . . . 58
Syntax Designs . . . 32, 33, 39, 46, 48, 84

Table Rock, Niagara, view of . . . . 22
Table Ware . . . . . . . 8, 12
Tams, S. & Co. . . . . . . 70, 71
Tams, & Anderson . . . . . . 70, 71
Tams, Anderson & Tams . . . . . 70, 71
Tea, Tea-pots . . . . . 243, 248
Templeton, Lady . . . . . . 17
Texas Campaign, The . . . . . 74
Thompson's "Seasons" . . . . . 120
"Tobys" . . . . . . . 241
Tomb Designs . . . . . . 54, 56
Tortoise-shell Ware . . . . . . 6
"Tournament" Pitcher . . . . . 44
Transfer Printing . . . . . 143, 144

Trinity Church . . . . . . 51
Trumble-Prime Collection of China . . . . 96
Troy from Mt. Ida view . . . . . 46
Tunstall . . . . . 12, 64, 65, 66
Turner, John, Potter . . . . . . 170
Turner, J. M. W. . . . . 120 ; designs 122
Turner, Thomas . . . . . . 162
Twymouth Haven . . . . . . 114

Unknown Makers . . . . . 75—81
United States Hotel, Philadelphia, view . . . 70
University Hall view . . . . . . 52
Urn, Niagara . . . . . . . 94
Utica view . . . . 70 ; inscription 78

Valentine, The, Wilkie design . . . 33, 46

Waldegrave, Lord . . . . . . 10
Wall, W. G. . . . . . 27, 28, 31
Wall, J. . . . . . . . 145
Walpole, Horace . . . . 10, 130, 133
Warren, General . . . . . . 113
Warwick Castle view . . . . . 25
Washington, George . . . 30, 53, 55-57, 68, 84, 86,
    . . 88, 89, 90, 91, 97, 107, 108, 109,
    . . . 110, 111 ; portrait 182
" Washington etc.," inscription . . . . 21
Washington Memorial . . . 22 ; tomb 63 ; vase 22
Webster, Daniel . . . . . . 21
Wedgewood, Josiah . . 5, 12, 14, 58, 66, 83, 96, 101
    . . 102, 103, 123, 142, 156, 166,
    . . 167, 169, 173, 175, 182, 185 ;
    . . catalogue 210, 211, 219–229
" Weehawk " by Wall . . . . . 28
Wells Cathedral view . . . . . 34
" Wellington " boots . . . . . 136
Wellington, Duke of . . . . . 169
Wesley, Rev. John . . . . . 15

West Point, N. Y.  .  .  .  .  .  . 20
Whieldon, Thomas  .  .  .  .  . 6, 170, 187
White House at Washington .  .  .  .  . 30
White Ware  .  .  .  .  .  . 44, 166
Whitfield, John  .  .  .  .  .  . 15
" Willow " pattern  .  .  .  .  . 10, 13, 59
Wilkie, Sir David  .  .  . 32 ; designs 31, 33, 39, 46
Windsor  .  .  .  .  . 57 ; Castle 25, 91
Wolfe, General  .  .  .  .  .  . 112
Wood, Aaron  .  .  .  .  .  . 14
    Enoch .  .  .  .  .  . 12, 14–28
    E. and Sons  .  .  .  . 15–56, 83, 89
    Ralph .  .  .  .  .  . 14
Wood & Caldwell  .  .  .  .  . 16, 17
Worcester  .  .  . 7, 125, 142–147 ; Royal 147

Yale College .  .  .  .  .  . 52, 73
Yarmouth  .  .  .  .  .  . 25
Young, Arthur  .  .  .  .  .  . 246

" Zoölogical Gardens " Series .  .  .  . 47